BITCOIN BILLIONAIRES

BITCOIN BILLIONAIRES

A TRUE STORY OF GENIUS, BETRAYAL, AND REDEMPTION

BEN MEZRICH

FLATIRON
BOOKS
NEW YORK

www.flatironbooks.com

Photograph on page 180 courtesy of the author.

Library of Congress Cataloging-in-Publication Data

Names: Mezrich, Ben, 1969– author.
Title: Bitcoin billionaires : a true story of genius, betrayal, and redemption /
     Ben Mezrich.
Description: First edition. | New York : Flatiron Books, 2019. | Includes bibliographical
     references.
Identifiers: LCCN 2019002977 | ISBN 9781250217745 (hardcover) | ISBN 9781250239389
     (international, sold outside the U.S., subject to rights availability) | ISBN 9781250217752 (ebook)
Subjects: LCSH: Winklevoss, Tyler. | Winklevoss, Cameron. | Venture capital. | Bitcoin. |
     Entrepreneurship.
Classification: LCC HG4751 .M499 2019 | DDC 332.4 [B]—dc23
LC record available at https://lccn.loc.gov/2019002977

Our books may be purchased in bulk for promotional, educational, or business use.
Please contact your local bookseller or the Macmillan Corporate and Premium Sales Department
at 1-800-221-7945, extension 5442, or by email at MacmillanSpecialMarkets@macmillan.com.

First U.S. Edition: May 2019
First International Edition: May 2019

10 9 8 7 6 5 4 3 2 1

To Asher, Arya, Tonya, and Bugsy:
HODL. It's all an adventure, and it gets
more fun every day.

CONTENTS

Author's Note   ix

ACT ONE

1. Into the Tiger's Cage   3

2. Dead in the Water   15

3. Damaged Goods   32

4. In the Beginning There Was Foam   41

5. The Basement   46

6. Finding Love in a Hopeless Place   52

7. August 30, 2012   59

8. Charlie   77

9. Stepford, Connecticut   83

10. Buyer's Market   97

11. The Reverse Heist   102

ACT TWO

12. The Spark — 117

13. Bayfront Park, Downtown Miami — 122

14. On the Road Again — 129

15. In the Air — 140

16. The King of Bitcoin — 150

17. The Morning After — 157

18. Bright Lights — 163

19. This Side of Paradise — 168

20. The United Front — 175

21. Behind the Door — 182

22. Bitcoin 2013 — 191

23. Going Mainstream — 205

ACT THREE

24. A Pirate's Tale — 217

25. The Day After — 221

26. The Fall — 227

27. Across Town — 238

28. Men of Harvard — 243

29. Judgment Day — 250

30. Launched — 256

31. From Dumas to Balzac — 265

EPILOGUE: Where Are They Now . . . ? — 269

Acknowledgments — 273

Bibliography — 275

AUTHOR'S NOTE

Bitcoin Billionaires is a dramatic, narrative account based on dozens of interviews, hundreds of sources, and thousands of pages of documents, including records from several court proceedings. There are a number of different and often contentious opinions about some of the events in the story; to the best of my ability, I re-created the scenes in the book based on the information I uncovered from documents and interviews. Other scenes are written in a way that describes individual perceptions without endorsing them. In some instances, details of settings and descriptions have been changed or imagined.

In 2010, I published *The Accidental Billionaires: The Founding of Facebook,* which was soon adapted into the film *The Social Network.* I could never have guessed that one day I would revisit two of the characters from that story—Tyler and Cameron Winklevoss, the identical twins who challenged Mark Zuckerberg over the origins of what would soon be one of the most powerful companies on Earth.

In the world *The Accidental Billionaires* was published into, Facebook was the revolution, and Mark Zuckerberg the revolutionary. He was attempting to change the social order—how society interacted and how people met, communicated, fell in love, and lived. The Winklevoss twins were his perfect foils: buttoned-down "Men of Harvard," privileged jocks who, in many ways easy to see, appeared to represent the "Establishment."

Today things seem different. Mark Zuckerberg is a household name. Facebook is ubiquitous, dominating much of the internet (even as it seems to be constantly embroiled in scandals ranging from hacked user data to fake news items and providing a platform for political-based disruptions). Meanwhile, Tyler and Cameron Winklevoss have reappeared in the news—in an unexpected way—as leaders of an entirely new digital revolution.

The irony of the situation is not lost on me; not only that Zuckerberg's and the twins' roles as rebels and Evil Empire seem to have been reversed, but also that my book and the film that followed helped enshrine an image of the twins that is in need of revising. It is my opinion that Tyler and Cameron Winklevoss didn't just happen to be standing in the exact right place at the exact right time—twice—by chance.

Second acts, in literature as in life, are rare. And as I hope to show, there is every chance that the Winklevoss twins' second act will eventually overshadow their first. Bitcoin and the technology behind it has the capacity to upend the internet. Just as Facebook was developed to enable social networks to move from the physical world to the internet, cryptocurrencies such as Bitcoin were developed for a financial world that now functions largely online. The technology behind Bitcoin isn't a fad, or a bubble, or a scheme; it's a fundamental paradigm shift, and it will eventually change everything.

ACT ONE

Moral wounds have this peculiarity—
they may be hidden, but they never close;
always painful, always ready to bleed
when touched, they remain fresh and
open in the heart.

—ALEXANDRE DUMAS,
  The Count of Monte Cristo

1

INTO THE TIGER'S CAGE

February 22, 2008.

The twenty-third floor of a nondescript office tower on the outskirts of San Francisco's Financial District.

The usual glass, steel, and concrete sliced and diced into overly air-conditioned, brightly lit cubes. Eggshell-colored walls and industrial-beige carpets. Fluorescent strips bisecting tic-tac-toe tiled dropped ceilings. Bug-eyed watercoolers, chrome-edged conference tables, faux-leather adjustable chairs.

It was a little past three on a Friday afternoon, and Tyler Winklevoss stood by a floor-to-ceiling window overlooking a pincushion of similar office buildings piercing the midday fog. He was trying his best to sip filtered water from a tissue-thin disposable cup, without spilling too much onto his tie. After so many days, months, hell, years, the tie was hardly necessary. The longer this ordeal dragged on, the more likely it was that sooner or later he'd show up to the next endless session wearing his Olympic rowing jacket.

He managed to get the barest taste of water before the cup folded inward beneath his fingers, rivulets missing his tie but drenching the sleeve of his dress shirt. He tossed the cup toward a trash can beneath the window, shaking his damp wrist. "Another thing to add to the list. Paper cups shaped like ice-cream cones. What kind of sadist came up with these?"

"Maybe the same guy who invented the lights. I've gotten two shades tanner since they moved us to this floor. Forget pits of fire, I'm betting purgatory is lined with fluorescent tubes."

Tyler's brother, Cameron, was stretched out across two of the faux-leather chairs on the other side of the room, his long legs propped up against the corner of a rectangular conference table. He was wearing a blazer but no tie. One of his size fourteen leather shoes rested perilously close to the screen of Tyler's open laptop, but Tyler let it slide. It had already been a long day.

Tyler knew the tedium was by design. Mediation was different from litigation. The latter was a pitched battle, two parties trying to fight their way to victory, what mathematicians and economists would call a zero-sum game. Litigation had highs and lows, but beneath the surface there lurked a primal energy; at its heart, it *was* war. But mediation was different. When properly conducted, there wasn't a winner or a loser, just two parties who compromised their way to a resolution, who "split the baby." Mediation didn't feel like war. It was more like a really long bus ride that ended only when everyone on board got tired enough of the scenery to agree on a destination.

"If you want to be accurate," Tyler said, turning back to the window and the gray on gray of another Northern California afternoon, "we're not the ones in purgatory."

Whenever the lawyers were out of the room, Tyler and Cameron did their best not to dwell on the case itself. There had been plenty of that in the beginning. They had once been so filled with anger and a feeling of betrayal that they could hardly think of anything else. But as the weeks turned into months, they had decided that anger wasn't doing their sanity any good. As the lawyers kept telling them, they had to trust in the system. So when they were alone, they tried to talk about anything but what had brought them to this place.

That they were now on the topic of medieval literature, specifically Dante's conception of the many circles of hell, showed that the avoidance strategy was beginning to fray; trusting the system had seemingly trapped them in one of

Dante's inventions. Even so, it gave them something to focus on. As teenagers growing up in Connecticut, Tyler and Cameron had both been obsessed with Latin. With no courses left to take by senior year of high school, they petitioned their school principal to let them form a Medieval Latin Seminar with the Jesuit priest who was the director of the Latin program. Together, the twins and the father translated the *Confessions* of St. Augustine of Hippo and other medieval scholarly works. Though Dante hadn't written his most famous work in Latin, they'd both also studied enough Italian to play the game of updating the scenery in his inferno: watercoolers, fluorescent lights, whiteboards . . . lawyers.

"Technically," Tyler said. "We're in limbo. *He's* the one in purgatory. We didn't do anything wrong."

There was a sudden knock. One of their own lawyers, Peter Calamari, entered first. His receding hairline framed a protruding forehead and under-size, jowly chin. His palm tree–patterned Tommy Bahama shirt was poorly tucked into the waistband of a pair of blue jeans so big for him they made him walk funny; Tyler wouldn't have been surprised if the tag was still on. Worse yet, Calamari was actually wearing sandals. He'd likely purchased them at the same place he'd bought his jeans.

Behind their lawyer came the mediator. Antonio "Tony" Piazza cut a much more impressive figure. Trim to the point of being gaunt, he was im-peccably dressed in suit and tie. His snowflaked hair was shorn tight and proper, his cheeks appropriately tanned. In the press, Piazza was known as "the master of mediation"—he had successfully resolved more than four thousand complex disputes, supposedly had a photographic memory, and was also an expert in martial arts—believing that his training in aikido had taught him how to channel aggression into something productive. Piazza was indefatigable. In theory, he was the perfect bus driver for this seemingly endless ride.

Before the two lawyers had even shut the door behind them, Cameron had his legs off the table.

"Did he agree?"

He'd aimed the question at Piazza. They'd begun to think of Calamari, a partner at the ever-boastful, chest-pounding Quinn Emanuel law firm, as little more than a messenger between them and the aikido master. If his roomy jeans and sandals were an attempt to connect with the Silicon Valley atmosphere, Cameron felt that they marked him as more gimmick than lawyer.

In fact, he wasn't even supposed to be there. Calamari was standing in for Rick Werder Jr., the lead lawyer on their case, who couldn't make it at the last minute because he had decided to represent a company in a $2 billion bankruptcy action. Despite the entire fate of the twins' case resting on his shoulders, Werder hadn't shown up to the mediation, the case's defining moment. The twins' understanding was that he was busy chasing what he thought was the bigger, better deal.

The twins had hired the Quinn Emanuel firm in an effort to add muscle to their legal team, as discovery was coming to a close and trial was on the horizon. Founded in 1986 by John B. Quinn, the firm had a reputation for being tough litigators dedicated solely to business litigation and arbitration. The firm had also pioneered a lack of a formal dress code—something unheard of in the world of white shoe law firms. This innovation was to blame for Calamari's sartorial failure.

"It's not a no," Piazza said. "But he has some concerns."

Tyler looked at his brother. The request they'd made had originally been Cameron's idea. They had spent so much time going back and forth through their lawyers—and now Piazza in the middle, a silvery sphinx constantly searching for middle ground—Cameron had wondered if maybe there was a way to cut through all the theater. Hell, they were three people who not long ago had met in a college dining hall. Maybe they could sit down again, just the three of them, no lawyers, and talk this thing through.

"What sort of concerns?" Cameron asked.

Piazza paused.

"Security concerns."

It took Tyler a moment to realize what the man was saying. His brother stood up from his chair.

"He thinks we're going to take a swing at him?" Cameron asked. "Really?"

Tyler felt his cheeks growing red.

"You've got to be kidding."

Their lawyer stepped forward, placating. "The important thing is, other than the security concerns, he's amenable to the idea."

"Seriously, let me understand this," Tyler said. "He thinks we're going to beat him up? During mediation. In the corporate offices of a mediator."

Piazza's face didn't change but his voice shifted lower—to an octave so soothing it could put you to sleep.

"Let's try to keep focus. He's agreed to the meeting in theory. It's just a matter of working out the details."

"You want to handcuff us to the watercooler?" Cameron asked. "Will that make him more comfortable?"

"That won't be necessary. There's a glass conference room at the end of the hall. We can set the meeting there. Just one of you will go in for the face-to-face. The rest of us will sit outside and watch."

It was utterly absurd. Tyler felt like they were being treated like wild animals. *Security concerns*. He had a feeling the words themselves had come from *him*. They sounded exactly like something only *he* would say, or even think. Maybe it was some sort of ploy; the idea that he'd be any physically safer facing just one of them was almost as ludicrous as the idea that they'd beat him up, but maybe he thought talking to only one of them would give him some sort of intellectual advantage. The twins felt he'd judged them from the very beginning because of the way they looked. To him, they had always been nothing more than the cool kids on campus. Dumb jocks who couldn't even code, who needed to hire a nerd to build their website, a website only he, the boy genius, could have, or rather should have, possibly invented. *Because if they were the inventors, they would have invented it.* Of course, in this logic, they'd want to knock him out if they could get him in a room alone.

Tyler closed his eyes, took a moment. Then he shrugged.

"Cameron will go in."

His brother had always been a little more rounded at the edges, less alpha, a little more willing to bend when bending was the only option available. No doubt this would be one of those situations.

"Like a tiger in a cage," Cameron said as they followed Piazza and their lawyer out into the hallway. "Keep the tranquilizer gun ready. If you see me going for his throat, do me a favor and aim for the blazer. It's my brother's."

Neither the lawyer nor the mediator cracked even the slightest of smiles.

W alking into the fishbowl forty minutes later was one of the most surreal moments in Cameron Winklevoss's life.

Mark Zuckerberg was already seated at the long, rectangular table in the center of the room. It seemed to Cameron that his five-foot-seven-inch frame was propped up on a thick extra cushion placed on his chair—a billionaire's booster seat. Cameron felt vaguely self-conscious as he closed the glass door behind him; he could see Tyler and his lawyer taking seats directly behind him on the other side of the glass. Farther down the hall, he saw Piazza, and then Zuckerberg's lawyers, an army of men in suits. Most of them, he recognized; certainly he couldn't forget Neel Chatterjee, of the firm Orrick Herrington & Sutcliffe LLP, a man so protective of his precious client (and what the twins might have to say about him) that when the twins had been invited to take part in a fireside chat at an internet conference in 2008, Chatterjee had appeared in the audience, presumably so that he could keep tabs on what they said. Chatterjee and the rest of the lawyers had yellow legal notepads, though Cameron had no idea what they would be writing down. As far as he could tell, the glass conference room was soundproof, and to the best of his knowledge, none of them were lip readers. The conversation would be between him and Zuckerberg: no mediator, no lawyers, nobody listening in, nobody to get in their way.

Zuckerberg didn't look up as Cameron approached the other end of the conference table. The strange chill running down Cameron's spine had little to do with the overzealous air-conditioning. This was the first time he and his former Harvard classmate had seen each other in four years.

Cameron had first met Zuckerberg in the Kirkland dining hall in October of 2003, when he, Tyler, and their friend Divya Narendra had sat down with him to discuss the social network that they had been building over the previous year. Over the next three months, the four of them had met several more times in Zuckerberg's dorm room, and exchanged over fifty emails discussing the site. However, unbeknownst to the twins and Narendra at the time, Zuckerberg had secretly started working on another social network. In fact, he registered the domain name thefacebook.com on January 11, 2004, four days prior to their third meeting, on January 15, 2004.

Three weeks later, he'd launched thefacebook.com on February 4, 2004. Cameron, Tyler, and Divya had only learned about it soon after, while reading the campus paper, the *Harvard Crimson*. Cameron soon confronted Zuckerberg over email. Zuckerberg had responded: *"If you would like to meet to discuss any of this, I am willing to meet with you alone. Let me know. . . ."* But Cameron had passed, feeling the trust had been irreparably damaged; what good could come of it, reasoning with someone who was capable of acting the way he did? The only thing Cameron had felt they could do at that point was rely on the system—first, by petitioning the Harvard administration and Harvard president Larry Summers to step in and enforce the honor codes pertaining to student interactions clearly delineated in the student handbook, and then, when that failed, reluctantly turning to the courts—and now here they were, four long years later. . . .

Cameron had reached the table and lowered his oversize frame into one of the chairs before *he* finally looked up, the tiniest sliver of an awkward smile touching his lips. It was incredibly hard to read someone who had no discernable facial expressions, but Cameron thought he detected a hint of nervousness in the way Zuckerberg rocked forward, his legs crossed beneath the table at the ankles, a mere glimmer of human emotion. Surprisingly, he was *not* wearing his signature gray hoodie; perhaps he was finally taking this seriously. Zuckerberg nodded at Cameron, mumbling some sort of greeting.

Over the next ten minutes, Cameron did most of the talking. He started by extending an olive branch. He congratulated Mark on all that he had accomplished over the past few years since Harvard. How he'd turned theface book.com—a college-based social network that had started as a small, exclusive website connecting Harvard kids with one another—into Facebook, a worldwide phenomenon that had moved from school to school, and then country to country, engaging at first millions, then billions of users, eventually drawing in more than one-fifth of the people on planet Earth, who were now willingly and regularly sharing their personalities, pictures, likes, loves, and lives on a network that showed no signs of slowing.

Cameron held himself back from saying the obvious: he, Tyler, and Divya believed, deeply and firmly, that Facebook had actually risen out of their own idea—a website initially called Harvard Connection, later renamed ConnectU, that was a social network of its own aimed at helping college students connect with one another online. Cameron, Tyler, and Divya had come up with the Harvard Connection out of their frustration with how narrow their campus experience had become. Freshman year was one big melting pot. Hell, it was during freshman week that Divya met Cameron by chance in Harvard Yard and invited him to his dorm room to play electric guitar. From that day on they were fast friends. Over time, however, these serendipitous social collisions seemed to fade on campus as everyone got busier and busier. It was hard to extend your group of friends beyond your dorm, your sport, or your major. The twins and Divya lamented this and set out to fix it. The Harvard Connection—ConnectU—a virtual campus—would recast campus life online with none of the physical barriers and rigid, impermeable social bubbles that existed in the off-line world. Freshman year could start all over again, but this time everyone would be much the wiser—youth wouldn't be wasted on the young.

In the spring of 2003, the codebase was nearing completion; however, their original programmer, Sanjay Mavinkurve, was graduating and heading to Mountain View, California, to work for Google. This forced the twins and Divya to find someone else to help them complete the codebase. Victor Gao worked on it through the summer, but his upcoming senior thesis commitments were too demanding for him to continue once the school year started, so he introduced them to a sophomore computer science major who seemed to have an interest in entrepreneurial projects.

By this point, the Harvard Connection, ConnectU codebase had been built out to organize users according to the domain name of their email address. So, for instance, if a user registered with a Harvard.edu email address, he or she would be automatically organized and placed in the Harvard network. This would bring order to the chaos of lumping everyone into one large network. Like a Russian nesting doll, ConnectU would be a network of smaller networks, which in turn would be networks of smaller networks and so on, regressing all the way down to the individual user.

Divya and the twins had designed ConnectU this way based on their epiphany that a person's email address was not only a good way to authenticate their identity but also a good proxy for his or her real-life social network—your email address was your virtual passport. The Harvard registrar only issued @harvard.edu email addresses to Harvard students. Goldman Sachs only issued @goldmansachs.com email addresses to Goldman Sachs employees. Chances were, if you had one of these email addresses, you were in some shape or form a part of those networks in real life. This framework would give the ConnectU network an integrity that other social networks like Friendster and Myspace lacked. It would organize users in a way that allowed them to find one another more easily, and connect in a more meaningful way. It was in fact the same framework that would soon launch the sophomore computer science major they hired into worldwide fame and internet dominance.

In the twins' opinion, the only networks Mark Zuckerberg was familiar with were computer ones. From the twins' own social interactions with him, it was clear that Mark was a lot more comfortable talking with machines than with people. Seen this way, it actually made a lot more sense if the world's biggest social network was in fact the offspring of an unlikely marriage between the twins and Zuckerberg, as opposed to Zuckerberg's brainchild alone. The idea of the solitary genius who invents something brilliant all by himself is the stuff of movies, a Hollywood myth. In reality, the greatest companies in the world were started by dynamic duos; Jobs and Wozniak, Brin and Page, Gates and Allen, the list went on and on. And, Cameron believed, should have included Zuckerberg and Winklevoss. Or Winklevoss and Zuckerberg.

Sitting at that conference table, Cameron had to acknowledge to himself what Zuckerberg had done was truly impressive. Whatever he'd taken from them, he'd grown it into a true revolution. Somehow that diminutive, pale kid sporting a hairstyle that looked like the work of Supercuts had changed the world. And so he made sure to tell him so. He talked about how what Zuckerberg had created was incredible, the sort of innovation that happened maybe once in a generation.

When Cameron paused, Zuckerberg added his own congratulations. He seemed genuinely impressed that Cameron and Tyler had become national rowing champions while at Harvard and were now in a position to make the US Olympic rowing team and compete for gold at the Beijing Olympics later that summer. He oddly reminded Cameron of the timid kid they had first met in the dining hall back at Harvard. A socially awkward computer jock who was elated to step into their orbit, even for a moment.

Cameron did his best to chase dark thoughts away as he took in the compliments: he tried not to remember what it had felt like to first read about Zuckerberg's website in the *Harvard Crimson*. At one point, Zuckerberg's job description posted on thefacebook.com was "Founder, Master and Commander [and] Enemy of the State."—*How about thief,* Cameron thought.

But going down that mental path wouldn't do him any good.

None of that really mattered now.

Glancing back at his brother and the men sitting outside the glass fishbowl—all those lawyers furiously tending to their notepads—Cameron kept his emotions in check.

"Mark, let's bury the hatchet. Let's let bygones be bygones. We're not saying we created Facebook."

"At least we agree on something."

An attempt at humor? Cameron couldn't be sure but plugged along anyway.

"We're not saying we deserve a hundred percent, we're saying we deserve more than zero percent."

Zuckerberg nodded.

"Can you really say that you would be sitting where you are today if we hadn't approached you?"

"I'm sitting here today because you're suing me."

"You know what I mean."

"I know what you think you mean."

"We approached you with our idea. We gave you unfettered access to our entire codebase. I saw that lightbulb turn on inside your head."

"You weren't the first person in the world to have an idea for a social network and neither was I. Friendster and Myspace existed before Facebook, and last time I checked, Tom from Myspace isn't suing me."

Exhausting, exasperating. Cameron pressed his callused fingers against the boardroom table between them. He pictured an oar being pulled through the water, stroke after stroke after stroke.

"This could go on forever, and it's not doing either of us any good. I'm a person, you're a person. You've got a company to run, and we have an Olympic team to make."

"Again, something we agree on."

"Life is too short to keep going back and forth like this."

Zuckerberg paused, then pointed to the lawyers through the glass behind them.

"They might disagree."

"Let's find some common ground, shake hands, and move on with our lives to the great things we all have ahead of us."

Zuckerberg stared at him for a full beat. He appeared as though he was about to say something else but instead simply twitched, and again attempted the briefest of smiles.

Then, in a manner that could only be called robotic, Zuckerberg reached across the table and offered what appeared to be an attempt at a handshake.

Cameron felt the hair rise on the back of his neck. Was this really happening? The conversation hadn't seemed to be getting anywhere—and yet out of the corner of his eyes he could see Zuckerberg's lawyers behind the glass rising to their feet.

Cameron reached out and shook Mark Zuckerberg's hand.

And without another word, the Facebook CEO hopped off his chair and headed for the door. Cameron had no idea what was going through his inscrutable head. Maybe Cameron had somehow reached him, and he'd decided to finally give the Winklevoss twins what they believed they deserved.

Or maybe Zuckerberg would retreat to the conference room where he and the Facebook lawyers had been camping out during the mediation with another idea.

"How'd it go?" Zuckerberg's lawyer Neel Chatterjee would ask.

"Good."

"Good as in . . . ?"

"Good as in I'm going to fuck them in the ear. . . ."

2

DEAD IN THE WATER

———————————————————————————————————•

September 9, 2011.

Five A.M.

Rays of umber, ocher, and gold that only people who wake up ungodly early see slipped through the Technicolor trees and shone on the winding scimitar of glassy water.

"Pull, goddamn it! *Pull!*"

Every cell in Tyler's body surged as he put his weight against the oar. He groaned as his broad shoulders opened like the wings of a bird, his frame stretching into the stroke with near perfect precision. Directly in front of him, Cameron moved in parallel, two parts of a coordinated, well-oiled machine. From afar they were a duet of smooth, controlled motion, but up close, inside the carved-out, fiberglass shell slicing across the crystal water, it was all sinew and sweat and grime, knots of muscle rising and falling beneath skin bruised and blistered and torn.

The oars bit into the water, propelling the boat forward in sudden surges. The brothers weren't just synchronized in form, in the mechanical motion of their muscles against the carbon fiber oars; they were physically identical. Born to work as two halves of a whole, an advantage that had helped push them from a curiosity—identical twins who rowed crew together—to a world-class team of two that could compete at the Olympic level.

Except today, the machine wasn't perfect. Something in the invisible gears that connected them was perceptibly *off*.

Without even glancing, Tyler could sense the five other boats alongside them, gliding neck and neck like gulls in a formation toward the finish line just a few meters ahead. From the shore it would almost be imperceptible, but from his position, he could tell they were half a foot behind the closest of the other pairs . . . six, maybe seven inches behind the pair who had won gold in Athens in the men's eight. That pair was trading back and forth with a pair of University of Washington alums, who had won Nationals three years in a row.

The armada roared toward the finish line. Tyler's eyes narrowed as he pulled with every ounce of strength he had left, but he knew, deep down, it would not be enough. Seconds later, an air horn sounded as each boat's bow ball breached the finish line.

The race was over.

The twins had finished dead last.

The inches that separated the six boats may as well have been miles.

A crew race was a battle that was almost always decided long before those last few meters. Rowing wasn't so much something you won, but something you managed not to lose; it was a war of breaking points. Whoever could swallow the most pain usually crossed the finish line first. And going into the well again and again was the only way to raise your tolerance for pain.

The twins slumped over their oars, utterly exhausted. Lactic acid, a by-product of intense exertion, coursed through their muscles. Every cell in their bodies was on fire, their lungs were burning. The puddles left by their oars, the exhaust of the energy they had poured into moving their boat down the racecourse, dissipated quickly into the surface of Lake Carnegie in Princeton, New Jersey.

They knew they should start cooling down and make their way back to the boathouse, but at the moment, they didn't even have the energy to lift their oars, let alone their bodies, and start paddling back home.

"It's just one practice," Tyler said. "Next time we'll get it back."

Cameron didn't lift his head.

"If we bump the stroke rate up a few beats, we'd be on the right side of that finish."

He could tell from Cameron's tone that the morning's loss was weighing much heavier on him (and maybe both of them) than it should have. Certainly they had fared poorly in race pieces before. The ability to compartmentalize the bad practices, leaving them on the water, was an important skill in the sport of rowing—a skill that had allowed the twins to litigate against one of the biggest companies in the world while simultaneously training for the Olympics. At the level they were rowing, the slightest hiccup in rhythm or technique could translate to defeat, and against the sort of competitors who were training for the Olympic team, every stroke mattered. The pristine setting of Lake Carnegie, four miles of sheet-flat water in Princeton, New Jersey, that had served as the national training center for the Olympic rowing team for decades, was the rower's version of an even playing field, which meant every practice came down to a combination of muscle, technique, training, and willpower. Victory was a matter of the horse, not the chariot.

Lake Carnegie was literally made for rowing. Before 1902, the Princeton team had rowed on the nearby Delaware Canal, a busy waterway jammed with cargo boats and pleasure cruisers, but the rowers had grown tired of dodging freighters and Sunday sailors. In a fortuitous stroke of timing, a former coxswain and alumnus was commissioned to paint a portrait of the steel baron Andrew Carnegie, and used the time he was supposed to be concerned with brushes and oil paints to pitch the idea of creating a lake for the use of the Ivy League college's crew team. Tickled by the idea, the financier had donated over a hundred thousand dollars, a fortune at the time, for the construction project. With the help of a handful of rowing alumni, Carnegie had secretly bought up all the land in the area, then damned off the Millstone River, moving earth and water to create the perfect rowing playground.

It wasn't long before the Olympic national team had recognized the value of the private, protected strip of water next to one of the most storied educational centers in the world; soon the best rowers from all over the country were being invited to train on the lake that stretched past the century-old boathouse.

Tyler and Cameron had spent countless mornings gliding beneath the stone arch bridges that straddled the lake at its narrower points, reminiscent of the stone abutments that punctuated the snakelike Charles River in Cambridge, Massachusetts. There they had cut their rowing teeth under the legendary Harry Parker. By the year 2000, when the twins matriculated to Harvard, Parker had been coaching the Harvard men's team for nearly forty years. Harvard oarsmen coached by Harry Parker had competed at every Olympic Games since 1964. The twins would continue this tradition by representing the United States in the men's coxless pair at the 2008 Olympic Games in Beijing, China.

At Harvard, the twins had been undefeated national champions. Cameron, the southpaw twin, had rowed port and sat in 6-seat of the heavyweight varsity crew, while Tyler, the righty twin, had rowed starboard and sat behind him in 5-seat. In an eight-man boat, the twins' seats were located in the "engine room"—the term for the middle of the boat, where the biggest and most powerful rowers sat. The college newspaper sports writers referred to Cameron and Tyler as the "Twin Towers" and nicknamed their crew the "God Squad"—because some of them were devout Christians who believed in God, while the rest believed they *were* gods.

The God Squad was the most famous Harvard crew since the storied "Rude and Smooth" crew of the mid-1970s, which was chronicled in David Halberstam's book *The Amateurs*. This crew earned its nickname because of its smooth rowing and rude antics. Many of these larger-than-life oarsmen went on to compete in the Olympics and become wildly successful after their rowing careers. Dick Cashin, the crew's 6-seat, became a private equity tycoon in New York City and donated the funds to build the Harry Parker Boathouse, a community boathouse open to the public and located on the Charles River upstream from Newell and Weld, the Harvard men's and women's boathouses.

The twins' high school rowing coach had given them a copy of *The Amateurs* during their first season when they were freshman in high school back in 1997. It was no coincidence that they ended up applying to Harvard a few years later. When they arrived at Harvard as freshmen in 2000, they hoped to one day fill the shoes of this fabled crew.

And fill them they did. The God Squad never lost a collegiate race. In fact, they never really had a close race. They were so fast that they went to the 2004 World Cup in Lucerne, Switzerland, and placed sixth, beating the Olympic team eight-man boats from Britain and France. After Lucerne they competed at the Henley Royal Regatta, the pinnacle of the British rowing season, an event on par with tennis at Wimbledon and horse racing at Ascot. At Henley, the God Squad defeated Cambridge University on their way to the Grand Challenge Cup finals, then raced gallantly against the Dutch Olympic team, losing by two-thirds of a boat length. A month later, the same Dutch eight-man boat went on to win Olympic Silver in the 2004 Olympic Games in Athens, Greece. This put into perspective just how fast the God Squad really was and forever immortalized them in the pantheon of collegiate rowing history.

After the twins graduated from Harvard in 2004, they made their way from the shores of the Charles River to the banks of Lake Carnegie, which was home to the United States National Rowing team.

Perhaps even more so than the Charles River, Carnegie was a magnificent setting. Unfortunately, this didn't make the loss that morning any easier to swallow. To Tyler, it wasn't just a meaningless race in another practice; the moment felt *existential*.

The London Olympics were ten months away. They could train day and night, push their bodies to an extreme they'd reached before, maybe even get on form enough to medal. It would be an incredible honor, a true victory, and it wouldn't change anything. Not who they were, not how they were viewed by the world. They were a book cover that had already been judged, and judged again. First by a court system they believed had been stacked against them from the very beginning, and then by public opinion, a popular conception and social conscience fueled by a movie that had told only enough of the story to paint them as caricatures, weighed down by how they looked and what they were supposed to represent.

Only they knew the true story and what really had gone down after Cameron's one-on-one meeting in that glass cage. How, in the blink of an eye, they somehow lost by winning.

Sixty-five million dollars!" Calamari, their lawyer, was nearly shouting at them. He held the one-page, handwritten settlement offer in one hand and a slice of pizza in the other. "This is incredible. Don't you see that this is incredible?"

Teardrops of melted cheese were falling from the end of the pizza as he waved it toward the twins. The casual dress lawyer was clearly excited about the settlement offer.

Tyler stared at the settlement offer dangling from Calamari's hand. Sixty-five million dollars sounded great until you juxtaposed it with Zuckerberg's fifteen-billion-dollar (and growing) slice of the pie.

"There's something missing here," Tyler started, when Calamari cut him off, that damn slice of pizza swinging so hard it threatened to break free from the man's fingers and rocket toward the twins.

"Are you kidding? Guys, it's Christmas in February! He's agreed to settle. And it's a fortune!"

Tyler looked at Cameron, who looked just as exasperated as he felt. Sure, Zuckerberg had offered to settle. As stubborn as he was, he was probably *always* going to settle. He might wait until the eve of trial and settle on the courthouse steps, but he was going to settle. Even if deep down the Facebook CEO didn't think the Winklevosses' claims had merit, they had always assumed that he knew they had enough—the atmospherics alone were too much—and there were the emails. There were a lot of emails, and the twins thought they were damaging enough to tie him up in knots and turn him into a human pretzel on the stand. A public trial had to be too risky to consider. Fraud was not something to leave to twelve jurors to decide. Worse yet, Zuckerberg knew that the other side was pushing for forensic discovery—electronic imaging—of his computer's hard drive, the same computer he'd used while back at Harvard. As the twins would find out later, Zuckerberg had good reason not to want to let that happen.

Facebook was a monster, a true Silicon Valley unicorn that was gaining millions of users by the day. Zuckerberg had become internationally famous, the young CEO of a company that was rapidly becoming one of the biggest success stories in the world. Soon, no doubt, Facebook would seek an IPO, and the last thing Zuckerberg or Facebook's board of directors needed before offering its stock up to the public was the unearthing of potentially damning documents.

Zuckerberg had to know where such a process would lead. The hard drive from his college computer contained a trove of instant messages (IMs) that

Zuckerberg had written while he was a student at Harvard. Some of them were to Adam D'Angelo, a friend and talented computer programmer who had attended CalTech and was now Facebook's CTO. These messages had been discovered during a court-ordered forensic analysis of Zuckerberg's hard drive, but Zuckerberg's attorney Neel Chatterjee had so far refused to provide them to the other side. It was a classic example of Schrödinger's cat—these IMs didn't exist if he settled—they existed if he continued to dig in his heels. And even if they were produced to the other side under a protective order, there was no way of guaranteeing they wouldn't find their way onto the internet, a medium written in pen, not pencil.

Eventually, of course, Zuckerberg and his team's fears would be realized, but luckily for him not until years *after* he settled with the twins. A particularly intrepid journalist at *Business Insider*, Nicholas Carlson, got a hold of a number of those IMs, which were later confirmed by Zuckerberg himself when they were republished by *The New Yorker*.

In one message, Zuckerberg spoke with D'Angelo about the Harvard Connection/ConnectU website he was working on for Tyler, Cameron, and Divya. As reported by Carlson in the *Business Insider*, Zuckerberg remarked to D'Angelo:

> So you know how I'm making that dating site. I wonder how similar that is to the Facebook thing. Because they're probably going to be released around the same time. Unless I fuck the dating site people over and quit on them right before I told them I'd have it done.

From there, Zuckerberg's thoughts only got more damning:

> I also hate the fact that I'm doing it for other people haha. Like I hate working under other people. I feel like the right thing to do is finish the facebook and wait until the last day before I'm supposed to have their thing ready and then be like "look yours isn't as good as this so if you want to join mine you can otherwise I can help you with yours later. Or do you think that's too dick?

D'Angelo later asked Zuckerberg what path he was going to pursue in terms of dealing with the twins. Zuckerberg responded:

Yeah, I'm going to fuck them Probably in the year—*ear

In legal terms, the IMs may have been in a gray area—they were not a smoking gun—but they were still dangerous. With respect to Zuckerberg's moral character at that point in his life, they were less gray than black-and-white. When in another IM he told his friend *"You can be unethical and still be legal—that's the way I live my life,"* he was voicing a philosophy that would make future Facebook stockholders rightly nervous. No doubt, in the years since college, Zuckerberg had changed—how could someone go through what he went through and not change in all sorts of ways, most of which would remain unknown to most of the world? Perhaps, as he'd later tell *The New Yorker*, he truly regretted the sentiments in those IMs. But the IMs were only part of the story; there were also actions that went along with those words.

Before the Winklevoss twins had approached Zuckerberg, his bold venture at the time was facemash.com, a Harvard version of the website Hot or Not? This site scraped photos of Harvard female students from the online Harvard directory and, without their consent, displayed these photos, two at a time and side-by-side, on facemash.com so visitors to the website could rate who was the "hotter." In one IM exchange, he even considered whether or not he should allow these photos of Harvard females on facemash.com to be compared side-by-side to photos of *farm animals*. This resulted in charges that he breached the Harvard computer network security, violated copyrights, and violated individual students' privacy and almost got Zuckerberg expelled by the Harvard Administrative Board, but in the end he was put on probation.

After being left in the lurch by Zuckerberg and surprised by the launch of Facebook on February 4, 2004, the twins and their friend Divya scrambled to find programmers to finish ConnectU, which finally went live on May 21, 2004. Not content with merely sandbagging his classmates and the enormous first-mover advantage it afforded him, Zuckerberg appeared to be determined to add insult to injury. As reported in the *Business Insider,* Zuckerberg recounted to D'Angelo via IM:

We've exploited a flaw in their [the ConnectU] system and created another Cameron Winklevoss account. We copied his account like his profile and everything except I made his answers all like white supremacist.

The fake account Zuckerberg created to impersonate Cameron was not just an assault on Cameron's character. It is also a revealing insight into how Zuckerberg had seen—and judged—the pair from the moment he'd met them in the Kirkland dining hall.

CAMERON WINKLEVOSS

Hometown: "I'm fucking privileged. where do you think I'm from?"

High School: You're not even allowed to speak its name.

Ethnicity: Better than you.

Height: 7′4″

Body type: Athletic.

Hair Color: Aryan Blond

Eye Color: Sky Blue

Favorite Quote: "Homeless people are worth their weight in paper clips—I hate black people."

Languages: WASP-y

Clubs: My dad got me into the Porcelain

Interests: Squandering my father's money . . .

If he had indeed hacked into the website he was supposed to have helped build, in the twins' opinion, Zuckerberg had potentially violated federal law. And the fake profile was just the start. In later IMs, Zuckerberg bragged about further hacking ConnectU's code and deactivating user accounts, just for fun.

And there was more. In the spring of 2004, Cameron sent an email to the "tips" email inbox of the *Harvard Crimson* to notify them about Zuckerberg's duplicitous behavior. A reporter named Tim McGinn was assigned to the story and began to investigate. Tim met with Cameron, Tyler, and Divya to hear their story and to review emails sent between Cameron and Mark. He then reached out to Zuckerberg for his side of the story. As Cameron was later informed, Zuckerberg went into the *Harvard Crimson* offices and tried to convince McGinn and his editor, Elisabeth Theodore, not to run with the story. When McGinn and Theodore decided to continue the investigation, Zuckerberg apparently hacked into McGinn's Harvard email account to try and keep track of the investigation and whether or not a story would be written.

As Cameron learned, Zuckerberg was able to hack into McGinn's email by exploiting the data in the Facebook database and violating the trust and privacy of his own users. More specifically, apparently he looked in the Facebook database for McGinn's Facebook account password, in hopes that McGinn used the same password for his Facebook account as he did for his Harvard email account. He also reviewed Facebook logs for all of McGinn's failed login attempts, thinking that McGinn had at some point mistakenly entered his Harvard email account password into Facebook when trying to log in. Armed with McGinn's private information dug out of the bowels of Facebook, Zuckerberg was able to break into McGinn's email and read all of his emails, including the ones he'd had with Cameron, Tyler, and Divya. Mark also saw email communication between McGinn and Theodore, in which Theodore recounted their meeting with Zuckerberg at the *Harvard Crimson* offices: "[Zuckerberg] did seem very sleazy. And I thought that some of his answers to the questions were not very direct or open. I also thought that his reaction to the website was very very weird."

While Zuckerberg's hack of ConnectU was arguably outside the university's jurisdiction, Zuckerberg's hacking of another student's Harvard email account was not. In fact, it breached the Harvard computer network security and violated an individual student's privacy (not to mention Facebook's own

privacy policy today) and Zuckerberg was already in trouble for similar violations as a result of the facemash.com debacle earlier that school year.

At the time, Harvard was unaware of Zuckerberg's additional violations.
A few years later, however, Zuckerberg's second offense became public. Despite the fact that Zuckerberg was, and still is, a Harvard student to this day—
he left indefinitely on a voluntary leave of absence to run Facebook after his
sophomore year—Harvard has never taken any public action related to this
hacking.

In total, the existence of that hard drive from Zuckerberg's college computer must have meant he'd never risk a trial, and not just because his IMs
regarding the twins would blemish his sterling reputation as a boy wonder
CEO, but more importantly, because they would call into question the very
basis of the revolution he was creating:

> If you ever need info about anyone at Harvard just ask.
> I have over 4000 emails, pictures, addresses, SNS.
> People just submitted it. I don't know why. They "trust me."
> Dumb fucks.

Private IMs between any other college kids could perhaps be explained
away as the digital equivalent of "locker room" talk. But in the context of a
college dropout whose mission was to "connect the world" and by doing so
would hold the privacy of millions of people in the palm of his hand, they had
the potential to permanently derail him. And certainly, to the twins, the IMs
proved what they had been saying all along: Zuckerberg had knowingly
wronged them. The image of a likable nerd who wore a hoodie and talked about
building things that are "cool" was not the Mark Zuckerberg they knew. Those
stark words and actions revived an anger in them that made it difficult to let
things go, even when it seemed, to their legal team, that they had won.

"This is bullshit," Tyler said, still looking at the paper covered in chicken
scratch. "We deserve to be rightful owners."

Calamari was still grinning over his celebratory pizza. He had just finished
a call with John Quinn, the Quinn in Quinn Emanuel, presumably to brag
about the potential settlement result. They didn't get it; these lawyers didn't

get a lot of things. Calamari could barely operate the PowerPoint presentation that their lead lawyer had prepared for the opening mediation argument. The irony of a lawyer who could barely operate a computer being a principal in the fight over one of the largest technology companies in the world was almost too much. Calamari mispronounced Zuckerberg's name a handful of times, calling him "Zuckerberger," and now he was doing an end zone dance with John Quinn before the ink on the offer sheet had even been applied, much less dried.

To Tyler, this wasn't about money; this had never been about the money. As Zuckerberg had so delicately pointed out in the fake profile he'd made of Cameron, Tyler and Cameron had been born into money. But what Zuckerberg didn't know was that their father had built that privileged childhood for them through sweat, brains, and character. He'd propelled himself upward from a heritage of hardworking German immigrants, a family of coal miners, and he'd made it his mission to instill in the brothers a sense of right and wrong so strict that it could often be blinding. Winning didn't matter if it didn't happen the right way, for the right reasons.

Tyler simply couldn't just walk away, not even for $65 million in cash.

"We'll take it in stock," he said suddenly. Cameron nodded. Calamari's face blanched. His greasy slice of pizza made a wet thud on the table.

"Are you crazy, you want to invest in that putz?!" Calamari exclaimed, looking incredulous, then glaring at his associates to nod their heads in disapproval. Immediately, he and his team embarked on a campaign to convince Tyler and Cameron that they were being foolish, batshit crazy, that they should take the cash and run. It appeared that lawyers didn't like getting paid in stock, the price of which could go up or down. For them, cash was king. All of a sudden Quinn Emanuel's 20 percent contingency fee, a cool $13 million for six months of work, looked a lot more uncertain.

All five Quinn Emanuel lawyers in the room pleaded with the twins, but they would not be swayed. In the twins' minds, taking stock was a way of going back in time and righting a wrong. As founders, who hadn't been cut out by Zuckerberg, they would have had stock. Here, after all these years, was their chance to get back, at least in part, to where they should have started. A hundred lawyers in Hawaiian shirts and sandals wouldn't be able to convince them otherwise.

Ultimately, the twins and their lawyers reached a compromise; the twins would take 20 million in cash, and the rest of the $65 million settlement (approximately $45 million) in stock. For the foolish, batshit crazy twins, this proved to be one of the greatest investments of all time. Their lawyers saw none of that upside.

After Facebook's IPO, the twins' $45 million in shares soared. It appreciated fifteen times and went on to be worth more than $500 million. If Quinn Emanuel had taken its fee in stock, the firm would have earned upward of $300 million for six months of work.

Sitting in that boat, drifting in near silence down the center of that man-made lake in New Jersey, watching the other boats head for the boathouse, Tyler was palpably aware of the toll that the fight had taken on them. The more public their battle had become—culminating in the movie that had made them household names—the more they had come under assault, both legally and in the public eye.

Shortly after they'd settled, the twins learned that Facebook had received a valuation that had been conducted by an independent, third-party valuation firm. This valuation, which Facebook used to comply with IRS rules and the US tax code, valued the twins' Facebook shares at a quarter of the price they had used in reaching the settlement—was it another ear fucking?

It certainly sounded like securities fraud to the twins, the withholding a material, independent valuation during a settlement agreement that involved a securities transaction, but Facebook maintained that they had not withheld anything, or deceived anyone.

Armed with both the valuation and the leaked IMs that had come out via *Business Insider*, the twins had tried to get the case reopened—an effort that was shot down by a California federal judge, and the verdict was later upheld by California's Ninth Circuit Court of Appeals. Both courts rejected the twins' arguments. The result hadn't been surprising to the twins; they were fighting Facebook, now a hundred-billion-dollar monster, in its own backyard. The stakes had become enormous, and the twins and Zuckerberg weren't the only ones at the table. President Obama had visited Facebook's headquarters after being elected in 2008—a win credited in part to Zuckerberg's site, which his campaign had used to connect with millions of voters dubbed the "Facebook Generation" and earned him the title of the "Facebook President." And it didn't hurt that one of Obama's campaign gurus was Chris Hughes, one of Zuckerberg's roommates, who had run marketing and communications for Facebook prior to joining the Obama campaign. This all culminated with Zuckerberg adorning the cover of *Time* magazine in 2010 as Time Person of the Year—"For connecting more than half a billion people and mapping the social relations among them, for creating a new system of exchanging information and for changing how we live our lives." Battling a tech colossus in California did not exactly get you favorable odds. The twins felt that the decks were stacked against them, and it was all aces for Zuckerberg.

They believed Zuckerberg had wronged them in 2004 by stealing their idea for what became Facebook, had wronged them a second time by deep-sixing the damaging IMs during litigation, and had wronged them a third time on the settlement agreement's stock valuation—they had indeed lost, by winning.

Despite receiving stock potentially worth hundreds of millions of dollars, an enormous sum by any standard, the twins felt like losers—Zuckerberg had managed to fuck them in the ear over and over again. And not only that, going up against Zuckerberg in such a public fashion had taken its toll on their image in the court of public opinion. They were torn apart in the media and ridiculed by the blogosphere as spoiled and entitled brats with a nasty case of sour grapes. Whereas each time another example of Zuckerberg's Shakespearean betrayals became public, the media seemed to look the other way.

Even Larry Summers, the former president of Harvard, took a shot at them, publicly calling them "assholes" while onstage at *Fortune*'s Brainstorm Tech Conference, hosted at the Aspen Institute. The twins' offense? Wearing jackets and ties when they'd attended President Summers's office hours in April of 2004 to discuss Zuckerberg's duplicitous behavior—behavior they believed was a direct violation of the *Harvard Student Handbook,* specifically the part of the *Handbook* that stated: *All students will be honest and forthcoming in their dealings with members of the Harvard community.* In addition, there was an expectation of "intellectual honesty" and "respect for the dignity of others."

Summers's public attack seemed so unfair, so disgraceful for an educator, let alone a current Harvard professor, that the twins wrote an open letter to then Harvard president, Drew Faust, expressing their concerns regarding Summer's conduct:

. . . At [March] office hours, we [Cameron, Tyler, and Divya] waited in his [President Summers's] reception area but were told that we would have to return next month because there were more students in the queue than time allowed. In April of 2004, we returned to office hours and were successful in meeting with President Summers. His manner was not inconsistent with his reputation and present-day admissions of being tactfully challenged. It was not his failure to shake hands with the three of us upon entering his office (doing so would have required him to take his feet off his desk and stand up from his chair), nor his tenor that was most alarming, but rather his scorn for a genuine discourse on deeper ethical questions, Harvard's Honor Code, and its applicability or lack thereof.

We now further understand why our meeting was less than productive; someone who does not value ethics with respect to his own conduct, would likely have little interest in this subject as it related to the conduct of others. Perhaps there is a "variability of aptitude" for decency and professionalism among university faculty.

Regardless, it is deeply disturbing that a professor of this university openly admits to making character judgments of students based on their appearance. It goes without saying that every student should feel free to bring issues forward, dress how they see fit, or express themselves without fear of prejudice or public disparagement from a fellow member of the community, much less so from a faculty member.

Ironically, our choice of attire that day was made out of respect and deference to the office of the President. As the current President, we respectfully ask for you to address this unprecedented betrayal of the unique relationship between teacher and student. We look forward to your response.

Despite Summers openly admitting to making character judgments about the twins, his students, based on their appearance, the media snickered and President Faust sidestepped their letter and declined to admonish him.

Perhaps it was no surprise that Summers's tenure as president of Harvard was quick and judged by many to be a failure. In January 2005, at an academic conference on diversity in the sciences and engineering, Summers caused an uproar when he called into question the innate aptitude of women—as compared to men—in the sciences. Three months later, the Harvard faculty passed a "no confidence" vote in his leadership, and less than a year later, on February 21, 2006, Summers resigned. No one since the Civil War had served a shorter term as president of Harvard.

After Harvard, Summers landed a job in the Obama administration, though Obama would soon pass on him for chair of the Federal Reserve, instead choosing Janet Yellen—a woman. Ironically, despite not appreciating Facebook's enormous potential in its earliest days when it was sitting right in front of him in Harvard Yard—dismissing it during his meeting with the twins as an inconsequential student project—Summers managed to find his way onto a few boards of tech companies in Silicon Valley, including Square. This was thanks to some help from Sheryl Sandberg, who had joined Facebook as its chief operating officer in 2008. She was a former student of Summers—and later worked for him when he was secretary of the treasury under President Clinton. Perhaps Summers's friendship with Sandberg had inspired him to lean in against the twins and try to even the score. Who knew?

"No matter how many times we win this race," Cameron said, from the stern of the boat, "it isn't going to matter."

He was right. They had ended up with a vast amount of money; but to the world, they were losers. They weren't going to change anyone's minds by competing in another Olympics. Even standing on a podium wasn't going to get them any sense of justice. They would just be dumb jocks who rode off into the sunset.

"It's not personal," one of their lawyers had told them, "it's business." This was when they'd started questioning the number of Facebook shares Zuckerberg had given them. To Tyler, that was just as bad as Zuckerberg's IM: *you can be unethical and still be legal.*

It had never been just business between them and Zuckerberg, it had *always* been personal. And they had lost. If they wanted to change that narrative, they couldn't do it with an oar.

They needed to go back to the arena where it had all started and begin to fight all over again.

3

DAMAGED GOODS

Four weeks later, Cameron's thoughts were moving at a thousand rpms as he stepped out of the taxi that had taken them straight to the heart of Silicon Valley from SFO. It was "a thirty-minute ride" that never took less than an hour but was at least pretty pleasant if you took the 280 instead of the crapshoot that was the 101. Then again, Cameron had barely noticed the scenery as he sat next to his brother in the back of the cab, going through the heavy folder of company pitch decks they'd brought with them from New York City.

After hanging up their oars and officially retiring from U.S. Olympic Crew, they'd dived headlong back into the high-tech entrepreneurial scene that was centered in Silicon Valley. But unlike Zuckerberg years earlier, they hadn't moved west. Manhattan had been the easy choice for their home base of operations. Not only was it a more familiar setting for them (they'd grown up just outside of the city), but their father had made his fortune building a consulting firm that counted many New York–based Fortune 500 companies as clients. To them, no matter where ideas came from or where companies built their fancy campuses, New York City was the financial engine of the world.

Since everything they did these days seemed to make the news, when they leased office space in the Flatiron District—the center of New York's burgeoning tech scene, colloquially referred to as Silicon Alley—for their venture firm Winklevoss Capital, the deal was splashed all over the real estate section of the *New York Post*. With five thousand square feet of prime commercial real estate a few blocks from the Empire State Building, the twins were definitely looking to make their mark.

Becoming angel investors—the name given to investors who provided early money to entrepreneurs with no strings attached—seemed like the quickest way for the twins to get their feet back into the startup game and give them the best chance of changing the ending of the story that had been forced upon them.

Their colleague and co-plaintiff in their battle with Zuckerberg, Divya Narendra, had already begun his next chapter. After receiving his law degree and MBA from Northeastern University, he'd gone all in on his new venture SumZero—a social network for investment professionals. Instead of sharing photos, users shared investment ideas. SumZero didn't have billions of users—its users had billions of dollars. The company was quickly becoming the world's largest network of its kind, and the twins were excited about investing in it. They wondered: How many more Divyas were out there hiding in plain sight? As an entrepreneur, you had one, maybe two, but usually not more than three chances to catch lightning in a bottle; as a venture capitalist, however, you could chase lightning as long as you had cash to invest.

Cameron and Tyler had grown up around financiers. They understood that money was the lifeblood of any company. Without, first, Eduardo Saverin's $1,000, then PayPal billionaire Peter Theil's $500,000—Facebook would never have grown to be more than a few kids in a dorm room poking each other. It was money that had allowed Zuckerberg to feed Facebook's voracious appetite for engineers and servers, resulting in world domination.

Cameron's feet hit the sidewalk in front of a multistory, wood-framed building that squatted between a small, paved parking lot and a semienclosed beer garden. Just ahead, a brightly colored sign took up one corner of the building, emblazoned with a picture of a palm tree that declared their destination in bulbous, orange letters: *Oasis*, and beneath that, maybe slightly less dramatically, *Burgers & Pizza*.

Although as tech VCs he and his brother weren't going to be coming up with the next Facebook themselves, maybe they would find it. Maybe they would even find it here; Cameron could feel a familiar thrill rising inside of him. They were opening a new chapter in their lives, and he could think of no better starting place than Oasis, the hamburger joint right smack in the center of Menlo Park.

He knew that Tyler, sliding out of the taxi behind him, carrying the folder stuffed with business plans of companies looking for venture cash, would have told him to take a breath, temper his optimism. Although most people thought the Winklevoss brothers were completely identical, in fact, they were mirror image twins, the result of a fertilized egg splitting later than usual in the process, around the ninth day, and then developing as two separate embryos. Where fraternal twins were dizygotic—developing from two different eggs fertilized by two different sperm—identical twins were monozygotic—a single egg fertilized by a single sperm separating into two viable embryos. Mirror twins began in a similar fashion—a single egg fertilized by a single sperm— but remained intact for much longer; normal identical twins split between the second and fifth day. In fact, it could be said that mirror twins were two individuals who had remained a single entity as long as was biologically possible— beyond the tenth day, a monozygote that split would most likely end up a conjoined twin, attached forever.

Like identical twins, mirror twins had the same physical features, but they were perfectly opposed, as if they were staring at each other in a mirror. If one twin had a birthmark on his left thigh, the other would have the exact same mark—on the right thigh.

Like two pages in a book torn at the seams: Tyler was right-handed and more left-brained, analytical, measured, and strategy minded. Cameron was left-handed and more right-brained, tactical, operational minded, goofy, artistic, sometimes more empathetic, and sometimes more optimistic.

Often Tyler focused on the stairs, not the steps, and Cameron was more willing to let his imagination roam past the data they had at hand. Neither of them would have described themselves as poets; but where Tyler focused on the black and white, Cameron tried to let himself see more color. They were both creative in their own intuitive way, and together they knew their minds had the potential to create something great.

Now that they were centimillionaires because of their Facebook settlement, few people would understand why they were bothering themselves with trying to start again. The twins never needed to work a day in their lives; yet they chose to work every day of their lives. Why? What made them tick?

The twins were driven by *curiosity* and the desire to explore. They thrived off of challenges and got a thrill out of testing their limits. To them, that was exciting, electric. Complacency was just not in their blood.

At their core, Tyler and Cameron were *builders*. As kids they built LEGOs, as teenagers they built webpages, in college they built a social network. They weren't on this Earth to exist. They were here to create.

Despite what Zuckerberg thought of them—his misreading of them as simple, dumb jocks—at the age of thirteen, they had taught themselves how to code in HTML and had made money over the summer by building webpages for small businesses. At the time, their high school had not offered computer science, so instead they had loaded up on every advanced placement course possible. They had planned to study computer science at Harvard, but the time commitment of the rowing team had made it impossible, so they'd majored in economics instead. Zuckerberg had gotten lucky—in another world, the twins never would have had to approach him for coding help. In any event, Tyler and Cameron didn't believe they were on the earth to exist; they were here to create, to build.

And there was no greater place to build the future than Silicon Valley. It was more than a place filled with entrepreneurs toting pitch decks: Silicon Valley was a living, breathing organism.

It had a circulatory system, represented by the big name VCs in their low-rise California ranch-style office parks, lined up along nearby Sand Hill Road: first settled by Kleiner Perkins in 1972, the proverbial "Sand Hill" was now home to the likes of Sequoia, Accel, Founders Fund, and Andreessen Horowitz, to name a few. Sand Hill pumped cash into the veins of fetal startups, helping them uncurl their tiny fingers and toes.

It had its vital organs, the megacompanies that had taken that lifeblood and grown viable and strong: Google, up in Mountain View, with its massive campus called the Googleplex, sixty buildings teeming with engineers and software developers and AI experts; Apple in Cupertino, on its way to becoming the most valuable company in the world, in the midst of constructing a new headquarters built to look like a massive spaceship that had crashed down to Earth; Facebook, of course, which had first opened its doors just blocks away from where Cameron was standing, and was now located at 1 Hacker Way, spitting out newly minted millionaires every week, inflating the local housing market to the top of the national charts and making the zip codes around Sand Hill the wealthiest in the United States; Intel and Tesla, and Twitter, on and on and on, each as important to the system as a liver or a kidney or a lung. Then there were the vestigial organs, like the famous HP and Apple garages, tourist spots where visitors could imagine themselves as young genius engineers on the cusp of changing the world.

The organism even had its brain: Stanford University, in Palo Alto, every year emitting dozens of brilliant young computer scientists and engineers like neurotransmitters moving along the neurons of the Valley's nervous system, teaming up to leap across the various synapses in their paths.

And, of course, it had its digestive system, the eateries, breakfast spots, and coffee shops where the Valley's royalty congregated, sharing innovations over scrambled eggs, chai lattes, and french fries.

The Oasis might not have been quite as famous as nearby Buck's of Woodside, where PayPal was first demoed and a VC was once pitched something called Yahoo!, but the burger joint and beer garden around the corner from the original Facebook offices had played host to entrepreneurs, investors, and wide-eyed, bushy-tailed Valley dreamers for decades. Opened right after prohibition ended, the casual spot had become one of Cameron and Tyler's favorite places for meetings. In fact, it had originally been a favorite of their parents when they had lived in Palo Alto before moving their young family to the East Coast after their father sold his first company to Johnson & Higgins, one of the largest insurance brokerage firms in the world. Though at first it had seemed strange taking meetings in the shadow of Zuckerberg's nearby kingdom, they were well aware that everyone in the Valley identified them with the boy CEO anyway, so there was no reason to try and hide from the association. And besides, Oasis served damn good burgers.

Tyler reached the door first, but let Cameron go ahead of him as they entered the restaurant. Cameron was struck by the smell of french fries, grilled meat, and spilled beer; even though it was past two in the afternoon, the place was packed. Everyone looked impossibly young; Cameron guessed that at least half were still students at Stanford, the rest barely past graduation. He couldn't help wondering how many of the tables he passed were taken up by Facebook employees. As he and Tyler moved through the crowd, people stared and pointed, and then pretended to look away. Nothing really unusual about that; people tended to stare and point wherever they went. Even before the movie, before Harvard, the twins always seemed to catch people's attention. But here was different.

Cameron was starting to feel a slight tug at the optimism that had filled him outside; it wasn't just Tyler's usual caution mirrored inside his mind, but something he'd allowed himself to push away during the long flight from New York and the ride from the airport. Although they'd set up Winklevoss Capital a few months earlier, and had put the word out that they were looking to invest in young tech startups, they had yet to close a deal. Although the folder in Tyler's hands was large, many of the companies inside had already moved from possible investments to missed opportunities.

Because it was just the two of them, they were able to move quickly when they liked something, setting up calls and flying cross-country at almost a moment's notice when something peaked their interest. But over and over again, mostly because of what appeared to be bad timing, they'd found themselves about to write a check, when they'd get a message from the entrepreneur that unfortunately, the funding round had just closed, or was "oversubscribed." Not entirely unusual in a world where multimillion-dollar rounds could come together in an afternoon, and there was so much money chasing the next big thing—but it was still incredibly frustrating. They had money ready to wire, but they could never seem to connect.

Cameron had refused to let his optimism fade. But as he followed Tyler through the crowd, passing tables weighed down by pitchers of beer, mountains of fries, charred burgers and dogs, he wondered if the stares he was getting were indicative of something new.

He pushed the nagging thought back down, as over his brother's shoulder he caught sight of a squirrely-looking kid. Freckled, skinny, a dagger-like face under a shock of red hair, wearing a bright green T-shirt, the kid was sitting alone at one of the round tables, a half empty pitcher of beer in front of him, three filled glasses at the ready.

Tyler reached the table first, and the kid was half out of his chair a second later, nervous and sweaty and shaking their hands like he was trying to pump water out of a well. He was smiling, but even before Cameron had taken a seat next to Tyler, Cameron could tell that something was wrong. He slid into one of the stained, wooden booths that was covered in the carved signatures of past patrons. Even here, entrepreneurs were striving for immortality, the chance to be remembered forever. Being memorialized on a few inches of wood in the heart of Silicon Valley was better than nothing.

Just a half day earlier, on a phone call before they'd boarded the plane for California, this same kid—his name was Jake, he was two years out of Stanford, and his company had just pivoted from mobile advertising into the realm of VR—had been exploding with enthusiasm. Jake was going to be the first real investment of Winklevoss Capital, to the tune of one million dollars.

But less than a minute into the conversation, before Cameron could even taste the beer in front of him, Jake had launched into an apologetic monologue, a sort of verbal yoga tied in so many knots it was hard to understand what the hell he was apologizing for. Until the end, the last few sentences, which were abundantly clear.

"See, guys, I'd really like to take your money. I thought we were going to take your money. I talked to the board about increasing the size of our round, and um," he sputtered, "they say we're already oversubscribed, and, like, we have to turn you down."

Cameron could see the splotches of red growing on his brother's cheeks. He decided to speak first, before his brother let his anger get ahead of them. Maybe there was a way to salvage this situation.

"But when we spoke earlier, you weren't oversubscribed. That was about eight hours ago. You wanted us on your cap table, we were already talking about giving you free office space when you expanded to New York. Are you saying something changed while we were in the air?"

The kid ran a hand through his hair.

"Yeah, um, yeah, we got like, oversubscribed."

"Just be straight with us. We flew out here to sign the stock purchase agreement. Out of respect, just tell us what the hell is going on."

The kid paused, then glanced around them at the nearby tables. People were looking, but nobody seemed close enough to hear. Then he leaned forward, lowering his voice.

"Between you and me, I want to take your money. I just can't. We're oversubscribed. Guys—I gotta go."

He started to rise from his chair. Tyler looked like he was about to reach out and grab the kid, but Cameron kept his voice calm.

"Come on, Jake, give us a minute. Oversubscribed? Our dollars are as green as anyone else's. Please, tell us what's going on. We deserve that much."

"It was a hell of a long flight out here," Tyler added, evenly.

The kid looked around again, then lowered himself back in his seat. He took a drink, rather gulp, from his beer mug, then shrugged.

"You see where we are, right? Facebook's first headquarters, you could throw a hard drive from here and hit it. Their new headquarters is about five miles down that road."

Cameron felt himself sinking farther into the booth. He had an idea of where this was heading.

"You see those kids at the table next to us?" Jake continued. "I know them, they were in my class at Stanford. They're working on a startup to make digital postcards. What do you think their endgame is? Those guys by the arcade machines in the corner? They're working on video compression. Their exit strategy? They've all only got six weeks of runway left before their startup runs off a cliff."

Entrepreneurship was a game with historically bad odds: most startups failed gloriously, which meant that every entrepreneur had to go into the business with a plan B, C, D, etc. Silicon Valley was a town made up of engineers who thought in frameworks, decision trees, and game theory. Everyone needed money—but just as important, optionality. When things went bad—and for 99 percent of the people in that restaurant, they would—a face-saving acquisition, or "acquihire," by a larger company like Facebook would ensure future funding for their next startup idea.

"It might be optics," he continued, "but optics are important in a land of dreamers. They might want your cash, they might not have anything against you, in fact they might *really* like you, but they don't want to cut off all the branches on their tree either. They have other investors too, as well as board members—you think the suits would let them take a penny from the two guys Zuckerberg hates more than anyone else in the world? Your dollars might be green, but they're marked."

"This is crazy," Cameron said. "You make it sound like we couldn't even give our money away if we tried."

The kid didn't even crack a smile.

"Not here. Right now, we might as well be sitting in Facebook's cafeteria. Every restaurant in the Valley—all anyone is talking about is Facebook. Who are they going to buy next? How many millionaires are they going to mint tomorrow? When are they going to IPO? You should be glad this place will even serve you a hamburger."

Silicon Valley may have been an oasis for tech entrepreneurs, but for the twins, even sitting literally in the Oasis, it might well have been a desert.

The kid took another chug of his beer. Maybe he hadn't meant it to come out so harshly, but his words hit Cameron like a ton of bricks. All his optimism—gone. The fire of redemption that had been growing inside since they'd left Lake Carnegie and the Olympics behind, the exuberance that they could start over and change the narrative and still be part of the entrepreneurial world—stripped away, smothered, left for dead.

This too somehow, Zuckerberg had taken from them.

Jake stood up again, his eyes apologizing, and then reached into his pocket and took a crumpled twenty-dollar bill out of his pocket. And Cameron and his brother watched as this kid, who probably didn't have enough money in his bank account to buy a proper wallet, dropped the crumpled bill on the table in front of them.

Because in this place, this young entrepreneur chasing his dreams was afraid to be seen even letting the Winklevoss twins pay for his beer.

4

IN THE BEGINNING
THERE WAS FOAM

J uly 2012.

Three A.M.

Ibiza.

A Mediterranean party island ninety miles off the coast of Spain.

When you're six foot five, 220 pounds, and there are two of you, you can't just curl up and disappear . . .

Tyler used his oversize shoulders to push his way through the middle of the crowded dance floor, lowering his head every few minutes to dodge half-naked acrobats swinging from rubber cords attached to the ceiling. The music was so loud Tyler could feel it in his bones, a throb of electronica that seemed to come right out of the ground. Along with the acrobats, giant neon cherries bobbed down over the mob of beautiful people that surrounded him, and every few minutes he had to shield his eyes against pinwheels of brightly colored laser lights playing across the undulating revelers. The crowd was young and lithe and perfect, but Tyler wasn't looking to meet anyone tonight and did his best to resist eye contact when he wasn't shielding himself from the retina-burning lasers. At the moment, he wanted nothing more than to be anonymous. As if that was even *possible*; at thirty, Tyler hadn't been anonymous for as long as he could remember.

To be fair, this hedonistic dance floor lodged along the coast of one of the most beautiful party islands in the world wasn't the sort of place you went to *blend in*; Pacha nightclub, a former "finca"—Spanish ranch—turned disco—had grown into the premier stomping ground of the European elite, as well as a decadent playground for Hollywood royalty. Young people from all over the world descended on the club, famous for its multiple dance floors, multimillion-dollar sound system, VIP rooms, and celebrity DJs. In fact, that very night's party was called "F@@k Me I'm Famous"; on the way to his and his brother's VIP table, he'd passed Naomi Campbell, Kate Moss, and Paris Hilton. And even Hilton had stared at him as he'd passed by. He'd done his best to pretend not to notice.

"Well, this is sufficiently insane."

Tyler stumbled through the lasers and the crowd toward the voice, and nearly ran right into himself. Cameron grinned, giving him a facetious thumbs-up. Cameron was wearing a ridiculous lei made of flowers and bright red cherries around his neck. There was also a fleck of foam on his cheek, the remains of another party going on next door—where, Tyler assumed, the dance floor was periodically flooded with white bubbles. Wonderful, he thought. I guess it could be worse. I could be miserable *and* covered in foam.

Now that he was with Cameron, Tyler felt even more conspicuous. When you were an identical twin, of course you got noticed; in high school, it had mostly been affable curiosity. Not only did they look the same, but they had also been rowers who had been training together since freshman year of high school, and pretty much everyone in Greenwich, Connecticut, knew who they were. At Harvard, it was much the same: they were big names on campus, varsity athletes who were also prominent members of the Porcellian Club, the most elite of the final clubs, a place that had groomed presidents and kings.

"What the hell are we doing here?" Tyler finally responded as his brother surveyed the crowd around them.

"Having fun, I think."

A glow-in-the-dark beach ball bounced perilously close to Cameron's head, then continued on its haphazard journey across the top of the crowd.

"Do I look like I'm having fun?"

"You could try the foam party," Cameron said. "But don't swallow any. I'm pretty sure that's how you get Legionnaires' disease."

Tyler pointed toward a bar at the far end of the hall, draped in women wearing bandoliers of glowing test-tube shots. Although alcohol seemed almost redundant in a place built on such sensory overload, Tyler figured it was the appropriate way to end their evening.

It felt strange, being on vacation. He and his brother hadn't taken a real vacation in their entire lives. Usually free time had meant training; after they'd graduated from college, they had trained six hours per day, six days per week, fifty weeks per year—taking only two weeks off to recharge after each season.

But that was over now; they weren't competitive rowers anymore. Likewise, apparently, they weren't investors either. After their meeting at the Oasis, after Jake had gone off script and told them the real reason why they hadn't been able to make any headway in their quest to become Silicon Valley venture capitalists, they had retreated back to New York. It seemed completely absurd; nobody would take their money, because everyone's endgame was the same. Facebook had become this huge vacuum, sucking up every entrepreneurial dream in the area, and that meant Tyler and Cameron were poison. They had a last name that nobody dared put on their cap tables, no matter how badly they needed cash. Winklevoss money was the kiss of death.

Tyler had thought they'd hit rock bottom before, but they had dived even lower. Back in New York, taking stock of the situation, they had tried to figure out what to do next.

Simply taking their settlement, no matter how much it was, and walking away wasn't a possibility. Maybe Eduardo Saverin, the other Facebook castaway who had successfully settled for much more than Tyler and Cameron—reportedly billions—could take the money and run, but they couldn't; it just wasn't in their DNA. Saverin was rumored to be living a high life in Singapore—but Tyler and his brother felt they were cut from a different cloth.

Even so, they had to face reality. They refused to give up, but maybe they needed to recharge, reset, and find a new path forward. It had been Cameron's idea to try to do that in Ibiza. Tyler had regretted the decision from the moment they'd gotten on the plane. They were single, young, and enjoyed a good party, but they had always had a plan. It was hard for Tyler to adjust to living in the moment.

He was halfway to the bar, staring at those evil-looking test-tubes, already thinking about hopping the earliest flight back to the States, when a stranger caught his arm, stopping him with a grin and a heavy Brooklyn accent.

"Hey, are you the Winklevii?"

It was a nickname that had been given to them in high school and later immortalized by the movie, one that had stuck in the press.

"We're actually on our way out," Tyler tried, but the guy wasn't going to give up so easily. Tyler looked at him: young, maybe early thirties, muscled and compact, pectorals pressing out against an open, short-sleeve shirt. He had wild eyes and a tightly shaved head, but his smile seemed friendly enough.

"I need to talk to you about something. Something important. Revolutionary, really."

Cameron had caught up and seemed more amused by the man's aggressive approach than Tyler was. Cameron was like that, sometimes. Tyler didn't suffer fools, but sometimes Cameron felt the fools were the most fun to hang out with. In Ibiza, that was probably truer than in most places.

"We've already taken part in a revolution. It didn't work out that great for us. But thanks anyway."

"Facebook?" the guy said. "Facebook isn't the revolution anymore. Facebook is the Establishment."

Sounded crazy, but Tyler knew it was true. What had started as a revolutionary idea, putting people's real-life social networks online, upending the way people met one another and communicated and shared, had once been new, almost indie and rebellious. But in the few years that had passed, even in the months since that meeting at the Oasis, Facebook had come to dominate the internet, sucking the oxygen out of the Valley, corralling massive amounts of data and monetizing information in such a way that for many, Facebook often seemed more Big Brother than Robin Hood.

"So what do you have in mind?" Tyler asked. "Another social network?"

The man smiled again, then did something truly confusing. He reached into his pocket and pulled out a U.S. dollar bill.

"Hell yeah, man. The oldest social network on Earth."

5

THE BASEMENT

Charlie Shrem descended the stairs two steps at a time, keeping one hand against the unadorned cinder block wall to his right as he navigated the narrow slabs of wood that went down, down, down into his basement command center, his operational headquarters, his corporate throne room—his bat cave.

Every nerve in his fragile, five-foot-five-inch frame was firing in tune to the freakishly loud EDM music piping through the plastic buds jammed into his ears. He'd been on an electronic music kick for two weeks straight, ever since a friend from college who'd taken a job at one of the investment outfits on Wall Street had taken him out to celebrate the impending launch of Charlie's new company. His friend had got him past the line at one of the clubs over the bridge in Manhattan, a place in Chelsea, Charlie believed, though the night had gotten hazy enough by 2:00 a.m. that the details were mangled. What he did remember was that the place was *banging, going off*, filled with city girls in tube tops and shorts and ridiculously high heels. Then again, Charlie was pretty sure he didn't actually talk to any of those girls; it was New York, after all, so most of them were a head taller than he was anyway, and besides, his buddy had a corner table stacked with vodka, and not the cheap stuff Charlie was used to. Working for an investment bank had its advantages, including a corporate credit card. And for the moment, plastic was still king.

Charlie hit the bottom step and launched himself over a pair of cardboard boxes overflowing with broken keyboards and injured wireless routers. Similar boxes were stacked up to his right and left, leftovers from one of his previous businesses, the one he'd actually started in high school. While the other kids at the nearby Yeshiva of Flatbush had been busy studying their Torah—and yes, a few of those boxes contained menorahs, prayer books, yarmulkes—Charlie had been sneaking away from the urban campus during his free periods to make house calls all over the neighborhood, picking up broken electronic equipment, computers, routers, DVD players, even cassette recorders and bringing them back to his bat cave to fix. He'd called the company Epiphany Design and Production, mainly because he liked the word "epiphany." Eventually, in the year between high school and college, his first business had morphed into a second one, a daily deal online retail site called Daily Checkout.

Hence the boxes, stacked all over this basement in Brooklyn, scaling the cinder block walls in pyramids so high they would have made Ramses himself proud. Beyond the boxes, there were also corrugated metal shelves lined with the tools of his old trade: soldering irons, circuit boards, pliers, wire cutters, and extension cords running in every direction, like living creatures.

Charlie picked his way through the chaos, finally approaching his desk—a small wooden affair, barely big enough for his equipment: a computer, three monitors standing side-by-side, and his keyboard. He didn't care that it was the same desk he had been using since junior high, then in high school at the Yeshiva, and then while he'd made his way back and forth to Brooklyn College for his undergraduate degree.

He knew that one day this place was going to be on the cover of magazines, maybe even carefully chopped up and carted off to the Smithsonian, to sit right next to George Washington's teeth and Steve Jobs's first Mac.

Okay, he wasn't sure that Jobs's Mac was in the Smithsonian, but it damn well should have been, and Charlie's desk was going to end up right next to it. In California, they launched revolutions from garages: Jobs and Woz building personal computers next to a rack of pocket wrenches in a garage in Los

Altos, Bill Hewitt and Dave Packard making oscillators behind barn-like doors in a garage in Palo Alto, and Larry Page and Sergey Brin inventing Google as Stanford grad students in Susan Wojcicki's garage in Menlo Park. But in Brooklyn, there weren't many garages; there were basements. And in the part of Brooklyn where Charlie grew up, those basements were crowded, dark, dingy, and usually smelled a little bit like brisket.

From above, the urban neighborhood of narrow streets spanning Avenue I to Avenue V, Nostrand to West Sixth Street, might have looked like any other section of the borough, but in reality, Charlie's home sat right in the center of the seventy-five-thousand-member-strong Syrian Orthodox Jewish community—an ethnic, religious, and cultural island unto itself. Although the "SYs," as they called themselves, did not dress in the black garb of other Orthodox Jewish sects—a choice made in part to allow them to flourish entrepreneurially and financially in the wider community of other Jews and gentiles—the Syrian Orthodox Jews were held together by strict traditions and codes dating back generations. Most draconian of these codes—a law known as the "Edict" set down by a group of Syrian rabbis in 1935—made sure the sect would remain insular: "No male or female member of our community has the right to intermarry with non-Jews; this law covers conversion, which we consider to be fictitious and valueless." But despite these mostly successful blinkered rabbinical strategies, which had kept the Syrian Jewish community intact— all of Charlie's cousins, uncles and aunts, grandparents, and family going back generations lived within a quarter mile of his house—and are firmly lodged in the Brooklyn landscape—the SYs had simultaneously managed to extend themselves outward in financial empires, in areas including real estate, retail, electronics, and, more often now, technology.

Charlie reached the desk and dropped into his chair, yanking out the earbuds and resting his phone next to the keyboard. Then he powered up his computer, heading right for his Skype account.

It took less than a minute for his business partner to appear in the lower left corner, shrunk down so that Charlie could talk while simultaneously monitoring the computer code that was now free-flowing like a river down the center of his screen.

"You're late," his business partner croaked through the internal micro-phone of Charlie's computer. "Is this becoming a habit for you?"

Charlie kept his attention on the streaming code. He'd grown used to Gareth Nelson's conversational style: his usual lack of social conventions, his abrupt vocal patterns, and of course his heavy Welsh accent, which made half of what he said pretty much incomprehensible. This largely explained why most of their interactions had occurred over email or instant messenger. In fact, Charlie believed that in total, he'd probably spent less than seventeen minutes actually conversing by voice with his business partner in all the time he had known him. Over text, Gareth's accent didn't get in the way, and his Asperger's was a great benefit. The guy didn't waste any words; everything was business, which made him the perfect sort of partner and counterbal-ance to Charlie.

"This looks really good," Charlie said, jabbing at the code. "The transac-tions will go smoothly, and the servers look like they can handle a pretty large customer base. It's a great starting place."

He was nearly bouncing in his chair as he made the calculations in his head. Although he was small, he was constantly in motion, which made him often appear to take up much more space than his frame would have suggested. He also had a tendency to talk really fast; actually, everything about him moved fast. His feet, his mouth, his brain. Even his hair follicles; his cheeks and chin were in a constant state of overgrowth and, even at noon, were covered by what could only be described as something several hours beyond a five o'clock shadow.

The speed at which his mind moved was probably the reason why during college he'd shifted his focus from tinkering with electronics to computer cod-ing, eventually teaching himself to become a world-class hacker. Working on hardware was slow, meticulous; but when you were coding or hacking, you traveled at the speed of electricity. Of course, hacking had its risks, and you could get yourself into a lot of trouble if you weren't careful.

When Charlie had hacked into the University of Ghana, he'd actually sent them a private briefing afterward, detailing their security vulnerabilities. It was a courtesy in security circles known as "responsible disclosure." He'd also worked his way into an airport's security system in Germany and grown a following on hacking forums under the avatar "Yankee," a nod to his New York roots.

Charlie wasn't a black hat, a malicious hacker in search of monetary gain; he was something closer to a white hat, drawn in by the puzzle and the challenge of finding security flaws. It was hacking that had actually led him to the new business he was about to launch with Gareth, his autistic Welsh partner, a man he'd never met in person. A business that Charlie considered a truly revolutionary moment in tech history.

His newest adventure had begun almost three years earlier, while he was still a college senior. After an uneventful day spent commenting on a variety of hacking forums, Charlie had suddenly seen a strange little email that had been sent out to a cryptography mailing list. The email had come from someone named Satoshi Nakamoto. In the email, Satoshi had stated that he'd developed a brand-new virtual currency, which he'd then described, in detail, in an attached "white paper."

At first, Charlie had thought the email was a joke. Stupid bullshit, he'd told himself. Who was this Satoshi Nakamoto, anyway? Charlie looked around hacker forums for more background on this Satoshi character but could find nothing. Stranger still, Satoshi, who claimed to be a Japanese man in his midthirties, wrote his emails in perfect, idiomatic English. Once Charlie read the white paper, however, it was obvious that Satoshi was a polymath, a multidisciplinary genius who was an expert in cryptography, math, computer science, peer-to-peer networking, economics, and more. How could this person be that smart and accomplished and yet be a ghost to the internet, a complete phantom? How could Charlie not at least even know of him?

Or her.

Or them.

Charlie would have gone on with his life, ignored the email and the white paper, if it wasn't for the enthusiasm of a new, online friend he'd met while perusing crypto boards and forums under the handle "Yankee": the autistic Welshman Gareth Nelson. From their many exchanges, Charlie knew that Gareth wasn't the type to get excited easily; hell, before Satoshi and his white paper, Charlie hadn't thought the guy was even physically capable of getting excited.

But Gareth was certainly excited now: this was something big, important. *Revolutionary.*

Over the ensuing years, Charlie had realized that the Welshman was right.

He moved his face closer to the screen as the last few lines of code flowed upward. He was totally in the zone, barely listening as Gareth offered comments from his Skype corner, as the EDM music still leaked, in tinny twists, out of the earbuds on the desk by Charlie's cell phone, as footsteps reverberated through the basement ceiling above him: his mom, working on that brisket.

Almost three years after reading Satoshi's white paper, Charlie was certain: it was going to change everything.

And Charlie was going to ride that change right out of his mother's basement and into history.

6

FINDING LOVE IN A HOPELESS PLACE

Money as a social network. Well, it's certainly an interesting take." Tyler propped himself up on one elbow, his body stretched out awkwardly on an eggshell-white daybed. He was decked out in a crisp, white linen shirt, a brightly colored Vilebrequin swimsuit, and a woven straw fedora. Cameron was on a similar lounger to his left, shirtless, wearing equally brightly colored swim trunks. A canopy offered some respite from the sun beating down, while a Mediterranean breeze cooled the scalding beach as it rolled off the sea.

"You know a thing or two about social networks—and I know money. Money connects people. It's a form of communication. And it's about time that it truly went virtual."

The muscled guy they'd met at Pacha the night before—David Azar, an entrepreneur from Brooklyn who, it turned out, owned a chain of check-cashing businesses—was directly across from them, white shirt open past his sternum, squatting cross-legged on a piece of furniture that was somewhere between a beanbag chair and an ottoman. Right beside the daybed a wooden, sun-streaked table supported a metropolis of rosé bottles, glass champagne flutes, and trays piled high with fruit.

The three were smack dead in the middle of Blue Marlin Ibiza, arguably the most famous VIP beach club in the world, a mixed-use slice of paradise that was part high-end restaurant and part European day party. A daybed ran four hundred euros, just for the afternoon, and the ones behind the DJ went for three times that. Nobody hit the Blue Marlin on a Sunday afternoon to talk shop; this place was all about sun, top-shelf alcohol, pulsing music, and some of the best people watching and celebrity spotting in the Eastern Hemisphere.

The crowd, whether splayed out on matching daybeds, dining at the attached five-star restaurant, or undulating in sarongs and espadrilles on the roped-off dance floor, was mostly European and almost universally stunning. The women glimmered in tiny bikinis, tops sometimes missing. The men, shirtless or draped in white muslin or linen, were almost universally chiseled and tan. There were models everywhere, some with names and faces the mono-zygotes recognized. One girl, two beds over, had been featured in the inflight magazine tucked into the airplane seat magazine holders of the Iberia Airlines flight they'd hopped from Barcelona to the Spanish island. Maybe she'd arrived at Blue Marlin by way of the long, fashion runway–like wooden path that led directly from the center of the beach club to the sea, where the tenders and Jet Skis shuttled guests back and forth between the hotspot and the mega-yachts parked farther out in the protected bay. Each new arrival warranted whispers, but nobody reached for cell phones. At Blue Marlin, even the most famous people in the world were simply part of the scenery.

"If whatever you're selling can help our deposit make its way over the Atlantic to our villa's landlord, I'm all ears," Tyler said, shifting his attention from the wooden runway, where a pair of Italian Instagram stars strolled by on impossibly high Louboutins.

In fact, the trouble with their villa deposit, which still hadn't arrived two days into their trip, underscored just how money worked—or didn't work—in the year 2012. You could connect with anyone anywhere in the world using Facebook; you could speak with anyone anywhere in the world using Skype; you could communicate with anyone anywhere in the world using email, and all for next to no cost. But good luck if you wanted to send them money—it wasn't much easier to send money around the world in 2012 than it was when Pacha first opened its doors in 1973. You still had to use the Balkanized, legacy banking system, which was built before the internet even existed, littered with middlemen and rent-seekers all along the way. And only if the central authorities of this network allowed it to happen, would your money move at a snail's pace from point A to point B. The truth was, even in 2012, if you wanted to get money from New York to Ibiza, the fastest and surest way was to hop a plane from JFK with a bag full of cash.

Instead the twins had arrived in Ibiza well before the deposit on their rented villa; thankfully, their landlord—an always smiling Italian transplant, who apparently would also be acting as their chauffeur, picking them up at the airport in a tricked-out SUV, smartphones in each hand, and a Bluetooth headset lodged in his hair—understood how the international economy worked, and just as often didn't.

"What I'm talking about," Azar said, sipping his wine, "is something completely new. Truly digital money, decentralized, that's exchanged like email. There's no middlemen. There's no authority. Money that moves at the speed of electricity, over the internet. A system that does for money what Napster did for music."

Tyler glanced back toward the DJ booth, where a young Frenchman was bouncing up and down behind his computer system. The crowd on the dance floor moved with him, lithe bodies so close together it was hard to see where one limb ended and another began.

Less than a decade ago, a DJ would have had to lug hundreds of vinyl records in heavy metal cases around with him to every gig. Today the same DJ could carry his entire set on a USB stick or thumb drive in his pocket. If music could transcend the physical world into the digital world then why couldn't money?

In fact, in many ways, money had already gone digital. When you deposited money—say, a hundred dollars—into a bank, that bank didn't store your money in some vault somewhere, waiting for you to retrieve it. That hundred dollars immediately went digital; in fact, banks hardly stored any actual money at all. By federal banking law, banks in the United States only needed to keep

10 percent of the money deposited in actual, liquid reserve. Which meant if you deposited a hundred dollars into a bank, you only actually had ten real dollars on hold in some vault. The other ninety dollars? Digital, ones and zeros on some computer hard drive, or off in the cloud.

The only physical money anyone really had was what was in his or her wallet. The rest had already been turned into data, by the middlemen, who took a fee.

The new form of money Azar was talking about skipped that step. It was already data.

Digital, decentralized, no authority. It was a sales pitch—and there was no doubt, Azar came on like a compelling salesman. In fact, the way he talked, his enthusiasm—he seemed like he'd just walked off the lot of an auto dealership back in Brooklyn. But, like the French DJ, he was hitting all the right notes.

Money, as it currently stood, ran through a system controlled by powerful arbiters: Visa, MasterCard, Western Union, governments near and far. It was a system that could seem arbitrary, with obvious flaws—lag times, unexplained fees, bureaucratic logjams.

Tyler and his brother had just fled to Ibiza after facing off against other types of arbitrary systems; first the California federal courts, where the central authority was a judge named James Ware, who had decreed that the twins couldn't reopen their case against Facebook. (Never mind that for years, Ware had lied about having a younger brother who was the victim of a racially charged murder during the civil rights movement—an untruth that had led to a judicial reprimand.) And then their case had shifted to the Ninth Circuit Court of Appeals, where the central authority was Chief Justice Alex Kozinski, who had upheld Judge Ware's ruling. (Never mind that for years, Kozinski had been accused of sexually harassing his female clerks—pulling up pornographic photos in front of them on his computer while they were in his chambers, and previously, allegedly, maintaining a server that contained sexually explicit images, including one of naked women on all fours painted to look like cows.)

Digital, decentralized, no arbitrary authority.

Whether it was the setting, or the timing—Tyler felt drawn to the Brooklyn salesman's pitch.

"Like Napster," Azar continued, "it's peer-to-peer. And it's all out in the open. There's no inside baseball, no insider information, it's all open-source and democratic. And this new system of money is based on math, not humans."

Azar refilled his glass from one of the bottles on the table between them.

"It's called Bitcoin," he finished, holding his glass up to the sun. "It's a form of cryptocurrency."

"Cryptocurrency," Cameron repeated, from his daybed. "It sounds criminal. Is it legal?"

"I don't think the word applies. That's part of Bitcoin's brilliance. It functions without government approval. There's no headquarters to raid, and it can't be stopped without stopping the internet itself."

Stopping the internet? Tyler could tell the muscled salesman was spinning dialogue at them; he didn't seem to be technically minded, or really have a deep knowledge of what he was selling, beyond his pitch. But, as he'd said, he knew money. Not Wall Street money—but the sort of money you come across from owning a chain of check-cashing businesses extending outward from the Syrian Orthodox Jewish section of Brooklyn. He understood the emotional connection of currency, the desperation of those trying to cash checks who were unable to access the traditional banking system. He knew all about velocity and liquidity.

"Traditional cash is all about trust," Azar continued. "You have to have faith in the machinery of the system, and you have to trust the middlemen. With Bitcoin, you don't have to trust a-n-y-b-o-d-y. Because, like I said, it's all based on math."

Tyler glanced at his brother, who seemed as focused on the salesman and his pitch as he was. This was something that neither of them had ever heard of before; not in any of the startup pitch decks they'd been sent, not during any of those Silicon Valley meetings. Not at the Oasis, not anywhere on Sand Hill Road. It wasn't clear, yet, how this . . . cryptocurrency worked—or how math was involved. But a system that didn't rely on trust, that didn't involve an authority—it seemed too good to be true.

"Tyler! Over here! I thought I saw you guys at Pacha last night! Come join us for a drink!"

Tyler looked past Azar, in the direction of where the voice was coming from, and recognized a group of Americans waving at him from four daybeds down. He recognized at least two of them from back in New York: a tall art fiend named Josh, or Jason, who Tyler believed ran a gallery downtown, dedicated to early 1970s graffiti masters, and a brunette in what looked to be a macramé bikini. The rest of the group looked similarly hip, none of them over the age of twenty-five, none of them strangers to this party island, halfway around the world from where they'd grown up. Wealthy millennials with big bank accounts and a dozen credit cards between them; no doubt, this crew of "influencers" had helped build Facebook with their bare thumbs. Tyler was certain that none of these people had ever heard of Bitcoin. The money they knew best was the type that was passed down from generation to generation, worn around their fingers, necks, maybe even toes.

"Be there in a minute," Tyler called back. Cameron was already getting up from his chair, hooking one of the bottles of rosé with his fingers. Come to think of it, maybe his brother had dated the brunette back in the city? Tyler couldn't be sure, but he was willing to bet that Cameron wasn't going to try to explain cryptocurrency before he poured the pretty girl a drink.

"Friends of yours?" Azar asked. "I get it, you're on vacation. But I'd love to pick this up when you're back in New York."

Tyler pointed to the bottle in his brother's hand.

"How many Bitcoin would that go for?"

"Right now? Not sure. Would have to check my phone. This morning, Bitcoin was trading at around seven dollars a coin. At the moment, it's really volatile, because not enough people know about it yet, and you can't really buy anything with it. It's Facebook before anyone was really on Facebook."

No doubt Azar was hoping for an emotional connection by throwing in the Facebook reference. And, of course, it had worked. Tyler's mind did go back to Facebook, to the situation that had led them to Ibiza in the first place. Tyler and his brother had put their trust in the judicial system, only to be beaten. A system that had relied on trust in humans had failed them.

There was something about a system that relied on math, not trust, that was intensely appealing. Math was built on rules that no one, not even Zuckerberg, could break.

Although Tyler knew they were just scraping the surface—he didn't yet know anything about this new currency beyond Azar's pitch, nothing about what this technology really was, or what it might represent—he had come to a conclusion: *either this Bitcoin was complete bullshit, or it was a really big deal.* A new currency, seemingly invented out of thin air. Bitcoin was either worth nothing, or it was going to one day be insanely valuable.

"Say we do want to get involved," Tyler said as he rose from the daybed, feeling the pulse from the DJ booth through bare feet. "What do we do? Buy up some of this Bitcoin?"

"You could. Or you could go one step deeper. As I said, at the moment, Bitcoin is volatile. Buying Bitcoin is like gambling. And everyone knows, you don't get really rich by being a gambler.

"You get really rich," he continued, with a Brooklyn car salesman's grin, "by being the house."

7
AUGUST 30, 2012

T he analogy is a little off—they aren't so much the house as they are the bank. Or to keep with the casino metaphor, the cashier's cage."

"Pay attention to the road, Cam. We're not going to be the house or the bank if we're wrapped around a telephone pole."

Cameron lightened up on the gas pedal as he pulled their SUV into the slow lane. Tyler was right, Cameron had gotten so caught up in the conference call they'd been on since they'd pulled onto the Long Island Expressway forty minutes back, he'd been driving by reflex alone. Which meant driving fast, grand prix style, in synch with the thoughts racing furiously behind his eyes.

"I don't think there are any telephone polls on the LIE anymore," he said, his thumb hovering over the mute button on the car's speaker console.

Who the hell needed telephone poles anymore? The smartphone on the seat next to him was Bluetoothed to the car's onboard computer, which was invisibly linked to the closest cell tower. Once he pressed the button, undoing the mute function, which he'd made liberal use of whenever he and his brother needed time to digest whatever the disembodied voices on the other end of the line threw at them, every word he uttered would be turned into digital information, 1s and 0s bound together in electronic packets that would piggyback through those cell towers into larger data streams beamed straight up into space, bouncing from satellites to another cell tower miles away, ricocheting again to another smartphone sitting in an office on West Twenty-Third Street in downtown Manhattan, the destination of their morning drive.

Sure, it would probably have been more prudent to wait until they had reached the address, just a block from where they were still constructing their own offices, the headquarters of Winklevoss Capital, before starting the meeting, but Cameron had been on fire since they'd reconnected with Azar after they'd returned from Ibiza.

Azar had followed up with Cameron on Twitter. Cameron couldn't remember if he had given the guy his email at the Blue Marlin; day drinking on a beach filled with models was distracting, and it didn't help when you had a villa with a private pool. Thankfully, Azar had been resourceful. His first direct message on Twitter had made Cameron laugh out loud:

> **Not sure if I was discussing virtual currency with you or your brother in Ibiza at blue marlin. Let's meet up in NY . . .**

But it had quickly led to more formal conversations and finally an in-person meeting. Although Cameron and Tyler both owned loft apartments in the city, they'd been spending most of the summer at their parents' house in the Hamptons. Although the area had a reputation for being a bit of a party destination itself—not on par with Ibiza, but speckled with exclusive restaurants and summer outposts of notable Manhattan nightclubs—the twins had spent most of their time relaxing on the beach and devouring anything they could find on the subject of Bitcoin. At the time, not a single book on Bitcoin had been published; but by diving deep enough into the internet, the twins were able to find blog posts, Reddit posts, and articles written by early adopters, known as "Bitcoiners,"—as well as Satoshi Nakamoto's original Bitcoin white paper. They'd also reached out by email to former professors at Harvard and Oxford, where they'd earned MBA degrees, to get more academic opinions on this new virtual currency.

None of the professors they'd contacted—some of them among the most elite economics professors in the world—had ever heard of Bitcoin. When the twins had explained what they had learned so far, some responded in a knee-jerk way, labeling Bitcoin as some sort of scam or Ponzi scheme. But when Cameron pressed them on those notions, the professors couldn't exactly say what the scam was, or *why* it was a Ponzi scheme.

Settling their SUV just below the speed limit, Cameron hit the button to unmute the conversation.

"The party is just getting started," blurted a voice, words coming so fast they threatened to run right into each other. "The market cap of the entire Bitcoin economy is only about a hundred and forty million. That's million, with an *m*. Gold is seven trillion. And gold is pretty much useless. Walk into a store and try to buy a pack of gum with gold."

Sometimes it was hard to distinguish voices on a conference call, and doubly hard in a car going sixty miles per hour, with the blare of a siren from an emergency vehicle racing past on the other side of the median separating the lanes going in the opposite direction. But Cameron had no trouble identifying the voice of Charlie Shrem, the youngest member of the team they were on their way to meet. Not just because Charlie had a habit of talking fast, but also because his energy level was completely on par with his age. The kid was barely twenty-two, and from what Cameron had gathered from the emails they'd traded, still lived in his mother's basement, in an Orthodox Jewish–Syrian neighborhood deep in Brooklyn. But he was obviously some sort of prodigy. The company he had cofounded, the business that Azar was trying to assemble a group to invest in, was already making waves in the Bitcoin community.

But before they could decide on whether or not they wanted to invest in a Bitcoin company, Cameron and his brother were going to have to better understand what Bitcoin was in the first place. What made it good, viable money? What made it better than gold? What was money anyway?

"Okay, but gold has some intrinsic value," Tyler said. "It's used in jewelry, and in transistors."

"But what about cash?" Charlie responded. "It hasn't been backed by gold since the 1970s, and the government can print as much of it as it wants. Talk about a Ponzi scheme. No intrinsic value there."

"Cash has intrinsic value," Cameron responded. "If you were freezing on top of a mountain and all you had was cash, you could burn it to keep warm."

"Ah, the *Cliffhanger* maneuver," Azar's voice came through the car's speakers. "Love that movie."

"The intrinsic value of gold is overrated," emerged another voice over the line.

Cameron glanced at Tyler. The new voice belonged to Erik Voorhees, Charlie's head of marketing. Voorhees was a few years older than Charlie, soft spoken but obviously incredibly sharp, and well versed in Bitcoin. Born in Colorado, Voorhees was a staunch libertarian who had traveled all over the world before migrating to New Hampshire as part of the Free State Project, a political movement whose goal was to create a community based on libertarian ideals. Voorhees, who had recently joined Charlie in New York to help run his fledgling company, was an acolyte of the Austrian School of economics; a philosopher and an activist, he had gravitated toward Bitcoin in part because it was a form of money that did not rely on any state actors and was truly borderless.

"I suppose gold wouldn't do you any good if you were shipwrecked on an island," Cameron said in response to Voorhees. "You'd take food or water over a bar of gold, or a mountain of cash, any day of the week."

"In that situation," Voorhees said, "Bitcoin would have very similar intrinsic value to gold or cash. But the difference is, if you were trapped on that island with your cash and your gold and your Bitcoin, if you had your smartphone with you, you could still *use* your Bitcoin. Because Bitcoin has *technological* intrinsic value. Bitcoin has the potential to change the game entirely."

Thirty minutes earlier, right before Cameron and Tyler had gotten onto the expressway, they'd stopped at a gas station attached to a 7-Eleven. Five miles later, Tyler had realized he'd left his wallet on top of the gas pump, and they'd had to turn around. Like the delayed deposit on their villa in Ibiza, it was another stark reminder of the inherent flaws of physical money and again begged the question: What was money, anyway?

Was it pieces of green paper, emblazoned with the pictures of dead presidents and luminaries, sitting in a leather wallet on top of a gas pump off the Long Island Expressway?

Was it some shiny rock pulled out of the earth, molded into bars or coins, then buried again in some vault somewhere?

Or could it be something else, something that kept pace with a rapidly changing world?

Something new, a form of technology as practical and current as the technology behind the smartphone on the seat next to Cameron, spouting out voices that already had been to space and back?

Welcome to the 'Bakery,' gentlemen. If these walls could talk—well, they'd sound pretty fucked-up. There's been a lot of secondhand smoke in this room. This is where most of our best thinking takes place. Lighting up neurons today, for a better tomorrow."

Charlie Shrem certainly fit the mental image Cameron and Tyler had been building of the boy wonder CEO; miniature in stature, slightly bearded, curly hair plastered back against his small head by a coating of gel so thick it shimmered. But homunculus that he was—he was small enough to be the twins' coxswain—his presence dominated the offices of his eight-month-old startup. He'd been playing the circus master since he'd met them outside the front door on Twenty-Third Street, arms wide at his sides, a grin plastered ear-to-ear. Then he'd grabbed each of them in an awkward, hipster hug. Cameron couldn't help but feel the nervous energy bleeding out of the kid—Charlie was actually trembling—or smell the hint of marijuana seeping from his plaid short-sleeve shirt and distressed khaki pants.

The energy level had only risen from there; Charlie was practically bouncing out of his Converse Chuck Taylors by the time he'd led them through the main office, a mess of desks and computers and spaghetti twists of wires leading everywhere at once. Charlie had paused beneath a flat screen attached to an exposed brick wall, showing the current price of Bitcoin—seven dollars and forty-three cents—and made some comment about how he'd gotten in so early, something about the ass crack of Bitcoin's dawn. Then he'd led them straight to the room he called the Bakery, for reasons that were obvious even before he'd made the joke about the talking walls.

Small, cramped, with windows overlooking Twenty-Third Street, the paraphernalia of what appeared to be Charlie's favorite hobby was visible in every corner, and on every shelf. Cameron counted at least three bongs, as well as ceramic ashtrays littered between computer equipment and open file folders. He also saw a device that he didn't recognize; eventually, Charlie would explain that it was called the Magic Box, a prototype of what would later be known as a vaporizer. It was—basically a wooden box with a glass tube coming out of it, within which you could burn marijuana and turn it into vapor— an invention that he was certain would catch on within a year or two, or maybe three. Cameron followed his brother and Charlie into the room, where they were joined by Voorhees—skinny, average height, with thinning reddish hair and angular features—and their old friend from Ibiza, Azar. Seeing a pair of canisters that looked like miniature oil drums, Cameron peered closer, only then noticing that the drums were covered in letters from the Cyrillic alphabet. They formed words that he couldn't read, but he knew enough from taking Linguistics 180 back at Harvard to tell that it was Russian.

"Oh yeah, these are really cool," Charlie said, grabbing one of the cans and offering it to Cameron. "Vodka in miniature oil barrels. Look at what it says on the other side."

"'NEFT, we support the Bitcoin economy,'" Cameron read out loud.

"You can scan the bar code on the back, and buy it with bitcoin. It's freaking brilliant."

To Cameron, this introduction to Charlie and his company was part funny, part WTF. The kid was something else; he was clearly smart and scrappy but a total whirling dervish. One thing was for sure, this wasn't some startup in the Valley looking to court seed funding from the cabal of pleated khaki pants on Sand Hill Road—this was different.

"Bitcoin, the digital currency, with a lowercase *b*," Voorhees said, pointing to the miniature barrel. "As Charlie implied, you send bitcoin with a lowercase *b* from your digital wallet to the address embedded in the QR code printed on the side of the can. It's that simple, but that's only a tiny part of the story."

Cameron knew from his research that the first documented time bitcoin had ever been used to purchase a product happened on May 22, 2010. On that historic day, a Florida programmer named Laszlo Hanyecz was hungry for pizza and had decided he would use some of the bitcoin he'd accrued to quash his hunger; there was only one problem: no merchants accepted bitcoin as payment at that time. Undeterred, Hanyecz had posted a message titled "Pizza for bitcoins?" on Bitcointalk forum, the main congregating point online for Bitcoiners at the time:

> I'll pay 10,000 bitcoins for a couple of pizzas. like maybe 2 large ones so I have some left over for the next day. I like having left over pizza to nibble on later. You can make the pizza yourself and bring it to my house or order it for me from a delivery place, but what I'm aiming for is getting food delivered in exchange for bitcoins where I don't have to order or prepare it myself, kind of like ordering a "breakfast platter" at a hotel or something, they just bring you something to eat and you're happy!

An eighteen-year-old named Jeremy Sturdivant, who went by the online handle "jercos," decided to take Hanyecz up on his offer. They'd finalized the details over Internet Relay Chat (IRC), and then Hanyecz had proceeded to pay jercos 10,000 bitcoin, worth roughly thirty dollars at the time, for two Papa John pizzas. Hanyecz confirmed the transaction on the Bitcointalk forum:

> I just want to report that I successfully traded 10,000 bitcoins for pizza. Thanks jercos!

That day would be forever known and commemorated as Bitcoin Pizza Day. Since then, numerous Twitter accounts, such as @bitcoin_pizza, had been set up by Bitcoiners to track the current USD value of the two pizzas that Hanyecz had purchased. As of this writing, those two pizzas were worth approximately $36.6 million.

"But Bitcoin with a capital *B* is where the real action happens," Charlie said.

Talking seemed to be the only thing that kept the kid's energy at bay. In one of their earlier conversations, Azar had told the twins a bit about Charlie's background as a socially awkward kid from the Syrian Jewish community in Brooklyn, which was Azar's home, as well. The two of them had grown up within blocks of one another, and Charlie had always had a flair for computers. Now the kid who'd never been picked for dodgeball was suddenly the center of attention, and he was taking full advantage of the moment. He was not an entirely unfamiliar type of character to the Winklevoss brothers.

"'Bitcoin' with a capital *B* refers to the *protocol,* in other words, the entire Bitcoin Network," Voorhees said, his more measured tone a stark contrast to Charlie's verbal sprint. "While 'bitcoin' with a lowercase *b* refers to the digital asset that travels along the Bitcoin Network."

"Same word, two different meanings, case dependent," Charlie inserted.

"Protocols are the digital plumbing of the internet," Voorhees continued. "They are the pipes that your emails travel through, the tunnels that carry your voice to a listener halfway around the world. The Bitcoin protocol allows bitcoin to move from point A to point B, and allows you to buy this miniature oil can of NEFT Vodka."

"The analogy seems dangerous," Cameron said. "If 'Bitcoin' with a capital *B* is plumbing, what makes 'bitcoin' lowercase *b* anything more than digital sewage?"

Voorhees smiled. "The same properties that make gold valuable, make bitcoin valuable."

Cameron and his brother may have just started climbing the learning curve of this new digital currency, but as economics majors at Harvard, they were well versed in the world of old-fashioned money. At Harvard, they'd studied under Martin Feldstein, former chief economic adviser to President Ronald Reagan and the real-life inspiration for the character of Mr. Burns on *The Simpsons.* The brothers were steeped in the works of Adam Smith, Milton Friedman, and John Maynard Keynes. They understood that gold was worth what people were willing to pay for it—a case of classic supply and demand. They also understood what drove that demand—what made gold "good" money. They'd even once presented on the topic with a PowerPoint slide show.

Initially, gold's chemical properties made it the natural choice; going down the elements on the periodic table and analyzing their properties, you could first cross off the gases—right from the get-go. Since whatever substance was going to be used as money couldn't be highly reactive—otherwise it might explode in your hands—and it couldn't be corrosive—otherwise it would rust—that disqualified another thirty-eight elements. And since money had to be rare, but not too rare—a metal like copper was too abundant, while a metal like osmium was too rare, being found only in meteorites—that ruled out another twenty-six elements.

Which left only rhodium, palladium, platinum, silver, and gold—five of the eight noble metals. Rhodium and palladium wouldn't be discovered until the 1880s, well after money had been in use for thousands of years; and platinum's melting point would have been too high for preindustrial furnaces. By process of elimination you were left with silver and gold. Silver tarnished easily and had a much greater industrial application—too useful to make good money—leaving gold just useful enough.

"Gold is valuable because of its naturally occurring properties: it's scarce, durable, portable, divisible, fungible, hard to counterfeit, and easy to authenticate," Tyler said.

"Exactly," Voorhees responded, "and bitcoin has all of those properties too—"

"But Bitcoin is better at being gold than gold," Charlie interrupted.

"Correct. Bitcoin is not just scarce like gold, but its supply is also fixed," Voorhees said. "By the design laid out in Satoshi Nakamoto's original white paper, there will never be more than twenty-one million bitcoins created, whereas the supply of gold increases as new deposits are discovered. And bitcoin is more divisible than gold. Each bitcoin can be subdivided into one hundred million pieces, and you can own as little as .00000001 bitcoin. And you can send it to someone instantly, like sending an email. Try emailing someone a bar of gold."

"It's gold with wings, gold 2.0!" Charlie said.

"All enforced by computer source code," Tyler added.

Charlie seemed to be so enjoying how things were going, he decided to reward himself by grabbing for a large bong.

"Code is law," Voorhees said. "Mathematical law."

"What prevents me from spending the same bitcoin twice?" Cameron asked. "If I can email the same picture to more than one person, what prevents me from doing that with my bitcoin?"

"The double-spend problem," said Voorhees.

This was a unique issue for digital currency that did not exist in the physical world of cash. If you gave someone a twenty-dollar bill, you couldn't turn around and then give another person the same twenty-dollar bill. In the digital world, however, where 1s and 0s were plentiful, there were no such physical limitations. Historically, this problem had always been solved by invoking some central authority—the Federal Reserve, Visa, MasterCard—that monitored transactions and made sure the same digital dollars weren't spent twice by the same person. But Bitcoin had no authority, no referee. It was also known as the "Byzantine Generals' problem" in computer science circles and was a problem that was thought to be unsolvable: How do you create consensus in a completely decentralized system?

"That's where this gets really cool." Charlie looked up from his bong. "Satoshi solved the problem in his white paper, which started it all. The answer is what makes the whole Bitcoin system work: *mining.*"

Cameron had only had a few hours of internet reading to wrap his thoughts around the "mining" system, which acted as the engine to the Bitcoin ecosystem. He still didn't have a complete grasp of how it all worked—but what he already knew fascinated him.

Voorhees explained how Bitcoin "miners"—people with computers running specialized software—validate and audit bitcoin transactions by solving complex math problems generated by the transactions themselves. Once a miner has solved the math puzzle for a new "block" of transactions, the block is added to the Bitcoin "blockchain," the global ledger of every bitcoin transaction since the beginning of time. For their effort, miners were rewarded by the network with newly minted bitcoins. This is known as the "block reward." And the more computing power a miner brings to the network, the greater the chance they have of solving the math problems and winning the block reward. The more you mine, the more likely you are to win.

"Or to put it in more technical terms," Voorhees said. "The greater a miner's *hashrate,* the greater their chances."

Cameron had learned the term years ago, in a computer science class. Hashrate, or hashes per second, was a measurement of computational power: how many computations (i.e., hashes) a computer could perform in one second. Miners were furiously competing with one another to solve the mathematical problems that validated the current block of bitcoin transactions; the more these miners invested in their hardware—buying faster chips, housing their computers in coolant data centers, and so forth—the better their chances of winning a reward of newly created bitcoins. And then the race began all over again.

In trying to understand the process, Cameron had actually come up with his own simple analogy, which he decided to share with the room:

"Remember *Charlie and the Chocolate Factory*?" he started.

Charlie burped out a cloud of smoke as he took a pause midway through his hit.

"Never watch that movie high. The Oompa Loompas will scare the shit out of you."

"The little boy in the movie," Cameron continued, trying not to be distracted by the real-life Charlie getting higher and higher next to him, "is looking for a golden ticket inside candy bars. Charlie is a like a miner. And the golden ticket, which will grant him a tour of Willy Wonka's factory, is like the block reward. Now suppose that by searching for this golden ticket, Charlie is also simultaneously validating purchases of candy bars and recording them in the factory's business ledger—the Willy Wonka blockchain. And suppose there are many Charlies all around the world doing the same thing, searching for that golden ticket. As they open Wonka bars, they are auditing the Wonka blockchain and checking one another's work. Willy Wonka's contest has miraculously incentivized children around the world to work together to validate and record transactions of Wonka bars, helping Willy keep track of who paid for what, thereby protecting his profits and ensuring that his factory stays in business and can continue to make chocolate for everyone."

Voorhees smiled.

"That's very good. And it perfectly illustrates the magic of Bitcoin. Instead of middlemen, or gatekeepers, you have an open competition of miners, individually incentivized to validate transactions. No bank or government sits in judgment of transactions, or takes a piece of each slice of pie. Middlemen are replaced with math, or in the case of your example, an army of Charlie Buckets."

"And the Willy Wonka of Bitcoin," Tyler said. "Who set all of this in motion: Satoshi Nakamoto."

Cameron knew from his reading that the creator of Bitcoin was no less mysterious than the fictional character from his analogy. On October 31, 2008,

Satoshi Nakamoto had published his famous white paper titled: *Bitcoin: A Peer-to-Peer Electronic Cash System,* to the Cryptography Mailing List—"*a low-noise moderated mailing list devoted to cryptographic technology and its political impact,*" laying out "a new electronic cash system that's fully peer-to-peer, with no trusted third party." The white paper detailed bitcoin's specific features:

- *Double-spending is prevented with a peer-to-peer network.*
- *No mint or other trusted parties.*
- *Participants can be anonymous.*
- *New coins are made from Hashcash-style proof-of-work.*
- *The proof-of-work for new coin generation also powers the network to prevent double-spending.*

And then three months later, the first version of the Bitcoin software was released into the wild. In thirty-one thousand lines of code, Satoshi was able to achieve what no one else before him had: the elimination of the need for trusted, central parties. On January 3, 2009, Satoshi verified the first Bitcoin block, block 0—the "Genesis Block." Embedded in the Genesis Block was the headline of the London *Times* newspaper of that day:

CHANCELLOR ON BRINK OF
SECOND BAILOUT FOR BANKS

The headline itself was a sobering reminder of human fallibility and the impact it had on the financial system.

And soon after, Satoshi vanished, never to be heard from again.

Over the years, numerous journalists had tried to track down the elusive founder, but they had very little to go on. Satoshi Nakamoto appeared to be a pseudonym. In Japanese, "Satoshi" meant "clear-thinking" or "wise," while "Naka" meant "inside" or "relationship." "Moto" was used to describe "an origin" or "a foundation." Strung together, the made-up name translated to "thinking clearly inside the foundation." Was it a clue? A mantra?

Between his white paper, source code, blog posts, and emails to Bitcoin core developers, Satoshi had left a total of eighty thousand words behind on the internet, approximately the length of a novel. Yet despite all of this, he had left almost no personal clues. If he was a Japanese man, he wrote in idiomatic, flawless English that alternated between American spellings and British spellings. The time stamps of his writings revealed no particular time zone. Investigative journalists had named at least fifteen people as possible alter egos to the mysterious inventor, including Elon Musk, the Tesla billionaire, and Hal Finney, a game designer and cryptographer who had received the first Bitcoin transaction from Satoshi in 2009; but none of these leads had led anywhere.

"To me," Voorhees said, "the mystery surrounding Satoshi is a feature of Bitcoin, not a bug. The beauty of Bitcoin is that it is not built around Satoshi, it's not built around anyone. To understand Bitcoin, you only need to understand *Bitcoin*."

Charlie coughed from behind an epic ring of pot smoke, then grinned.

"Gravity doesn't work because you believe in Isaac Newton."

Ten minutes later, the group had moved out of the Bakery and back into the front office of the small startup, so Charlie could finish his guided tour.

He was showing them some of his software, running on a pair of desktop computers. "Our company, BitInstant, is part of the Bitcoin economy's gravity. Specifically, we're in the business of helping people buy bitcoin in an easy way. We take their cash, turn it into bitcoin, and then send it to them—*instantly*."

"For a small fee," Voorhees clarified, from behind Cameron and his brother.

"See," Charlie continued, "if you buy bitcoin on an exchange—and at the moment, just one exchange carries most of the Bitcoin business, almost ninety percent—you have to go through the pain of opening up an account, filling out paperwork, wiring money overseas, and so on—waiting weeks for your account to be approved, waiting days for your money to arrive—it's a lot of heavy lifting. At BitInstant, we take care of all of that for you. You give us cash, we do the rest."

"You're the cashier's cage," Cameron said. "You deal with the exchanges."

"Correct. We turn cash directly into coin. You give us cash, and we can put bitcoins in your virtual wallet in under thirty minutes."

"These 'virtual' wallets. Are they safe? From hackers? If you lose your phone, or your computer gets jacked—"

"It's like your bank vault was just carried off, Wild West style," Charlie said. "You're right, Bitcoin brings about different security concerns; the thing about Bitcoin, it's digital but it's also physical."

Charlie held up his left hand, and Cameron saw a glint of silver around the young entrepreneur's pinky. Charlie carefully removed the ring and held it out so Cameron and his brother could see hundreds of tiny little alphanumeric characters etched along the inside of the ring.

"Is that your private key?" Cameron asked. He was referring to the "password" that gave you control of your bitcoin. Each bitcoin private key was a 256-bit number that could be any combination of 1s and 0s. It was a 256-bit number that allowed 2^256 possibilities; put in perspective, that was more possibilities than there were observable atoms in the universe. The chance of someone guessing a private key was 1 in 115 quattuorvigintillion.

"Almost, all but the last five alphanumeric characters, those are in my head."

"Did you imbed your private key on a ring yourself?"

"Actually, my dad did. He's in the jewelry business. I had him engrave it for me. I keep about twenty percent of my bitcoin right here, on my finger. This is what we call 'cold storage'—offline."

"Is this really practical?" Tyler asked. "Can't you just keep it on a USB drive? Put it in a safe somewhere?"

"Sure. Put some on a USB. Leave some in a password-protected wallet on your computer. Put a bunch on a pinky ring. Hell, tattoo it on your arm. The thing is, we don't really care what people do with their bitcoin. We just want to make it easy and fast for them to get them. Once they get their bitcoin, they should be free to do whatever they want with them."

Voorhees was nodding in agreement, and Cameron knew they were now touching on philosophy. The idea that people should be able to do whatever they wanted with their own money, independent of any government oversight, was a cornerstone of the libertarian ideology that had fueled much of the interest in Bitcoin up to that point. Early Bitcoiners were mostly made up of people like Voorhees, people who believed that nobody else should have a say in how individuals chose to act, as long as it didn't hurt anyone else. It was a philosophy that could extend in some dangerous directions.

"Storage is one thing," Cameron said. "Commerce is something else. People aren't buying just vodka and pizzas with bitcoin."

He glanced at the industrial-size bong across the room. Charlie laughed.

"You're talking about Silk Road."

It wasn't exactly an elephant in the room of Bitcoin, it was the room itself. Silk Road was an infamous, online bazaar that allowed users to buy and sell illegal goods and services. Its growth into a multimillion-dollar business, a sort of Amazon for illicit drugs, had coincided with the growth of virtual currency, and to the people who knew about either of them, they were inextricably intertwined.

"Not your typical due diligence," Tyler said. "We checked out Silk Road. Not just drugs, but also guns, murder for hire. Pretty dark stuff."

It hadn't been as simple as typing in a web address on his computer to get to Silk Road. Cameron and Tyler had needed to download special software called Tor to make their computer anonymous, and even then they'd felt concerned just browsing a few pages of the online bazaar. What they'd seen on the site was almost hard to believe. Page after page of mostly drugs for sale, complete with pictures. You could search for cocaine, heroin, marijuana; when you found what you wanted, you could buy it with bitcoin—and only with bitcoin—and have it delivered right to your doorstep.

Although Voorhees, a dyed-in-the-wool libertarian, might have seen it as simply a place where people could shop without government intervention, Tyler and Cameron saw it as something different—something obviously *criminal*. Even the term "dark web," the online subterranean world where sites like Silk Road existed, gave them the creeps. The fact that this was a potential first use case for virtual currency was troubling and a major potential hurdle if Bitcoin was going to go mainstream—something that could render the innovation dead on arrival.

"They also sell pretty good brownies," Charlie said.

"Silk Road is just a proof of concept," Voorhees said. "You can buy and sell real world goods with bitcoin. Our job at BitInstant is one step removed. We help people get bitcoin, no more, no less."

Cameron had read enough of Voorhees's opinions online to know that his views were much more fundamental than that: he was staunchly against the criminalization of drugs, of any sort of governmental regulation aimed at controlling how people behaved. In fact, when Charlie had hired him as BitInstant's first real employee, he'd been living in New Hampshire, where he had moved as part of the Free State Project, a political crusade to populate the state with libertarian believers who were fighting for freedom from overbearing government. Voorhees appeared to be against most forms of taxation, most forms of military action, and many—if not most—financial laws. And yet, just a few years older than Charlie, he also seemed to be a practical, thoughtful businessman.

"We're already moving about two million dollars a month through our system," Voorhees continued. "Three out of every ten bitcoin in existence were acquired through us, and that number is rising."

"We can't keep on top of it," Charlie said. "I've hired ten employees, but I need to double that, triple that. We're going to be the Apple of Bitcoin."

Cameron had been through pitch meetings before, so he was no stranger to hyperbole, but he could tell Charlie wasn't playing a part; this kid really believed he was hanging on to a lightning bolt. And why shouldn't he? He had started the company in his mother's basement, with the help of someone he had met online, a silent partner named Gareth Nelson, who was apparently autistic and still handled the technical aspects of the business from off-site—somewhere overseas. Charlie had begun by borrowing ten thousand dollars from his mother. It was just the kind of rags-to-billions story the tech world was famous for.

BitInstant was simple, and just maybe, as Charlie believed, a rocket ship. Cameron and his brother had hoped to find that rocket in Silicon Valley, but Silicon Valley had unfriended them.

Charlie was welcoming them with open arms—through Azar, who had grown up around the corner from Charlie in the same insular community, and who was now hoping to put together an investment team to fund Charlie's company—specifically, a team of identical twins with deep, deep pockets.

Cameron looked around. If there really were already ten employees at BitInstant, they were probably sharing desks and even chairs. So far, Charlie Shrem had raised $130,000. Ten thousand from his mom, and the rest in a single check from a colorful investor he had met after doing a live webcast at a conference in New York. Charlie had been telling the online audience about BitInstant, how none of the investors he'd approached understood Bitcoin and would fund him, how he just needed a little financing to make it work. Four hours after he was off the show, he'd received a Skype from a famous Bitcoin enthusiast named Roger Ver.

Ver, known in the Bitcoin community as "Bitcoin Jesus" because of his proselytizing and the many investments he'd made in the industry, had begun the brief Skype conversation by asking Charlie how much money he needed; when Charlie had thrown out a number, almost off the cuff, Ver had instantly agreed. And just like that, without ever meeting in person, they'd struck a deal; Ver had wired Charlie $120,000 for a 15 percent ownership of BitInstant.

From what Cameron had read about Ver, he held philosophical beliefs similar to those of Voorhees but seemed even more radical, even more of a fundamentalist. Ver had even once run for the California State Assembly under the Libertarian Party but then had immigrated to Japan after spending ten months in a federal prison back in 2006 for selling illegal fireworks over the internet.

Ver had begun buying bitcoin since the early days and had seeded more than a dozen fledgling companies like BitInstant. Cameron and Tyler had never met Ver, they had only been cc'd on a few emails with him; at present, there was no way to know whether he'd remain a silent angel investor, or become more vocal and involved as BitInstant grew.

Voorhees and Ver were driven by ideology, but they were also subject matter experts. Charlie was less driven by ideology, and more by passion, and was maybe a little deluded: all traits that good entrepreneurs shared. All of them were evangelists, talking about changing the world; and they meant it.

Despite some obvious concerns, Cameron knew that every early-stage startup deal had its warts. Something was telling him that getting his feet wet in Bitcoin by investing in BitInstant was the right move. This kid, Charlie Shrem, full of bravado, hubris, and a touch of deluded naivete, might just be the rocket ship they'd been looking for—even if it would just be them, Bitcoin Jesus, and Charlie's mom on the capital table.

Earlier in their conversations, Azar had mentioned that there were other suitors for BitInstant—specifically, investors with experience in the crypto space, who were already considering making a play for Charlie's term sheet. If Winklevoss Capital was going to be competing for BitInstant, then they had to move fast.

Cameron knew what steps he had to take next. He hadn't closed a venture deal yet, but they weren't in Silicon Valley, they were in the Flatiron District. This was New York, a city whose restaurants and clubs weren't shy about turning away even Silicon Valley tech-stars. This was downtown Manhattan—the Winklevoss twins' playground.

He thought he had a pretty good idea how to impress a kid like Charlie Shrem.

8

CHARLIE

S ometimes you ask and you ask and you ask for a sign, for just a little hint this way or that, for a bolt flashing down from the sky, lighting the way in front of you, and you get nothing, not a blink, not even a firefly.

And sometimes, you get a goddamn burning bush.

Better yet, Charlie thought to himself as he stepped through the oversize double doors that led into a living room surrounded by plate glass windows looking out on a balcony big enough to sport what appeared to be an actual apple orchard—not potted plants, not some terraced bullshit with vines poking through latticework from IKEA or Pottery Barn, but a real live orchard, apples and all—forget the burning bush, why not a SoHo loft filled to the brim with European runway models.

Then again, to call this place a "loft" was a truly unimaginative use of the English language. If he couldn't feel Voorhees a step behind him, practically pushing him through the threshold and down the short steps that led to the carpeted main level, Charlie would have thought he'd passed out in the short cab ride over from the Flatiron District, and had entered some sort of fugue state. Places like this weren't supposed to exist, outside of the tabloids. Everything around him was just so damn *glossy*.

From those ridiculous windows to the furniture, all of it modern, curved, *undulating*, beneath recessed lighting beaming down from a ceiling that had to be twenty feet above his head. And the people, my god, the people. There had to be a hundred people in the place, and yet it wasn't crowded, it was *social*. It was SoHo, the way SoHo was supposed to be when you read about it in a travel guide or watched it on Bravo; everyone was too tall and too thin and decked out in hip clothes that didn't need designer labels to show that they came from boutiques where you drank champagne while you shopped.

"Now this is a party," Charlie said as Voorhees moved next to him, taking it all in.

"It certainly is."

Charlie could tell that Voorhees was holding himself back; to be fair, Voorhees was always holding himself back. He was smart like that. Even though he was only five years older than Charlie, he was already a real businessman, a gifted speaker and salesman. Roger Ver had introduced Voorhees to him; shortly after wiring that business-saving six-figure investment, Ver had told him that he had a perfect guy for Charlie to hire. Charlie had first responded— "I'm not going to hire some random guy from New Hampshire!"—but the minute they'd met at a tech event in New York, Charlie had been sold. Voorhees understood the macroissues, he was one of the smartest economic theorists Charlie had ever met and was as eloquent as he was tough, when professionally necessary.

Voorhees was never going to see the world the way Charlie saw the world, which was probably a good thing. He didn't come from where Charlie came from, which was a lot farther than New Hampshire. Somebody had to keep them tethered to reality. Because at the moment, Charlie was lifting off, and damn it felt good.

"Our hosts," Voorhees said, pointing through the crowd.

And there they were again, like something out of Greek mythology. One was over by the fully staffed bar, talking to a guy with a goatee and dreadlocks, and a few feet away, Tyler, or maybe it was Cameron, who the hell could tell, was sitting on one of the leather banquettes, next to a brunette in a silvery cocktail dress that started halfway up her thighs and ended well before it should have. The woman's skin was so pale and shiny and porcelain she couldn't possibly be real, she had to be some sort of marionette that had escaped its strings.

But then Cameron, or Tyler, or Cameron, was waving Charlie over and saying something in the woman's ear, and she was smiling, actually smiling, and patting the banquette next to her. She was real, and she seemed to want to talk to *Charlie*.

He started across the carpet, doing his best not to run into any of the obstacles that seemed to suddenly be appearing out of nowhere. A huge, plastic chair shaped like an open palm, fingers reaching out at him, trying to grab him. A pair of waitresses, in what looked to be black-and-white French maid outfits, pendant curves billowing up out of leather bustiers, threatening to smother Charlie as he moved. A B-list cable television star, offering up a funny-looking cigarette, beckoning him to stop, to pause, to slow.

Truth be told, Charlie was already way too drunk. Not buzzed, he'd passed buzzed hours ago, somewhere between the short walk from the BitInstant offices, where he and the twins had met earlier that afternoon, for a second time, pregaming in a group circle with NEFT vodka shots, to Tyler and Cameron's still-under-construction headquarters, where the twins had offered up a guided tour. Though it was still a hard-hat site, an open jungle gym of Sheetrock, wooden beams, and plaster dust, the scale of the place was hard to ignore. Five thousand square feet looked like the Taj Mahal to Charlie, who had grown up in rooms where he could usually touch two walls at the same time. No doubt Winklevoss Capital was supposed to make an impression. Say what you wanted about the twins, but above all else, Tyler and Cameron *made* an impression.

"Charlie," whichever twin was on the banquette said, reaching to a sleek, Nordic-designed table and retrieving two champagne glasses, "meet Anya. She's from Bulgaria. And she wants to hear all about Bitcoin."

Charlie stuttered out some sort of hello, then took a deep sip of the champagne.

"It's the future of money," he finally managed, and the girl laughed. Then she launched into a story about the last time she was in Paris, for fashion week, and wanted this pair of shoes, but all she'd had was Bulgarian cash, and anyway, who wanted to calculate the exchange rate between a lev and a euro, and was Charlie going to do something about that? And then she laughed again, and Charlie realized this woman was actually interested in him.

"This is incredible," Charlie said, realizing a second too late that the words weren't just in his head. The twin laughed.

"No, this is a Saturday night. The really good parties are all midweek. But I think we can salvage something. It's not even eleven yet, and we've got a couple more stops to make."

He reached back to the elegant table and grabbed a bottle of Dom Perignon, then leaned toward Charlie's glass, topping it off, doing the same for the Bulgarian beauty between them.

"Buckle up, guys. The night's just getting started."

Three hours later, Charlie was steadying himself against the back wall of a speakeasy in the East Village, focusing on the shot glass full of rum that had somehow found its way into his other hand. Next to him, Cameron—now he was sure it was Cameron, because that had to be Tyler over by the jukebox, talking to a phenomenal-looking blonde whom Charlie was pretty sure was either Tyler's current girlfriend, ex-girlfriend, or soon to be girlfriend—was telling a story about the Olympic Village in Beijing, something that had to do with a South American rowing team, a Russian boxer, and a bout of food poisoning—but Charlie was having a hell of a time keeping everything clear. Not only because the shot was at least his third since they'd found their way into the hidden bar, through a door at the back of a loading dock, but also because the Bulgarian model was still with him, just a few feet away, dancing with two of her friends who had been with her in Paris that time she couldn't get those goddamn shoes. And every now and then, when she wasn't pressing her body up against one of her friends, she was smiling at Charlie.

Voorhees was never going to believe that things were going as well as they were. Voorhees had tapped out an hour earlier, cornering Charlie on his way out, telling him not to make any decisions until they were back at the office on Monday. Charlie knew that Voorhees had some reservations about taking the twins' money. He was impressed by them, and much preferred them to the Silicon Valley establishment, but they still weren't Bitcoiners, at least not yet.

It was one thing to teach them about Bitcoin and encourage them to invest in the ecosystem, but it was an entirely different thing to get into bed with them by taking their money.

Ver, on the other hand, was much more adamant. Since Azar had first advanced the idea of the Winklevoss twins getting involved, Ver had voiced his reservations: he had told Charlie that the Winklevoss twins didn't share the same vision that he, Charlie, and Voorhees did for BitInstant. As Ver put it— these were guys who loved to sue people who didn't see eye to eye with them. Plus, BitInstant didn't need their money, business was doing great, they didn't need any more cooks in the kitchen.

A recent Skype call with Ver over the twins had actually gotten heated, the first real disagreement Charlie had ever had with his initial investor. Ver had argued that dealing with the twins could only complicate things for them. But Charlie had dug in his heels. He agreed with Azar on this issue, that the Winklevoss twins were just the kind of jet fuel that BitInstant, and also Bitcoin, needed right now. Ultimately it was Charlie's company, and Ver had no choice but to concede.

Charlie believed that Ver was reflexively against the Winklevoss twins because of where they came from, what they represented, or what he thought they represented—the Establishment. But Charlie had now actually met them in person and spent time with them—unlike Ver, whose only impression of them came from a movie. Despite what they looked like, underneath they were fiery and determined. What else had driven them to the Olympics, to all of their accomplishments? Regardless of how they might have appeared, they had something to prove. To themselves, and to the world.

Ver was unbending in his views, almost combative toward anyone or anything that was in conflict with them. Erik Voorhees might have some offbeat opinions, but Ver's strain of libertarianism was on another level. Charlie thought it came from a good place—Ver truly believed that free markets would bring the highest standard of living and the greatest happiness to the greatest number of people—but it made him, and to a lesser extent Voorhees, see governments, states, borders, and regulation as something to fight. And as far as Ver was concerned, the Winklevoss twins, celluloid "Men of Harvard," were the Establishment's wet dream.

Charlie wasn't an ideologue. He was just trying to scratch his way out of his mom's basement. He respected Ver's and Voorhees's minds, but he believed ideology was something you had time for after you'd made it, not before.

He smiled back at the Bulgarian model. Shit, she had to be half a foot taller than him, and she had that skin, and that majestic, wavy, jet-black hair, and that silvery dress, hugging the angles of her body like the skintight scales of some sort of magical fish, and . . . damn, he was drunk, really, really, *really* drunk.

And suddenly he was on the move, right past Cameron (or Tyler?) and then past Tyler (or was that Cameron?), and then down a long, narrow hallway that led to a wooden door with a picture of a sombrero. He'd almost made it past the urinals to the stall when he vomited, right on his sneakers.

When he finally got control of himself, recovered enough to make it to the pair of metal sinks across from the urinals, he realized he was grinning. Drunk as he was, he was happier than he'd ever been. Voorhees could have all the reservations he wanted, and Ver could flat-out disagree, but Charlie knew that his decision was already made.

He ducked his face under the faucet and let the cold water put life back into his cheeks. He'd just thrown up on his shoes, but he wasn't going to let that slow him down.

9

STEPFORD, CONNECTICUT

I still remember when there was just one boat. All that blue water everywhere and just one boat with two crazy kids pulling on oars. Every time I think about it, it makes me smile."

Howard Winklevoss was leaning against the white wooden fence, elbows on the top rail. What was left of his distinguished-looking white hair shifted in the breeze, and his aviator-style glasses shielded his eyes from the glare of the midmorning sun. Although Tyler was a good head taller than his father, at sixty-nine his dad was still such a large presence in his life, he felt fifteen again, peering down to where the meandering coastline of Long Island Sound intersected with the park surrounding them.

The view from the peak of Tod's Point—a sprawling, 2.6-mile network of dirt trails, picnic areas, and parkland that was also the original site of the town of Greenwich, Connecticut (purchased from the Sinoway Indians for the princely sum of twenty-five fur coats in 1640), was like a painter's palette before the brush touched it and broke the colors at their seams. The yellows, greens, and blues were still intact: bright sand, lush grass, crystal water. Tyler could make out at least seven boats cutting across the current, white against the blue, the young men and women within the boats little more than blurs of synchronized motion.

"It's still surreal seeing so many boats," Tyler said.

The fact that the boats were out on the water—that the sport of rowing was growing and thriving in Greenwich, engaging hundreds of people every year—meant something to Tyler and his family, because it was something they had helped build from scratch. He and Cameron often thought of crew as their first real startup; those kids were out there on the water because Tyler and his brother had taken a risk years ago.

"It looks so easy from up here, doesn't it?" his father continued. "All the complexity, the hard work, the pain, the physics, hidden beneath the calm surface and all that beauty."

Tyler smiled. He looked over at Cameron—he knew they were both thinking the same thing—this was the way their father always saw the world. Everything in terms of the math behind it. Howard Winklevoss couldn't just look at boats on the water; he saw mechanical centers of gravity, torque, leverage, and thrust versus drag, friction, all of it combining to create balance, harmony. That was how his mind worked, always seeking to turn reality into mathematical problems that could be solved. Chaos into order, a sort of reverse entropy.

Howard Winklevoss hadn't been born in a place like Greenwich, Connecticut. His was a true American success story; he'd bootstrapped himself, and the whole Winklevoss line, up into the upper class by way of that mathematical, gifted mind.

Howard Winklevoss's great-grandfather August Winklevoss, the twins' great-great-grandfather, was a coal miner, a transplant from Hanover, Germany, who had settled in Pennsylvania Dutch country and then promptly died of black lung. His son, the twins' great-grandfather, became a coal miner at age eight. Toward the end of his years, he had a permanently fused, L-shaped back resulting from a life spent bent over, digging coal in caves and shafts with a heavy pick balanced over one shoulder. His brother, the twins' great-uncle, had lost a leg in a mining accident when a mine cart ran over it—his mangled leg was sawed right off on the family kitchen table by a county doctor.

Howard Winklevoss Sr., the twins' grandfather, hadn't been a miner his whole life, but he had started out as one. A self-taught mechanic, he had helped a wealthy man whose car had serendipitously broken down on a road nearby his family's homestead in Mercer, Pennsylvania, where he lived with his parents and eleven siblings: six brothers and five sisters. This wealthy man paid him so handsomely for fixing his car that day that Howard Sr. was inspired to leave the coal mines behind and start fixing cars full-time. Eventually, with the man's help, he put together just enough money from his mining days to open a makeshift garage with his brothers, earning themselves the nickname "Barnyard Garagemen." Howard Sr.'s father, the twins' great-grandfather, was very upset at the time, because he thought horses were far superior to the auto—you could rely on them, they didn't break down, and cars couldn't work in the field. But eventually Howard Sr. would go on to start multiple businesses, including a general store.

Howard Jr., the twins' father, had picked up a love for automobiles and an entrepreneurial spirit from his father, and had nearly flunked out of high school because he'd spent all his free time building a Model A Ford from scratch. He would work at his father's general store each day after school, then, after dinner, would work on the homemade car until late in the evening. Everyone around him had told him he was crazy and that it would never pass the Pennsylvania inspection requirements. He scrounged parts and pieces from junkyards, garage sales, and mail order catalogs, obsessed with getting the Model A perfect, down to the very last nut and bolt.

He'd finished the car in two years and managed to pass state inspection, making it road legal. But he barely survived his high school exams. Nonetheless, he drove his chopped and channeled hot rod down to Penn State and rolled into the admissions office, looking for a spot. The older lady behind the desk took one glance at his transcript and sent him packing. Undeterred, he headed to Grove City College, where he managed to impress their admissions director with what he had built.

At Grove City College two important things happened: he continued to develop the entrepreneurial skills that he had learned from his father, and he met his future wife, Carol Leonard.

During freshman week in 1961, Howard and his parents were in line for registration in front of Carol and her parents. Carol's mother, Mildred, playfully pointed out the handsome guy in front of them to Carol. Unknown to

Carol at the time, Howard's parents had pointed out the attractive blond girl behind them to Howard. A month later, when Howard and Carol phoned home, they both had "you'll never guess" conversations with their parents.

From then on, Howard and Carol were a picture-perfect match in a 1960s, collegiate, postwar kind of way. Carol, the daughter of a New York Police Department detective and a schoolteacher from New Hyde Park, Long Island, was a reserved prom queen who was more comfortable following the rules than breaking them. She was a quick study and possessed a wisdom of universal truths that you'd find in the Book of Proverbs, a book that along with the Bible, her mother often quoted. Howard was a handsome, athletic, and confident—bordering on cocky—upstart who was comfortable taking risks and getting creative about the rules. Together they were the perfect team.

When he wasn't spending time with Carol or his fraternity brothers, Howard was spending time on his entrepreneurial endeavors. He paid his way through Grove City selling pots and pans door-to-door. Soon he was hiring his fraternity brothers and running a mini cookware empire. Upon graduation, Howard decided he wanted to study business and better himself. Learning that San Jose State in California charged only $49.50 per credit and had few, if any, entry requirements, he headed west. At San Jose, the master's degree in business administration (MBA) program was already full, so Howard settled on studying for a master's degree in insurance, with the intention of working his way into the MBA program the following year.

At San Jose, and then even more so as he continued his studies, chasing a PhD at the University of Oregon, his love for building mechanical things transferred over to the new science of early computing. It was in Oregon that a summer course in pensions—a mathematically complex area of business so obscure at the time that he was the only student that registered for the class—would change the direction of his life. An innovative computer simulation he created to compare different ways to calculate pensions led to a professorship at the Wharton School, as well as a groundbreaking book: *Pension Mathematics: With Numerical Illustrations*. Meanwhile, Carol earned a master's degree and doctorate degree in education at the University of Pennsylvania, in between continuing to teach elementary school.

Eventually Howard would leave Wharton to start a consulting firm.

He hired a number of his brightest students to join him—the ones who didn't spend their time building cars and selling pots and pans.

Even though Howard's consulting firm, Winklevoss Consultants, had its office in Philadelphia, he was on the road so much making sales pitches and interacting with clients that he could have lived just about anywhere in the United States as long as it was close enough to a major airport. After living in Philadelphia for over thirteen years, he and Carol, looking for a change, decided on raising their young family in Palo Alto, California.

Back then, Palo Alto wasn't widely referred to as Silicon Valley. It's gorgeous weather and the fact that many of Howard's relatives had moved from dreary Pennsylvania to settle there and start their own families made it an ideal place. As a young family, they enjoyed the beautiful town, the wonderful parks, and the excitement of nearby Stanford University. Cameron and Tyler were so devoted to the playground at the end of the street where they lived that every day, rain or shine, they piled their toys into wagons and hauled them down the street to the playground.

While Howard worked in the home office above the garage, or was on the road starting to build his empire, Carol focused on raising young children and volunteering in the local community. Howard often remarked to his children that he owed all of his success in life to his wife. This was especially true in terms of raising his family.

A few years later, Howard sold his company to Johnson & Higgins, one of the largest insurance companies in the world and located in New York, and he and Carol moved their family to Greenwich, Connecticut, a nearby suburb. Howard worked for Johnson & Higgins as a senior vice president for two years, commuting between New York and Greenwich, but ultimately decided he was an entrepreneur at heart. So in 1987, at the age of forty-four, he decided to start all over again and found a new company called Winklevoss Technologies.

This company would be different from that last one. Instead of being hired as a consultant by a company to conduct a complex pension study and then deliver the finished product, Howard and his team would build the software necessary to run such studies and then sell it to companies so they could conduct the studies themselves. Winklevoss Technologies would be a software provider instead of a consultant shackled to the billable hour. At the time, the desktop personal computer was a brand-new idea. Howard's new company would bet on the nascent technology of personal computing rapidly growing, improving, and exploding with adoption. It was the kind of risk that he couldn't have taken without Carol's unwavering encouragement and support.

After school, the twins would often go to their father's office and do their homework. In between schoolwork, they would explore the office, talk with the software engineers, read the computer magazines lying around, play on the computers, and watch from the inside how a technology company worked. Cameron and Tyler literally grew up inside of a startup, before startups were even a *thing*.

The Winklevoss household was not a jock household in the traditional sense. While everyone was active and played sports, the dinner table conversations were not dominated by discussions of topics like the score of the Yankees game. Instead Howard enjoyed talking about the things that he was passionate about most—business, technology, computers, math, financial markets—while Carol rounded out the conversation with topics like literature, film, human interest, culture, and the arts. Howard and Carol were both intellectual heavyweights in their own unique way, and together they covered a huge swatch of knowledge and wisdom. Cameron and Tyler's role models growing up were not sports figures; they were startup founders like Steve Jobs and Bill Gates, the people who were in the business magazines they read in their father's office and who, like their father, were trying to change the world through technology.

While Howard taught his children everything he knew about business, Carol ensured that they got a much broader education in life. She was determined to provide them with the opportunity to find their passion, wherever it might lie.

Although Tyler and his brother had been raised in a family that now had money, their parents never let them lose touch with their family history, and not just their father's coal mining ancestry. Carol's forebearers were also German immigrants who came to the United States in the nineteenth century with nothing but their dreams. Carol's grandfather was a fireman and hotelier in Rockaway Beach, her uncle served in the U.S. Army during World War II and fought in the Pacific Ocean theater, and her father was a homicide detective. Like Howard's family, Carol's family embodied good Christian morals and believed that a person's word meant something. Howard and Carol had grown up believing that the world was a place where honesty and the ability to work hard were respected above all else. Winning was not what mattered: what mattered was that you gave your best effort and conducted yourself with the highest integrity and character. As Howard Sr. had always told his son: "I don't care how many follow in my tracks, I just want to be the first person making footprints in the snow."

"I remember when you and Cameron first started out," Tyler's dad said. "Everyone looked at you cross-eyed. Leaving campus and disappearing off into the woods to row."

Tyler laughed. He and his brother hadn't grown up in coal country—far from it—but that didn't keep them from cutting their own path—or trying to create those first footprints in the metaphorical snow. Two overly tall, identical kids stood out in the *Lord of the Flies* atmosphere of high school, and not always in a good way. Being obsessed with Latin, computers, and building web pages didn't exactly help. Nor did studying classical piano for twelve years, or teaching themselves how to code in HTML. The twins of this era were a far cry from the final clubs jock stereotype Mark Zuckerberg would later peg them as being at Harvard. But a quirk of geography had led to the passion that had eventually dominated their early life and changed their standing in the local, athletically centered community.

It had all started with their next-door neighbor, a kid named Ethan Ayer, who was six foot nine and ten years older than the twins. He had gone to boarding school at Andover, which had one of the best rowing programs in the country. He would later go on to row at Harvard and then Cambridge University. When he'd come home to visit, he'd told these great stories about rowing, about being out on the water, competing with other rowers from all over the world. Tyler and Cameron had been intrigued. Their mother had started checking the local yellow pages and realized that there were no rowing programs in Greenwich. Even though there was water everywhere, and adults in the town who had rowed back in boarding school and college, there weren't any local rowing programs for Tyler and Cameron to join. Calling marina after marina, their mother was told that the only rowing they did was when a motorboat ran out of gas.

Still, she'd persisted and eventually found a rowing club in Westport, Connecticut, thirty miles north. One summer day in August of 1996, she packed up the twins in the car and drove them to what turned out to be an abandoned wooden building—the original Westport Train Station—with a rowing club squatting inside. This humble club, sitting on the banks of the Saugatuck River, had been founded by an Irishman named James Mangan a few years earlier.

The twins entered the long wooden boathouse and, not finding anyone inside, made their way down the overgrown path to the water; there, in the middle of the path, they first ran into Mangan. When his eyes locked onto the two of them—fifteen-year-old mirror identical twins, already well over six feet tall and still growing—he'd broken out in an ear-to-ear grin. He'd made some comment in his thick Irish brogue about God dropping them on his front porch: a righty and a lefty who were exactly the same, growing every day. He immediately agreed to train them.

When they'd first started, they weren't really sure what the hell they had gotten themselves into. The old train station had no running water, no electricity, no heat, and you had to be careful where you stepped or you'd fall right through the floor; the nearest locker room was the restroom in the Mobile station across the street.

On their first day on the water, in an old, rickety practice shell that was partly held together with duct tape, Tyler and his brother managed to take a total of eleven strokes. Mangan, grinning the whole time, told them that one day they would take hundreds, sometimes more than a thousand, in a single practice. And never mind the duct tape or the condition of the hull: *this sport wasn't about the chariot, it was about the horse.* Most importantly, the boat didn't care who you were, where you were from, the size of your wallet—it cared only about what you *did*.

"We thought you were nuts when you said you weren't going out for any varsity teams," Howard said. "I thought your mom was nuts when she made me put an ergometer in the attic."

Tyler winced, remembering the brutal training device, more akin to a medieval torture machine, and how many winters he had spent up in that attic, pulling the chain on that mechanical monster. But it was the ergometer that had pointed them toward the Olympics. Every month, teenagers from across the country would submit their twenty-minute erg test results to US Rowing, which would post them to the US Rowing website. When Tyler and Cameron discovered that their own scores were in the top ten in the country for their age, they realized that there was a possibility they could compete on an entirely different level.

They then decided to lobby their private school's headmaster to create a varsity rowing program, the first ever in Greenwich. With the help of their father, they'd found a slip at a nearby dock in Long Island Sound and convinced a few of their classmates to sign up. The twins were two kids who had known nothing about the sport, who had trained and sweated (partially in their attic) until they were good enough to compete at the national level, making the US Junior National rowing team and competing at the 1999 Junior World Championships in Bulgaria. Then they'd built their first startup—a high school varsity rowing team—from scratch. That startup had helped get them into Harvard via early admission—because the twins weren't simply athletes; they were the definition of "scholar athletes," polymaths who had proven their mettle in both the classroom and on the water—and building their startup would put them on the strange path into another world where they were also starting from scratch.

To them, the art of crew really was a microcosm of startup life; it had taught them how to work on a team and succeed under pressure, where the difference between winning and losing could be razor-thin. Cameron had often remarked that some of the best lessons in his life he had learned at the boathouse—and they had very little, if anything, to do with the sport of rowing.

Tyler pivoted the conversation to the reason he and his brother had invited their father to Tod's Point. "We know more about Bitcoin right now than we knew at fifteen, when we took the leap into rowing. That was a big decision then, and this feels like a big decision now."

Tyler had always relied on his father for business advice and mentorship, not only because his father was a legitimate mathematical genius who had built a successful consulting company the same way he'd built a Model A Ford in high school, from the ground up, but also because he still considered his father to be the most ethical, high-integrity person he'd ever known. Maybe it was the coal country in the man, but Howard Winklevoss Jr. was the one who had taught them that right and wrong mattered, that a handshake was more important than any contract a lawyer could draw up. When the situation with Zuckerberg had first gone down, their father had been the most shocked of any of them about how the young Facebook CEO had acted. He wasn't a naive man, but he couldn't process how someone could behave so deceitfully, and with such disrespect. He'd supported Tyler and Cameron in their efforts to make things right, even when they'd turned down the cash settlement in favor of Facebook stock. And to them, it didn't matter how many lawyers had told them they were being fools; the fact that their father had stood behind them gave them the confidence to realize they were making the right decision.

"Cameron said it first—'this is either complete bullshit or the next big thing,'" Tyler said.

His father nodded, looking out at the water. They'd already discussed Bitcoin at length on the phone and during breakfast that morning. His father had immediately seen the mathematical beauty behind the now three-year-old cryptocurrency. The elegance of the blockchain—the open, decentralized ledger where transactions were permanently recorded—immediately made sense to him, and the brilliance of Bitcoin itself, of a currency backed by math and cryptography, with a fixed supply mined by computers running complex equations, certainly thrilled his mathematical mind. But he shared Tyler and Cameron's concerns about Silk Road, and the shady side of the Bitcoin world.

"I think Bitcoin is worth a deeper dive, but BitInstant is a bigger question. This kid, Charlie, is going to be a handful."

"It's not just him building BitInstant," Tyler said. "There's his head of marketing. And his seed investor."

"A libertarian philosopher and an anarchist."

"I don't think Roger Ver is an anarchist. I think he calls himself an individualist."

"I read my fair share of Ayn Rand in college. But someone needs to actually be in charge, grab hold of the reins and make sure this thing doesn't start to veer sideways. Someone needs to handle compliance, hire people, run the day-to-day. To manage the risks, and deal with the legal side of things. Right now, all of that falls on this Charlie kid, and that's who you'd really be investing in. Not the business plan, or the philosophy: a kid, running the show."

Tyler knew his father was right, that they wouldn't be investing in just the idea but in the person, the entrepreneur. That was what it meant to be a venture capitalist.

"He's smart. He's ambitious. He's got something to prove," Cameron said.

They were good starting points. But Charlie also seemed to be swayed by Voorhees's philosophies and taken with Ver's apparent ideology. Something he'd said had been worrisome: *We don't really care what people do with their bitcoin.* It had almost been a throwaway comment, but it had stuck with them. From a business perspective it made sense; BitInstant was an addendum to an exchange, it was just a way to help people get bitcoin for cash. But from a philosophical perspective, it was a fairly dangerous statement. Libertarians or individualists believed people should be free to do whatever they wanted with their money. But in reality, people had never been free to do whatever they wanted with their money. There were laws, regulations, criminal statutes.

Bitcoin was young, and at the moment, unregulated. But for a limited time only; eventually governments were going to care very much what people did with their bitcoin.

With BitInstant, they really would be betting on Charlie. It would be a risk. But wasn't that exactly what they were in the business of doing? Taking risks? Wasn't that exactly what they were looking for? The chance to take a risk on something with immense potential? To be part of a revolution, once again, only this time with no Mark Zuckerberg?

Even their mathematical father had to agree: a second act with the enormous potential of Bitcoin seemed like it was worth the risk. It wasn't often you got a second chance to catch lightning in a bottle.

An hour later Tyler was sitting next to his brother in their SUV as Cameron scrolled toward a contact on his cell phone. Tyler had the window rolled down next to him so he could feel the breeze against his cheeks. Their father was still at the end of the trail, leaning over Tod's Point, watching the boats row past. He and their mother came down to the Point often, and not just to reminisce about the twins and their rowing.

The Point had also been a favorite place of Tyler and Cameron's older sister, Amanda, who in many ways had embodied the best qualities of both Tyler and his twin brother. She was a brilliant student, star athlete, charismatic actress, with almost limitless energy; her talent while they were growing up easily overshadowed theirs. But most importantly, she was grace personified. A rising star when she went off to Williams College, suddenly she started suffering from debilitating bouts of depression. The family was deeply concerned about her well-being and tried to figure out what was going on. It was a hellish two-year journey into the world of mental health. They were suddenly in a land that science didn't understand, where synching up a diagnosis with the right treatment was like hitting a piñata blindfolded while walking around the Grand Canyon. It was also a deeply private struggle they faced—almost no one outside the family knew what was going on—and most wouldn't understand. This was not a broken arm, not something you could point to and easily process. This was the unknown, filled with stigma. At times, on her road to recovery, she sought relief from her pain through drugs—which ultimately took her life in New York in June 2002. She was twenty-three. She was never going to have her chance to catch lightning in a bottle.

Because her tragic end had taken place in a public setting—on a rainy night, around midnight on June 14, she collapsed on a street that was being used to film an upcoming Robert De Niro movie—the *New York Post* immediately ran several fabricated stories thrusting the tragedy into the tabloid sphere. It was a cruel airing of a private struggle that mischaracterized their fight, and more important who their daughter was—a star who burned brightly on Earth but was now flying high in the sky.

> *In one of those stars I shall be living. In one of them*
> *I shall be laughing. And so it will be as if all the stars*
> *were laughing, when you look at the sky at night.*

Prince, Antoine de Saint-Exupéry, ***The Little Prince***

The words of her favorite book were inscribed on her tombstone. Tyler and Cameron had been young, twenty years old, rising college juniors who spent most of their time rowing and thinking up business ideas in their dorm room. It had been a devastating time for them, and for their parents. Amanda was the only person in the entire world—including their parents—who had never mixed them up, always telling Cameron and Tyler apart perfectly. When they made the Olympics, they named their racing shell in her honor. As they raced at the Olympic Games in Beijing, beating medalists on their way to making the grand final in their first international regatta, a feat almost unheard of, Amanda's spirit was with them. And it had been only two years after Amanda's passing that the twins would be thrust into the torturous and circuitous series of events that had led them to where they were today.

"You ready to do this?" Cameron asked as his finger hovered over the contact on his phone.

Tyler nodded. To the outside world, it looked like things had always come easily to them. But Tyler knew that wasn't true. The thing their father, and his history, and their own family hardships, had taught them was that it wasn't about whether things came easily or hard, it was how you faced them. If you went down, you got back up.

And if you had a chance to do something great, you took it.

Cameron hit the number.

"So?" David Azar's Brooklynese reverberated through the car. "Are we gonna do this thing?"

"Draw up the contract," Tyler said. What Azar didn't know was that the eight-hundred-thousand-dollar investment they were about to make in BitInstant was nothing compared to what Tyler and Cameron had planned.

"Fantastic! And guys, I've got a perfect name for our investment group. You ready? Maguire Investments. Get it? Jerry Maguire? Show me the money!"

Cameron pressed the mute button and looked at Tyler.

"We can still change our minds," he said.

Tyler laughed.

In his mind, they'd already pulled the trigger.

10

BUYER'S MARKET

———————————————————————————•

Charlie put his cell phone down on his desk and leaned back in his chair. The air in his office felt thick and humid; the air-conditioning had conked out again, and Charlie had promised Voorhees and Ira Miller, his head software engineer, a redhead who could code like nobody's business, that he'd get the building manager over to fix it, but hell, the air-conditioning could wait. At the moment, Charlie's mind was spinning, his face was flushed, and it had nothing to do with the late summer heat.

He'd just gotten off the phone with Cameron for the third time that afternoon, the eighth time that day, the fifteenth time in the past week, and he could tell from the conversation that the twin wasn't even near done making this particular type of call yet. Which was entirely insane. If someone had told Charlie a month ago that soon he'd be sitting in his office, buying bitcoin on behalf of the Winklevoss twins—and the amount they were asking him to buy—he would have laughed them right out of the room.

Because it was crazy—crazy *awesome*. Not only had Charlie begun purchasing bitcoin for the twins, but he and Voorhees also had actually shown them how to set up a bitcoin wallet, acting as their guides and educating them on how the Bitcoin economy worked. Through that, the twins had also learned how BitInstant worked, and how Charlie was about to change the goddamn world.

At the moment, Bitcoin was still far from mainstream. Although maybe Charlie wouldn't have admitted it at their pitch meeting in the Bakery, for the most part the only ones who owned it in quantity were drug dealers, drug buyers, early adopting geeks who had heard about it from online message boards, and libertarians like Ver and Voorhees. For Bitcoin to work, and for BitInstant to become Apple, mainstream Americans had to get into the cryptocurrency game. And for that to happen, Bitcoin needed ambassadors.

Who would make better ambassadors than the identical twins, who always looked like they'd stepped off the cover of a Polo catalog?

But the twins hadn't been content just to make an investment in BitInstant— totaling $800,000 for a 22 percent ownership of the company. While they were closing the deal, they'd then asked Charlie to help them acquire some bitcoin itself. So Charlie had taken them through the first steps, that first virgin buy.

From the beginning, the twins were hyperfocused on security. Charlie thought they were a little paranoid; most people just downloaded a digital wallet and then didn't think twice about it. But it was their money, and they'd earned the right to be careful.

At their bidding, he'd gotten them two "clean" laptops from Best Buy; one "hot" and one "cold," and a dozen USB drives. He'd then helped them set up their digital wallet, which would require downloading the Bitcoin software client to the hot laptop, which was connected to the internet, and then transferring it via USB to the cold laptop, which was never to touch the internet. Once the software was on the cold computer, they'd created a digital wallet and generated their private key. Then a copy of the private key had been transferred to each USB drive, which the twins could then store securely.

Cameron had done his initial diligence on BitInstant by trying to purchase $100 of bitcoin through the service. After Charlie had printed him the first BitInstant deposit slip, for a hundred dollars, Cameron had taken the slip and headed off to the nearest Walgreens. At that moment, BitInstant had a deal with both MoneyGram and SoftPay, which meant between the two they had a network of ten thousand stores that could take their business. By simply generating a deposit slip through the BitInstant website, walking into any Walgreens, Duane Reade, CVS, or 7-Eleven, and handing the cashier cash, you could buy bitcoin. In fact, it had become a joke around the crypto community that if you bought your first bitcoin with a "red phone," you were a real OG. The "red phone" referred to the ubiquitous phones that were present at Money-Gram locations.

When Cameron got to that Walgreens, he'd picked that phone up and told the operator the code on his BitInstant deposit slip. The operator had confirmed the transaction, and then Cameron had gone to the cashier and given them a crisp one-hundred-dollar bill. He'd then taken the receipt, headed outside, called Charlie, and Charlie had told him that a hundred dollars' worth of bitcoin had just been transferred over to one of the Bitcoin addresses in Cameron and Tyler's digital wallet.

Those first bitcoin had come right out of BitInstant's reserve. An easy and quick transaction: BitInstant's proof of concept. But Cameron and his brother hadn't been done; not by a long shot.

That very afternoon, they'd told Charlie they wanted him to buy more, and that they were about to wire over a hundred thousand dollars from Winklevoss Capital's bank account.

A hundred thousand dollars. It was a staggering sum of money; the clients Charlie worked with daily, buying and selling bitcoin, were usually spending a few hundred dollars, maximum. Sure, there were a few big players out there, but nothing near a hundred grand.

But to Charlie's utter shock, that wire was only the *beginning.*

The wires kept coming in. The twins wanted bitcoin, so much, in fact, that eventually it became obvious they would need to go straight to the source, sidestepping Charlie and BitInstant and buying directly from the exchange itself.

For the amount they were talking about, that meant going directly to Mt. Gox.

Charlie could still remember the looks on Cameron's and Tyler's faces as he'd told them what, exactly, they'd be dealing with: 80 percent of bitcoin trading actually occurred through the big kahuna in the cryptocurrency exchange world—Mt. Gox. The ridiculous name had an even more ridiculous origin. Its owner, Mark Karpeles, a twenty-eight-year-old French émigré to

Shibuya, Tokyo, who called himself the King of Bitcoin and who had spent much of his twenties posting cat videos to YouTube, had purchased the company from an entrepreneur who had originally built the website as a trading hub for cards from the game Magic: The Gathering. Hence the name Mt. Gox, an acronym that stood for "Magic: The Gathering Online eXchange." It was a clunky, janky, totally unregulated exchange. Although millions of dollars in bitcoin were traded on the exchange daily, there was no regulatory oversight at all. Worse yet, on average it could take more than six days to get your money in and out.

Nonetheless, with the size of the investment position the twins were looking to take in bitcoin, Mt. Gox was the only choice they had. Charlie had already put $750,000 of Cameron and Tyler's money into bitcoin for them, and the twins' hunger for the virtual currency had not subsided. If anything, it had grown.

So they would have to go directly to the Japanese-based exchange, open their own account, and become customers. Which meant new headaches; to wire that kind of money to Mt. Gox, there were hoops they'd have to jump through. First, they had to scan their passports and mail physical legal documents to Japan—actually, to a P.O. box in Shibuya. Once their information made it over the ocean, they would still have to wait weeks for it to be processed, because the onboarding queue at Mt. Gox was so backed up. Luckily, because BitInstant was one of Mt. Gox's biggest customers, Charlie had a personal relationship with the French entrepreneur and was able to speed things up for the twins.

Karpeles was obese, difficult, and utterly strange; the man would disappear for days at a time, yet he was also a control freak and micromanager, who wouldn't let anyone else help out with even the most mundane parts of his business. He was still obsessed with cats and had a penchant for manga comics. Charlie pictured him in his office late at night, the neon of Tokyo flashing through the cracks in the drawn window shades behind him, a purring cat on his lap, a croissant in his pudgy hand; but Charlie had never actually met the man, he had only communicated with him over Internet Relay Chat (IRC).

Once their accounts had been set up, the twins could wire their money directly to Mt. Gox and start buying bitcoin on their own. And as far as Charlie could now tell, they were doing so, at a furious pace. Wiring half a million dollars a week, maybe more. Placing buy orders that were so large they could move the price of bitcoin, a price that was now hovering anywhere between $10 and $20 a bitcoin, if they weren't spread out over time. There was no doubt they were the biggest buyers of bitcoin in the world—the twins were fucking *whales*.

Charlie stared at the phone on his desk. His face was still flushed, and now there was sweat running in hot rivulets down his back. More than anything, he wanted to head over to the Bakery and power up his makeshift vaporizer. He could use something to calm his mind. Minutes ago, Cameron had finally told him the twins' endgame. Their investment in Charlie and BitInstant, even their initial purchase through Mt. Gox, was really just dipping a toe (two toes, come to think of it) in the water. But they were about to put their feet in.

11

THE REVERSE HEIST

P lease remove any laptop computers, large electronic devices, metals, liquids, shoes, jackets. . . ."

The drone of the bored TSA agent standing on the other side of the conveyer barely registered as Cameron unslung his black backpack from his shoulder. The TSA orders were, of course, redundant. Cameron had been flying since before he could walk. The poorly choreographed post-9/11 dance of airport security was second nature to him. His laptop was already on its way down toward the maw of the X-ray scanner. His high-tops were in the next bin, stacked on top of his leather wallet and keys. All that was left was the backpack.

The thing felt like it weighed a hundred pounds, as Cameron directed it toward the third bin he'd retrieved from the tower by the start of the belt, but, in reality, it was quite light; when it got to the X-ray machine, all that the TSA agents were going to see were a couple of magazines, a comb, and a paperback book. If they looked really hard, maybe they would see a dozen 8½-by-11—waterproof, fire-resistant, and tamper-proof plastic envelopes, resting between copies of that week's *Economist* and the most recent *Vanity Fair*. If the TSA agents got curious and decided to open the envelopes, they would see that each envelope contained a single sheet of paper. On each sheet, they would see what would appear to be a morass of random, garbled letters and numbers, printed by a computer.

And yet, even the slightest possibility of those TSA agents holding those plastic envelopes sent nervous chills down Cameron's spine. Even worse, just the thought of those X-ray scanners was enough to send him into a mini-panic. Could those machines actually capture legible images of the twelve pieces of paper in those twelve plastic envelopes? Did they store what they scanned? If so, where? On a local hard drive? In the cloud? Who had access to those scans?

As Cameron carefully placed his backpack and moved toward the short line of people waiting to go through the body scanner that led deeper into the Delta terminal at LaGuardia, he realized that he was actually shaking. He had nothing to be scared of; he wasn't smuggling guns, or drugs, or cash, just pieces of paper sealed in plastic envelopes.

He watched as a young woman entered the scanner, raising her arms above her head like she was about to leap off a diving board. Two more people were in line behind the woman: a guy who couldn't have been older than nineteen, in torn jeans and a black Megadeth T-shirt, and a middle-aged businessman whose suit pants were a little too short, making them look like clamdiggers above his argyle socks. Soon it would be Cameron's turn, and then he'd be on the other side, able to retrieve the backpack. Maybe then he'd be able to catch his breath again.

As the young woman moved out of the scanner and Megadeth moved in, Cameron wondered if his brother had suffered through the same mental anguish. Tyler had left their office a couple of hours before Cameron, so by now, he might already be in Detroit, heading toward his connecting flight. By this point, his matching backpack would be safely on his shoulder, well past the prying eyes of any TSA agents.

Megadeth was through the scanner, and it was now the businessman's turn to show off his diving form. Then Cameron was inside, arms up, imagining the tiny microwaves flitting through his skin and bones and organs. Finally, he was through too and back to the conveyor belt. He forced himself to go for his shoes and laptop first, then the backpack. Once he had it in hand, he started breathing normally again. Still, it wasn't until he was halfway to his gate that his heart rate started to settle down.

He wondered if it was going to be like this the whole three-day trip. Would he freak out at every airport, in front of every TSA agent, until all twelve pieces of paper reached their final resting place? He chided himself as he checked the information screens by the gate; his flight to Milwaukee was still on time, which meant everything was right on schedule. He'd have no problem making his connection to Madison. From there, it would be less than twenty minutes from the airport to the first bank. And when he was finished there, another twenty minutes back to the airport. Assuming the airlines didn't let him down (always a possibility), he'd soon be on the next leg of his journey.

Tyler had planned everything out to the minute: the flights, the connections, even the taxis in between. Left-brained Tyler was good at planning; he'd been in charge of putting together itineraries for their family vacations since he was in his early teens.

Heading toward the gate agent, phone out to show her the barcode of his e-ticket, Cameron realized a simple truth; fuck it, both he and his brother were built for this sort of thing. *High pressure, high stakes.* For Cameron, the next seventy-two hours were going to be some of the longest hours in his life. But they were a walk in the park compared to an Olympic starting line.

I think you're going to be very satisfied with our service, Mr. Winklevoss. We might not look as corporate as the banks you're used to, but we pride ourselves on our professionalism. We're sure we'll meet all of your local banking needs."

The customer service rep had a beehive hairdo that bounced as she walked. Her gray pantsuit swished with each step, in concert with the clack of her platform shoes against the tiled floor. She was a pleasant lady in her midforties, with round glasses that sat precariously on a button of a nose, and a bubbly smile to go with the hairdo. Everything about her personality seemed peppy, which was good, because Cameron needed the infusion of energy. She was the third bank manager he had met that day, and there were still two more to go, with multiple flights in between.

Following her down the long corridor that led past the teller windows of the Davenport, Iowa, branch of the Northwest Bank and Trust, Cameron had to slow his long legs and New York gait to keep from passing her. But he was thankful for the calmer, midwestern pace; at the moment he was fighting true exhaustion. Getting to the bank in Davenport hadn't been as easy as the ones in Madison and Minneapolis. Madison and Minneapolis were small cities compared to New York City, but compared to Davenport, with a population under 100,000 people, they felt enormous.

"At the moment," Cameron said as they reached the door to the vault, which the woman dutifully attacked with a set of keys, "my needs are pretty minimal."

The woman smiled back at him as she managed to swing the door open, then ushered him into a room with safety-deposit boxes stacked floor to ceiling on two walls.

"You never know. Just a safety-deposit box today, maybe an IRA tomorrow? We're here for you, Mr. Winklevoss."

She certainly liked saying his name. Cameron wasn't sure if the woman recognized him, but unlike some of the other banks he'd visited, she hadn't asked him any questions about the movie or about Facebook. Which he took as a very good sign. He wasn't wearing a baseball hat down low over his eyes, he hadn't painted on a mustache or dyed his hair, but he was certainly trying to keep as low a profile as possible. Renting a safety-deposit box in some small-town bank in the middle of Iowa wasn't suspicious on its own. Maybe he had family in the area, maybe he had met a girl on a business trip and wanted a place nearby to store an engagement ring, maybe he was thinking of opening a rowing boathouse on the nearby Mississippi River. People rented safety-deposit boxes all the time for all sorts of reasons.

Then again, if the woman had seen his entire itinerary, if she had known that his identical twin brother was, at that very moment, at a bank in a city two states away, renting a similar-sized safety-deposit box, she might have had some questions.

Even without that knowledge, if she really recognized Cameron's last name, she, or the bank's risk officer, might have had reservations about taking his business. The twins had already been turned down by a few banks over the phone when they'd called inquiring about opening an account and renting a safety-deposit box. Those banks were even smaller banks that didn't feel comfortable taking the twins' business because they were worried that whatever the hell the twins planned on depositing with them would be in-credibly valuable—making the bank a target for bank robbers and other bad actors.

Most small bank branches did not keep much cash on hand in their vaults; some as little as $20,000 at a time. This branch probably didn't even have that much, and why would they? Cash went digital the minute anyone made a de-posit. Why go to the trouble of hiring multiple guards, getting them bonded, and building hardcore security systems to protect what was ultimately a Microsoft Excel spreadsheet? But the safety-deposit boxes were different. The risks of holding something incredibly valuable, not just personal effects, but something liquid and fungible far outweighed the potential rental fees.

But if this particular bank manager was concerned, she wasn't showing it. If push came to shove, Cameron could try to put her at ease by reaching into his backpack and saying that all he was storing in the plastic envelope des-tined for this bank was his Harvard diploma, or transcript, or some original family portraits of his ancestors. If pressed further, he could show her the actual piece of paper inside the plastic envelope and explain that it contained secret intellectual property for a computer program he had written back at school, or something along those lines. Not that she would actually ask. Instead, he waited until she showed him to his deposit box, a rectangular one, halfway up the easterly wall, and handed him his key. Only when she'd gone back out through the door of the vault, locking it behind her, did he unzip his backpack.

Taking one of the remaining plastic envelopes out, he carefully placed it inside the box. As he did so, he contemplated the contents printed on the piece of office paper from Staples inside—the random letters and numbers that to the human eye were indecipherable. To a computer, with the right software client installed, this paper contained one-third of a bitcoin private key—a *shard*.

This shard, referred to as "alpha," when combined with two others, "bravo" and "charlie," formed a *private key*—the private key that controlled all of the twins' bitcoin. This meant that all three shards had to be separated from each other. Storing all three shards in one safety-deposit box would mean a thief could get control of all of the twins' bitcoin by stealing a single safety-deposit box—*a single point of failure*. And storing them in safety-deposit boxes at different branches of the same bank wasn't enough. An unscrupulous employee of that bank could pull off an inside job by accessing the vaults at different branches—another single point of failure. As a result, alpha, bravo, and charlie had to be stored in *different* safety-deposit boxes at *different* banks. With this security design, a thief would have to rob three different banks—or bribe employees at three different banks—or pull off some combination thereof to gain control of the twins' bitcoin. Either way, it would be a logistical nightmare—*Mission Impossible* shit that only worked in the movies—to get ahold of the three shards that made up the bitcoin private key.

Moreover, the twins had replicated this model four times across different geographic regions, to build redundancy into their system—removing the final single point of failure—and improving their overall fault tolerance. This way, if a natural disaster like a major tornado decimated the Midwest, there would still be other sets of alpha, bravo, and charlie spread across other regions in the country (the Northeast, Mid-Atlantic, West, etc.) that could be assembled to form the twins' private key. If a mega tsunami—or hell, Godzilla—hit the eastern seaboard, or a meteor hit Los Angeles, the twins' private key would still be safe.

A total of twelve safety-deposit boxes, held across three different banking institutions, and spread across four distinct regions in the United States, completed their security design. The twelve pieces of paper in these twelve safety-deposit boxes would make up the *only four copies of the twins' private key in the world*. No other copy would exist anywhere else, not on their laptops, not anywhere online, nowhere, only in twelve bank vaults spread out across the country. Cameron and Tyler's homemade, off-line or "cold" storage system, built of paper and metal lock boxes, was ironically state-of-the-art; it rooted the security of the twin's bitcoin in the physical world, outside the reach of online hackers.

The twins' security system made it unlikely that a thief could physically get ahold of their private key, but none of these bank vaults prevented a hacker from guessing it. Generated correctly, a private key was impossible to guess—1 in 115 quattuorvigintillion—but the trick was generating it correctly.

To securely generate their private key, the twins had to make sure it was completely random. As it turned out, picking random numbers wasn't as easy as it sounded; the human brain was not particularly good at creating random-ness. It had an innate tendency to embed nonrandom patterns and sequences, even if it was consciously determined not to. Computers also had challenges when it came to randomness. They were deterministic machines built to return the same result for a given input—the opposite of random. You could use a random number generator on your computer, but what if the algorithm used was faulty? What if it produced what appeared to be a random number but was, in fact, merely a complex pattern that was predictable to a machine and could be reverse engineered? What if a hacker or a government was sniffing the electromagnetic fields being emitted by your computer, reading all of the information on it, including the numbers being generated?

In the world of virtual currency, paranoia had no bounds—in the end, only the paranoid would survive. And the twins were hell-bent on surviving. To ensure the security of their private key, they would have to harvest random-ness from a sufficiently random and physical source that couldn't be inter-cepted or easily reverse engineered.

The twins had ended up going old school, settling on a physical random number generator—a pair of sixteen-sided *hexadecimal dice*. Each die looked like two miniature, eight-sided pyramids glued together at their bases. These were the kind of dice that kids in high school who wear black trench coats and play fantasy role-playing games like Dungeons and Dragons might carry. In addition, the dice had to be evenly balanced and the table had to be level—so that rolls of the dice weren't skewed to a particular letter or number, thereby defeating the randomness.

Cameron carefully placed the plastic envelope in the safety-deposit box, then slid the box back in its place, using the metal key the woman had given him to secure the lock. He placed the key to the safe onto a large ring—next to the two he'd received earlier that day—and placed the ring in the front pocket of his backpack.

And then he was back at the vault door leading to the rest of the bank. The woman opened it for him, springy and bouncy and friendly as ever.

"Are you sure you wouldn't rather have one of our larger deposit boxes? The monthly bill isn't much higher, and you get so much more room for your valuables."

Cameron smiled back at her as she shut and locked the door behind him.

"This one's more than enough for my stuff. Just some things that have sentimental value to me, but wouldn't mean much to anyone else."

It was true, to someone else that piece of paper wouldn't mean much. Just random numbers, picked by the roll of plastic dice. But if that piece of paper was somehow reunited with the other pieces of paper in his bag and some of those that were already safely hidden away by him and Tyler in safety-deposit boxes in banks all around the country—well, that would be a different story.

Those pieces of paper would suddenly be worth far more than whatever cash was kept in this bank's vault, maybe far more than all the cash in all the vaults of every branch of these local banks. Cameron couldn't be sure, because the value of what those pieces of paper represented changed every day, sometimes every minute. He didn't know how much they were worth, only what they had cost. And that number alone would have knocked the beehive right off his companion's head.

Cameron's taxi was still waiting on the street outside, ready to take him back to the airport, just in time to catch his next flight.

Efficient Tyler hadn't factored in friendly conversation to their timetables; this wasn't a pleasure trip, this was all business. They were on a mission.

On to the next city, the next bank, the next safety-deposit box.

A re we really going to do this?"

Cameron grinned at his brother as he lifted the heavy sledgehammer over his shoulder, his eyes hidden behind a pair of thick plastic safety goggles. He was wearing a raincoat over his Tom Ford suit, and a pair of disposable, polypropylene galoshes over his cap-toed dress shoes. He could have changed out of his expensive suit, put on some sweats, a T-shirt, jeans, but he'd been wearing the suit that morning when they'd met with their accountant, and he'd decided it fit the moment. It wasn't every day you got to use a sledgehammer while wearing a suit.

"It sure looks like we're going to do this."

Tyler was wearing a matching smock, but he still had his goggles up on his hair. His sledgehammer was resting on the cement wall behind him, its enormous head planted on the hardwood floor, inches beyond where the plastic tarp they'd laid out beneath the computer equipment ended. Tyler was looking at the hardware: the five laptops, already pried open, their hard drives gleaming against the tarp, the pile of USB drives, the pair of wireless routers, even the printer, up on its side to give them a better angle with the hammers.

"The routers are overkill," Tyler said. "The printer too. Nobody's going to be able to get anything off of a printer."

Cameron shifted the sledgehammer, getting a better grip with his gloved hands. The gloves, smocks, goggles, tarp, and hammers had all come from Home Depot. One of the computers had been bought by Charlie, along with the USB drives. The printer was from their home office, not the construction zone they were standing in, the future headquarters of Winklevoss Capital.

The construction site had seemed the perfect place for the business at hand. They'd drawn the shades, but even if the shades had been open, nobody outside would have looked twice at two guys swinging sledgehammers in a construction site. Not even Charlie, over at his office at BitInstant a couple of blocks away, knew what they were actually up to, the extent to which they were taking their security seriously. He probably would have thought they were crazy. When he'd first walked them through the process of acquiring bitcoin, he hadn't mentioned anything about sledgehammers.

The two clean laptops and the dozen USB drives were as far as Charlie had gotten. In the initial days, for the first $750,000 that they had Charlie purchase on their behalf, that had been enough, given the value at risk.

But when Cameron had explained to Charlie that the first $750,000's worth of bitcoin was only the beginning, and they'd moved their purchasing into high gear—Cameron and Tyler had begun buying through Mt. Gox on their own, moving much bigger amounts of cash into the virtual currency. And they had quickly realized that the dozen USB drives were nowhere near safe enough for what they had planned.

First off, there was no way they were going to leave any significant amount of bitcoin on Mt. Gox—a website that was once a magic card exchange and was now run by a crazy Frenchman who had made his mark putting cat videos on YouTube. Mt. Gox was a Dumpster fire waiting to happen.

The twins needed to store their bitcoin somewhere else. And with the numbers they were talking about, they'd decided to give their paranoia free rein. They'd already heard many stories about people having their digital wallets hacked, or their USB drives stolen, or people just plain losing their hard drives. Cameron had read about one guy in the UK who had actually spent months digging in vain through a garbage dump in search of a drive with a million dollars of bitcoin stored on it. The twins did not intend to dig through any garbage, or allow themselves to get hacked. Paranoia had its advantages.

So, one month earlier, in Cameron's apartment, they'd nailed towels up across all the windows, making sure there was no way anyone could peer in and see what they were doing, and locked their iPhones away, far out of reach and in airplane mode. *You never know who could be snooping through the camera or speakers of a smartphone.* They then had gone to work with the hexadecimal dice, creating a new private key—different from the one they had created with Charlie.

For this new private key ceremony, they'd bought two additional clean laptops, from different suppliers, one cold and one hot. They'd placed electrical tape over both laptops' cameras and speakers. The hot computer was used to download digital wallet software that was then transferred over via USB to the cold laptop; the twins had disabled the cold's Wi-Fi—by physically removing its Wi-Fi card. They then had entered their new private key—the one they'd generated using hexadecimal dice—into the digital wallet on the cold laptop. Once they'd had their digital wallet set up on the cold laptop, they could generate Bitcoin addresses, controlled by their new private key, to send their Mt. Gox funds to, and attach a lightweight printer via USB cable to print out their new private key into distinct shards. They'd then inserted these shards—alpha, bravo, and charlie—into the plastic envelopes and sealed them. Then they'd laid the envelopes out on Cameron's coffee table—ready for their backpacks and the long mission ahead.

Dividing them up between them, Cameron and Tyler had set off across the country, creating what they believed was the most secure storage system in the history of Bitcoin. USB sticks and computer hard drives could be stolen or hacked. Private keys on paper in a vault could be photographed or taken. But shards spread out all over the country, in a dozen different safety-deposit boxes—that was different. Only the twins themselves knew where the shards were, or how the shards went back together. Only they could retrieve their private key and get to their bitcoin.

It was like a bank heist in reverse. Instead of robbing a dozen banks, they'd filled them up. At some point in the future, what was once sitting on Cameron's coffee table, and now resting in those safety-deposit boxes, was going to be worth more than the entire balance sheets of those banks. Maybe.

All that was left were the loose ends. The hardware that had enabled them to pull off the reverse heist. And now it was time to eliminate the evidence. Erase any kind of digital exhaust, fingerprint, or traces of their private key, and destroy any surface area that a hacker could try and cling onto or digitally swab for DNA.

Cameron hefted the sledgehammer high over his head, and with a primal shout, brought it down as hard as he could on one of the laptops. The keyboard shattered into a thousand pieces, daggers of plastic ricocheting in every direction, clattering off of the cement walls. He lifted the hammer again, aiming at the printer. When the hammer hit, the crack of the plastic reverberated through his shoulders.

It felt so damn good. The rational portion of his brain knew that he was simply securing their investment, making it impossible for anyone or any technology to find or steal their bitcoin. But the rest of him was living in the moment. All the frustration of his past, of what they had been through with Zuckerberg and the lawyers and everything else, dissipating with each stroke of that hammer, with each implosion of plastic, metal, and glass.

The past was gone. Bitcoin was the future.

And Cameron and his brother had leaped headlong into that future. All told, they had spent a little over two million dollars so far, and they would eventually pour in over eleven million dollars to complete their goal. It was, perhaps, the largest bet anyone in the world had made on virtual currency. Maybe only Satoshi, if he was real, and still alive, had more bitcoin.

Either way, the Winklevoss twins were on their way to owning 1 percent of all bitcoin in existence.

All there was, and all there ever would be.

And that stash, that fortune—put them at the dead center of the crypto revolution.

ACT TWO

Life is a storm. You will bask in the sunlight one moment, be shattered on the rocks the next. What makes you a man is what you do when that storm comes.

—ALEXANDRE DUMAS,
The Count of Monte Cristo

12

THE SPARK

March 16, 2013.

A little after seven in the morning.

Cyprus.

A European island in the eastern Mediterranean, barely a hundred and fifty miles long, sixty miles wide, and fifty miles off the coast of Turkey.

The resort town of Larnaca on the southern coast, Cyprus's third largest city. A magnificent, stone-paved promenade running along Finikoudes Beach, embraced on either side by palm trees. A tourist haven, swarming with beach cafés, coffee shops, outdoor restaurants, and souvenir outposts. Crowded even on a humid Saturday morning; groups of Brits in bright-colored football jerseys intermingling with French couples holding hands, American teenagers escaping their tour groups for a latte and a walk along the sand, and, of course, Russians, gregarious and loud and breakfasting in the restaurants and smoking cigarettes beneath the weeping palms.

Marina Korsokov brushed the last remnants of a deep sleep out of her almond eyes as she turned off the promenade and strolled down a side street leading toward the town's center, a steaming cup of Greek coffee in one hand. She had a bag of croissants in the other, enough for her family of four, although she was sure that at least two of the pastries would be gone before either her husband, Nikita, or her daughter and son, Alexa and Mikhael, crawled out of their beds. It had been a late night the evening before; three neighboring families had been over for dinner, and the conversation had lasted well past even the adults' bedtimes. The discussion had been about politics and money, as usual; lately, every conversation in Cyprus seemed to revolve around politics and money. Marina figured that was to be expected when your country was on the verge of declaring bankruptcy.

Marina had slept soundly when she'd finally gotten to her bed; life was exhausting, not just raising two children under the age of nine, but also dealing with her husband's daily woes. Although most Cypriots had a view of the local Russian community as being dominated by oligarchs and gangsters, most were like the Korsokovs—working people who had scraped enough together to immigrate to Cyprus because it was safer than Moscow, warmer than Russia, and part of the European Union (EU)—a potential winning lottery ticket for their children, who would grow up far away from the hardships Marina and Nikita had lived through in the 1980s and 1990s.

Despite her new country's problems, she trusted that everything would work out. This wasn't Russia, this was a modern European country, a meeting place of many ethnicities, religions, and ideologies—a melting pot that was also a beachfront idyll. She liked to leave the worrying about politics and money to her husband and his friends. She was too busy building their life.

As Marina reached the end of the alley leading off the promenade and caught sight of a large crowd on a corner across the street, she was suddenly reminded of an old Russian proverb: *The less you know, the more soundly you sleep.*

Even from a distance, she could tell that the crowd was agitated and growing by the minute. It was made up mostly of men. Some she recognized from her nearby neighborhood, others were wearing aprons that marked them as workers from a café, or suits, which meant they spent their time in the office buildings or banks that spotted the narrow streets.

At first, she thought about avoiding the group, but then she recognized someone, one of the few women in the crowd, a fellow Russian named Natalya who with her husband ran a small clothing boutique next door to Marina's favorite bakery on the promenade.

Crossing the street, she waved to catch Natalya's attention, spilling some of her coffee on her sleeve. Cursing at herself in Russian, she reached the other side of the street just as her friend stepped to meet her.

"This is crazy," Natalya said. "I can't believe they are doing it. It's just not right."

Marina realized that the crowd was in front of one of the many bank branches that speckled the beachside town; she immediately recognized the bright red signs of LAIKA BANK, the country's second largest. Most of the storefront was brick, with large glass windows, a double wooden door, and three ATM machines perched on the stone sidewalk out front. Marina counted at least thirty people lined up at the machines, not pushing and shoving yet but clearly restless.

"What is this?" Marina said.

"It's the bank run before the bank run."

Marina realized she probably should have been paying more attention during the protracted conversation the night before. She knew that things were bad, that Cyprus, like many of the more economically challenged nations of the EU, was in major debt—and that the continent's financial leaders had been meeting in Brussels to figure out how to handle the situation. But beyond that, she was no expert; Cyprus was out of money, but its economy hadn't totally cratered like nearby Greece, which was in the process of being bailed out by the EU through an austerity package—lowered salaries and entitlements across the board, fired government employees, shuttered businesses—that had led to riots in the streets of Athens. Cyprus wasn't Greece; it was a small community of barely a million people. And besides, Cyprus had lived through troubled times before; they'd even survived a civil war between the Greek-dominated south and the Turkish-dominated north, which had resulted in the island being divided in two.

Marina's husband, Russian that he was, had a habit of shouting that the sky was falling; but they weren't in Moscow anymore, they were part of the EU, the civilized world. In the civilized world, the sky didn't fall. Did it?

Suddenly a kind of groan went up from the front of the line by the ATMs, and word quickly trickled back to the edge of the crowd.

"They've just run out," a man in a cream linen suit shouted. "The ATMs are empty. It's not even eight o'clock. This is a disaster."

"Can't you try another branch?" Marina asked.

The man looked at her like she was crazy.

"They're all empty. Not just the ATMs. The banks. It's all gone."

"He's exaggerating," another man said. "They aren't going to take all of it. Just a haircut. That's what they are calling it. A haircut."

"You're a fool," the first man shouted back. "They've already announced that the banks will be closed on Monday, and probably for the week. A banking *holiday*. Our money is gone!"

Marina felt the fear rising inside of her as she listened to the two men. Her family wasn't rich, not by a long shot. Her husband worked for his uncle's ceramics business, which was run out of Limassol, another resort town farther up the coast, where so many Russians lived that it was sometimes referred to as Limassolgrad. They had always been good at saving their money, a lesson they had learned growing up in Moscow, where things could turn ugly, and usually did, at the drop of a hat. They had put together a nest egg of a little over 120,000 euros.

Which, she now realized with a sinking feeling, was all in their account at Laika.

She grabbed Natalya by the arm and pulled her close.

"What's happening?" she hissed.

"The banks lost everything. And the EU won't bail them out. So instead, they made a deal. They put up some of the money, but the banks have to come up with the rest. They are going to take it from our accounts. From everyone's accounts."

"Just take it?" Marina said. "They can't do that. Can they? Just take your money like that?"

"Apparently they can. Not all of it, but it's not clear how much. Right now, they say six percent if you have under a hundred thousand euros, and ten percent if you have more. My husband says those numbers are lies. He heard that if your money is in Laika, you lose fifty percent."

She pointed to the crowd amassed in front of the ATM machines.

"ATMs are empty. They are going to keep the banks closed so nobody can pull their money out. They are calling it a one-time tax."

"But this is theft!"

"In Brussels, they call it 'burden sharing.' They are blaming the banks."

Marina's face blanched. As much as half her money—gone? Snatched right out of her bank account by the government? Could they really do that? Cyprus wasn't Greece, Cyprus hadn't gone bankrupt. Cyprus wasn't poor—but it was . . . different. It was well known that the banks in Cyprus were out of control; that between them, they held eight times the size of the entire GDP of the small island country. She also knew that a large portion of that was Russian money. Cyprus had turned itself into a tax haven, charging zero taxes, inviting money from everywhere, and had become the stomping ground of Russian oligarchs, and mobsters who were looking for a safe place to put their ill-gotten wealth. Supposedly, more than thirty billion dollars' worth of Russian money had found its way into Cyprus's banks. A full two-thirds of all deposits over a hundred thousand euros were Russian.

Apparently, the EU had decided to give that Russian money a "haircut," and along with the oligarchs and the mobsters, innocent bystanders like Marina and the crowd on the street around her were going to suffer as well.

"How could this happen?" Marina gasped.

She was still clutching the bag of croissants and the coffee, so she couldn't look in her wallet. But she doubted she had more than fifty euros. At home, maybe her husband had another hundred, two hundred at most. How were they going to eat?

What do you do when you wake up one day to discover that the money in your bank account is gone? That all you have is whatever's in your pocket? How do you survive?

"I have to get home," Marina said, pushing past her friend and the crowd, which had now grown twice as large. The coffee spilled again at the motion, but she barely noticed. She needed to wake up her husband, to tell him that for once, he was right.

The sky really was falling.

13

BAYFRONT PARK, DOWNTOWN MIAMI

O ne hour later, five time zones west.

Splashes of fire flashed overhead in a Technicolor arc, painting the night like neon graffiti, illuminating the bay and the dozens of luxury motor yachts jockeying for position along the floating dock. A throbbing, electric beat from the nearby outdoor "arena"—a massive, open pit, jammed with nearly 100,000 people, sprawled out in front of a huge, raised stage—reverberated through the air, so loud that, even from the dock behind the mainstage, each note threatened to crack the very air.

Now this is how you make an entrance, Tyler thought to himself as he stepped off the edge of a London gray, eighty-eight-foot *Riva* motor yacht and onto the dock. The humid breeze pulled at his white slacks and shirt, but he had no trouble navigating the short hop from the water onto land; the excessively tall girl in terrifyingly high heels next to him, holding on to his hand for balance, had it a little more difficult. When she too touched down, she let out what could only be described as a squeal, and Tyler laughed, because, given the moment, it was as appropriate a sound as any.

Tyler steadied the girl on the dock and started forward, toward the music.

Along with his slacks and shirt, his shoes were also white, because it was Miami, it was eighty-five degrees at night, and why the hell not. He had just spent the early part of the afternoon on the super yacht he had just disembarked from, a floating kingdom with tan leather interiors, a wet bar, a hot tub, and the woman next to him. Her name was Tiffany, and she was at least six feet tall in her bare feet, with hair streaked in purple and gold, eyelashes as long as a tarantula's legs, wearing a bikini top and white jean short shorts. She looked like a model and indeed had walked her fair share of runways. But she was a nursing student by day and could hold her own with any of Tyler's contemporaries.

Cameron was a few feet ahead of them, already on the dock, also wearing white, parenthesized by a Dutch supermodel with a name neither of them could pronounce and her famous DJ husband, both of whom were decked out in black leather despite the heat.

"Hold up," Tyler called to his brother, as he himself nearly tripped on one of the wooden slots beneath his feet. "I don't want to break an ankle before we even get inside."

The path that snaked out ahead of them toward the VIP entrance to the "arena" was really more runway than dock; held up by bright blue pontoons floating in the bay, it circumnavigated the waterfront, normally a jag of prime Miami real estate that bordered the Financial District, a good twenty-minute drive over the bridge from South Beach, where everyone who could afford to was actually staying—and ended at that covered entrance, which would assumedly spit them out so close to the stage that their ears would bleed.

Each step was a preview of the shattering volume and incredible energy that Tyler knew was coming; he could already see the top part of the stage, the hollowed-out half shell rising up beneath the fireworks engulfing the sky, a honey-combed, crisscrossed, metal monstrosity bristling with lights and speakers. He wasn't a huge EDM fan; he couldn't identify the DJ who was already onstage by the pounding music so loud now that it threatened to knock him right into the bay, but it was assuredly someone famous. He'd seen the lineup on the boat ride over: Calvin Harris, David Guetta, Deadmau5, Tiësto, Avicci, Swedish House Mafia—the list went on and on, every name more famous in the EDM community than the last.

"Welcome to Ultra," the Dutch model next to Cameron said over her shoulder as Tyler finally caught up. "Even if you broke your ankle the music would keep you dancing until five A.M."

It was the kind of thing someone married to a DJ might say, but Tyler doubted he would be dancing—or awake—at five in the morning. It had been a long month already, but Ultra was definitely something he and Cameron had to see. They had to be in Miami that second week of March anyway, part of a seven-city road trip down the southeastern seaboard of the country, pushing Bitcoin, and there seemed to be no better way to cap off two days of meetings in suits than a stop at one of the premier music festivals in the world.

Though tiring, the meetings had been extremely promising. In the past few months since they'd made their huge investment in the virtual currency, bitcoin had steadily risen in price and was hovering around the $40 mark. That meant their growing investment was now worth close to $40 million, and the entire market cap of bitcoin had gone from around $100 million in value to close to half a billion.

It wasn't hard to catch people's interest when talking about Bitcoin. And Tyler and his brother didn't have trouble getting just about anyone to meet with them; people were willing to sit down with them out of curiosity alone. But that didn't mean the businessmen they met with were willing or ready to invest in bitcoin. Bitcoin still seemed too speculative for people who worked at conventional banks and funds. Even managers of hedge funds, the types who had no problem plunking down tens of millions of dollars on modern art, odd commodities, gold, or sketchy mining outfits in undeveloped third world countries were afraid of a virtual currency created by a mysterious computer programmer.

Still, Tyler saw the cavalcade of meetings as a success. His immediate goal wasn't to convince anyone to buy bitcoin, it was to simply educate them on the new virtual currency, to act as an ambassador to what he believed, more and more, was the *future of money*. Success right now meant getting the conversation started and planting the seeds of the idea of decentralized virtual currency in the minds of some of the most influential business leaders in the world.

Still, it was a grueling schedule of meetings, and this was the perfect change of scenery. Ultra, in its fifteenth year in Miami, had grown from a few thousand attendees in 1999 to over 300,000 rabid electronic music fans. All in all, the Ultra stages, in combination with parties thrown all through the day and night at pretty much every hotel pool and club between downtown and South Beach, made for one big outdoor rave. The Delano, where Tyler and Cameron had booked a penthouse suite, was an art deco hotel located on Collins Avenue and was famous for its celebrity guests. Everything was white, from the minimalist furniture, to the walls, to the light fixtures. A wave of white, washing all the way from the hotel lobby, past the giant chessboard on the terraced lawn, to the candles in the candelabra sitting on a metal table that stood in the shallow end of the pool. The hotel had DJs stationed by the breakfast buffet, the pool, and the beach. Whether he liked it or not, Tyler knew he would be hearing trance-like, rising and falling electric tones in his sleep for days to come.

Their group reached the VIP entrance right behind a small crowd that had come off of one of the similar yachts crowding the waterway. Tyler recognized a few of the faces: Snoop Dogg, Michael Bay, Rob Gronkowski. All of a sudden, flashy plastic wristbands were slapped on their wrists, and they were whisked through the entrance—led through a break in the crowd—more of a tunnel weaving past arms and legs and bodies held back by steel barricades and security guards—toward a blocked-off area of tables for celebrities and people who were willing to spend like celebrities. Even though they were nonpaying guests, Tyler couldn't help but wince at the fact that these tables went for more than $20,000 for the night, and that most of the groups would be spending five times that on alcohol, served by women in skin-baring uniforms shuttling back and forth from a private bar tucked right next to the stage.

As they entered the table area, Tyler felt the ground shaking beneath his feet. The beat had gotten so loud that it was hard even to think, but that didn't stop him from noticing a smaller vibration in the pocket of his shirt. He realized it was his smartphone going off. As he reached for it, he saw that Cameron had also paused at the edge of the VIP area and was also reaching for his own smartphone. The fact that they were both getting blown-up messages at the same time—6:00 P.M. on a Saturday evening—meant that something important was going on.

Cameron got to his phone first. Sticking white earbuds in both ears, he tried to listen to a voice mail amid the ambient wall of sound, but he quickly gave up, looking at his screen instead. Tyler went straight to his own screen and saw text after text. Most were from the people they had met in the Bitcoin world, including Charlie, a variety of bankers they'd given presentations to in the past few days, and even their father. All the texts centered on the same topic, and many ended in multiple exclamation marks.

As Tyler read, then googled, then read more, the immense arena, the eardrum-shattering music, and the beautiful people receded around him. He could have been standing alone on a beach. All he could think about was what he was reading. He looked up and locked eyes with Cameron.

Cyprus.

At that moment, they both knew that this little island country on the other side of the world, which many of the three hundred thousand dancing people around them had never even heard of, was about to change *everything*.

Cyprus, according to some, was named for its rich natural veins of copper. Copper—once used for money by the Romans, still used by the United States in its pennies—was of little comfort to them now. Its banks had been swimming naked, amassing tons of bad debt, and the tide had just gone out.

The EU finance ministers—the central authority of this system—had agreed to help, but under one condition. The EU would lend Cyprus money, but only if Cyprus agreed to chip in itself by taking money directly from its people—a "bailout" predicated on a "bail-in." With the stroke of a pen, Cypriot banks had been ordered to confiscate all customer bank deposits in excess of €100,000 and send them to the Bank of Cyprus. In other words, if you held €500,000 in a Cyprus bank, you would lose €400,000 and be left with €100,000. And just like that, the government of Cyprus had agreed to pass the buck to its citizens—almost none of whom had anything to do with making the decisions that had gotten the country into financial ruin in the first place.

It wasn't the sheer size of the theft perpetrated by the Cyprian government against its people that had sent shock waves through the world—it was the fact that something like that could even happen. It was the exact thing that people like Voorhees and Ver prophesized: the capricious whim of government intervention.

The girl with the tarantula eyelashes leaned close to Tyler, glitter on her cheeks flashing from the lights of the stage and the glow of his phone.

"What's going on?" she asked, lips almost touching his ear so that he could hear over the music.

Tyler waved Cameron over.

"A whole country just got robbed by their own government," he shouted.

"That can happen?" the girl asked.

"It just did, in the EU," Tyler said. "And it can happen here too."

He and his brother were both thinking the same thing. What could happen in Cyprus could conceivably happen here. The U.S. government stepped in during economic crises all the time. Less than five years earlier, the United States had used billions of dollars of taxpayer money to bail out Wall Street banks during the 2008 financial crisis. During the Great Depression the government had prohibited U.S. citizens from owning gold: in 1933, President Roosevelt had signed executive order 6102, requiring citizens to turn in their gold for cash. It wasn't until 1975, when President Ford repealed this order, that it was again legal for Americans to own gold that wasn't jewelry or coins. And all bank deposits were only insured to the tune of $250,000.

"More than twenty thousand account holders at Laika, the second largest bank in Cyprus, are going to have half of their savings taken away," Tyler said. "The Bank of Cyprus, the largest bank, is going to take almost fifty percent of all deposits over a hundred thousand."

"They're calling it a tax, or levy," Cameron said. "They're closing all the banks to keep it from turning into a bank run."

"Look at this picture," Tyler said. "This is a mob outside one of the banks. A bunch of people got hold of a bulldozer. It looks like they're going to try to get inside."

"Nobody is going to feel safe keeping their money in an EU bank after this. No one is going to feel safe keeping money in any bank, period."

Tyler looked at him. The entire arena seemed to lurch under his feet as the DJ on the stage hit keys on his computer, launching off an artillery battalion of synthetic drumbeats.

If this could happen in an EU country, what prevented it from happening anywhere else? This was precedent.

Tyler was too young to remember the savings and loan crisis in 1987, but they had lived through the dot-com bubble in 1999, and the recent credit crisis, just four years earlier, in 2008. He believed that what was happening in Cyprus was exactly the sort of financial trauma that would open people's eyes to just how safe their money actually was—or wasn't.

Cyprus would scare the world straight. It was exactly what Bitcoin needed—the catalyst that would propel Bitcoin into the world's consciousness.

"If you don't keep your money in a bank, where can you keep it?" Tiffany asked.

Tyler felt his pulse rising in tune with the music, level after level after level, until it was a thunder in his ears.

Why keep any money, when there was something much better that was now available? Something that was about to get much easier to promote.

And much, much more valuable.

14

ON THE ROAD AGAIN

Charlie clung to the dashboard in front of him for dear life as the Mexico-blue Porsche 911 took the turn at sixty miles per hour, its tires hugging the asphalt as its entire chassis forcibly leaned onto one side, sending the two Korean girls sitting on Charlie's lap—bare legs, mini-skirts, tube tops, and all—flying toward the passenger-side door. He felt skin and leather and nails as the girls laughed and struggled to right themselves. On the other side of him, Roger Ver, the "Bitcoin Jesus," who was behind the Porsche's steering wheel, was laughing too.

"Keep it together, guys," Ver shouted over the loud K-Pop that was blaring out of the Porsche's speakers. "Don't want anyone breaking any laws before we make it to the restaurant. I've already seen the inside of a California prison, and I don't intend to see another one. At least not before Charlie tries the 'meat jun' at Omogari. It will blow his already blown mind."

Charlie helped the girls back on top of each other; it was a good thing that both of them were small—even smaller than Charlie—because when Ver had first told him they were stopping to pick up a couple of friends on the way to Omogari, he had thought the guy was joking. No way four people could fit in the front of a Porsche 911, and there was no backseat. When he and Ver had pulled up to the girls' apartment on the edge of Santa Clara's Koreatown—a stretch of the El Camino Real roadway dubbed "Soon Dubu Row" after the famous tofu stew in Korean cuisine and lined with Korean restaurants, supermarkets, dry cleaners, and other Korean businesses—Charlie had been relieved to see that neither of the girls was over five feet. Both were decked out in silk skirts and midriff-baring tops. The girls seemed perfectly happy sitting on Charlie's lap for the short ride over to the restaurant in nearby San Jose's Japantown—a historic, eight-block section of downtown, and one of only three remaining Japantowns in the country. Which put Charlie right in the middle, both knees jammed against the dashboard, and his left thigh pressing tightly against the gearshift.

"Sorry," one of the girls said, her voice heavy with a Korean accent, her bright red lips swollen beneath cliff-like cheekbones. "I hope I didn't crush anything important."

"Careful." Ver coughed. "Charlie is a nice Jewish boy. I should never have tried to mix him up with girls like you two."

The girls laughed again, and Charlie felt his cheeks growing red. Maybe it was the motion of the car, maybe the strong perfume the girls were wearing, or the bare legs next to him, but he was experiencing an uncharacteristic lack of words. Usually both he and Ver were fast talkers; when he and Ver spoke on the phone, it was a battle to see who could get more words in before the final bell. But tonight Charlie was definitely off his game. He'd always been a bit socially awkward around girls, but this was something different. Besides the car and the perfume and all that skin, he could think of a couple of reasons why that might be.

Things hadn't been going great at home in Brooklyn, which was part of why he had jumped at the chance to go west, to San Jose, for a series of BitInstant pitch meetings, all of which had been arranged by the Winklevoss twins, followed by a Bitcoin conference nearby, which they'd all agreed to attend. Ver, Bitcoin Jesus himself, had flown in to the conference from Japan, his home base.

Although Charlie had never met Ver in person when Ver had first invested in BitInstant, over the past few months they'd grown much closer—and had been face-to-face a handful of times. Still, he was thrilled at the opportunity to catch up. Charlie had begun to see Ver as more than just a business colleague and investor, but as a real friend, an adviser not just in the world of Bitcoin, but also in life. Life, for Charlie, was getting more complicated by the day.

"The operative word is 'Jewish,'" Charlie finally said. "Not Catholic. Our guilt has nothing to do with sex. It's all about our mothers."

Charlie's joke had more truth to it than he'd like to have admitted. At home, things between Charlie and his mother had been going downhill for months, coinciding with his company's rise. He was still living in the basement, but he'd stopped going to temple with his family every Saturday, and when he was out, usually at dinner with Voorhees or Ira or one of his other employees, he certainly wasn't keeping kosher.

Maybe it was all the time he'd spent hanging out with Voorhees or Skyping with Ver, or maybe it was his getting out of the basement more and more, but he had begun questioning everything that he had taken for granted growing up. People didn't think of Orthodox Jews the way they thought about other fundamentalist religious groups, but to Charlie, his mother's views and his Brooklyn community had begun to feel more and more suffocating, more and more like a cult.

It was back in college when he'd started to see travel as an escape from that life. Because of the relationships he'd made online, he'd had the opportunity to visit different areas of the world—and whenever he was in a different city or country, he'd reinvent himself as someone living without the restrictions of his religion. But as soon as he got back to New York, he would bend back to his upbringing. Lately, however, the invented Charlie was seeming more like the *real* Charlie.

"Here we go," Ver said, pulling the Porsche up to the curb and hitting the brakes hard enough to send the girls sliding off of Charlie's lap. "You think the valet takes bitcoin?"

It was something Ver asked before every transaction he made anywhere: *Do you take bitcoin?* Restaurants, supermarkets, convenience stores. So far, the answer was almost always . . . no.

"I'm kidding," Ver added as he opened the door and stepped out onto the sidewalk. "There's no valet. This place is real casual. They let in all the riffraff. I like to keep it simple, no pretensions. I'll let the twins wine and dine you at the Ritz."

Charlie couldn't see Ver's face because Ver was already coming around the car to let the girls out. But usually, when he mentioned Cameron and Tyler, it was followed by an eye roll.

And that was the second reason Charlie felt off that evening; when he'd left the twins earlier that afternoon, after their last meeting of the day, it was obvious that they weren't thrilled that he was heading to dinner with Ver. They'd warned Charlie about getting too close to Ver, about giving too much credence to what he had to say. They'd tried to be measured about it; they were well aware that Charlie and Ver were friends, and that a part of Charlie looked up to him—but they had made it clear they were starting to worry about the potential influence Ver could have, not just on BitInstant, but also on Charlie himself.

Ver started talking to the girls in Korean as he led them toward the restaurant's entrance. Charlie followed, uncurling himself from the front seat of the car and dusting himself off under the red awning. He wasn't surprised by Ver's fluency in Korean; Ver was obsessed with all things Asian, an observation confirmed by the fact that he was shuttling *The Fast and the Furious: Tokyo Drift*–style between Asia-town neighborhoods, only a few hours after stepping off a plane from Tokyo.

Ver was one of the smartest people Charlie had ever met, maybe the smartest, even if his views could be a little extreme. Lately Charlie had begun to think of him as his new "rabbi," to the twins' dismay.

Charlie didn't think the twins had anything to worry about. If anything, the meetings the three of them had that day should have put them at ease. Charlie had been on his game. Moreover, at that moment, life was good for all of them. After Cyprus, the price of a single bitcoin had skyrocketed to more than a $100, which had made the twins a whole lot richer than they already were. They had started their bulk purchase of bitcoin when it was below $10, which meant their investment had already appreciated by a factor of ten, a fantastic multiple by any measure; all the conversations they had had in the Bakery had been validated, and all of their predictions were coming true. The fact that Wall Street, and most of Silicon Valley, were still skeptical and dismissive of Bitcoin made everything even sweeter. When Wall Street and Silicon Valley discovered the massive bet the twins had made in the new currency, god only knew how they would react; the twins were building their new empire without anyone realizing they were doing it. Certainly the twins had to be pleased with how things were going, and especially with Charlie. . . . But were they?

As Charlie followed Ver and the girls into the half-full restaurant, watching them take one of the wooden tables by the window overlooking the street lined with Japanese groceries, magazine shops, and clothing stores, he realized what was really bothering him, even more than his troubles at home.

Something deep in him wanted to impress Cameron and Tyler. And he felt that just by hanging out with Ver, he was falling short in their eyes.

"You want beer? Sake? Whiskey?" Ver asked as he ushered Charlie to a seat between the girls.

Ver himself didn't drink. He didn't do drugs, or smoke. He was athletic, sported a near crew cut, and was built like a wrestler; he was actually a master at jujitsu who trained at a dojo right near his apartment in Tokyo. When you thought about it, he and the twins seemed to have a lot in common. The twins should have taken to him on sight; but the opposite had happened, as Charlie had seen, just twenty-four hours ago.

When Charlie had realized they'd all be in San Jose at the same time, he'd thought it was a perfect opportunity to get Cameron and Tyler together with Ver, and let them see that he wasn't as radical as his online persona.

That idea had been dead on arrival: the twins had turned the invitation down as soon as Charlie had brought it up, telling him that they needed to finish work and rest up for the following day ahead. That was when they'd both made it clear that they didn't love the idea of him continuing to hang out with Ver, even on his own. Tyler had put it simply: "Roger has said things, and done things—you've got to be careful."

Not having the twins approval had hit Charlie hard. He knew it was foolish, but it was like high school all over again, with him in the role of the little guy, cross-eyed and bad at sports, a total nerd, back in the corner of the gym, with all the other losers.

He shook the stupid thoughts away as he let Ver order him a whiskey. The twins weren't being bullies; they were being cautious. Their disapproval of his friendship with Ver wasn't some high-status thing; it was because they cared

about him, he told himself. In the twins' estimation, Ver came with dangerous baggage—not just his radical beliefs, but his past.

The way Ver told the story—and the facts seemed to back it up—Ver had
been railroaded by the U.S. government; but even so, he *had* spent ten months
in a federal prison for selling explosive pest control products online. This fact
alone was hard to look past, especially for two Harvard graduates from Greenwich, Connecticut.

"Why don't you tell the girls why you still believe in sky people?" Ver
started, once the drinks had landed and he'd ordered some food in his facile
Korean. "Or have I managed to finally win you over to reality?"

Charlie smiled. Ver had been teasing him about his religious beliefs almost
from the moment they'd finally met in person, just a few months ago. That
meeting had taken place in Austria, of all places; they had both been invited
to a Bitcoin summit by the Russian founder of the Mycelium electronic wallet,
who was also the entrepreneur behind NEFT Vodka, the mini oil cans that
Charlie kept on his desk back at the BitInstant offices in New York. Alexander
Kuzmin was another great character in the world of Bitcoin: He had previously
been a mayor in a small town in Siberia, where he had outlawed the use of "ex-
cuses" by any government employee. Kuzmin was now going all in on crypto
and had organized the summit in Austria to learn as much as he could.

Charlie had jumped at the invitation, since it had involved two things he
loved: Bitcoin and travel. He'd ended up sharing an apartment in Vienna with
Ver and Voorhees, right off the Vienna day market. They were already online
friends, but getting to spend time with Ver in person had opened Charlie's
mind in ways he hadn't expected. To Charlie, who was only twenty-two, Ver
seemed incredibly well traveled and knew so much about the world. He was
very open about his views, which Charlie liked about him; the guy wasn't just
trying to fit in, he was a true believer who wasn't afraid to say just what he
meant in every situation.

The first night out in Vienna, they'd ended up at a nightclub filled with
girls who weren't exactly prostitutes, but close enough. Ver had paid the women
little attention.

"I've never slept with a white girl before. I only sleep with Asian women.
I just can't break the habit."

Charlie assumed it was a joke, but that opening had launched them into a conversation about how this tall white guy from California had ended up in Japan in the first place, and it had all gone back to that stint in prison. The way Ver explained it, he'd been taken down because of his ideology. He'd been selling what were essentially fireworks over the internet; actually, firecrackers manufactured by a company called Pest Control Report 2000, that had been selling the product online for three years without problems. But Ver wasn't the only one selling them, just the only one arrested. Not coincidentally, at the ripe age of twenty-one he had just run for the California State Assembly as a candidate for the Libertarian Party. Already a big believer in individual freedom and the notion that the government used the threat of violence to get people to behave, he took part in a debate during the election, at which the local head of the DEA was present. During the debate, Ver had essentially called the DEA a bunch of Nazis and "jackbooted thugs."

Two weeks later, he had been arrested in brutal fashion. Surrounded by men with drawn guns, taken down by DEA agents for selling pest control that the government classified as illegal explosives. Ver had sold around 200 of the devices; the company he'd bought them from had itself sold 800,000, without permits, and nobody had gotten arrested. The company that manufactured the device had sold millions, and again, nobody had gotten arrested. But Ver did get arrested, and when he went to jail, it wasn't some cushy federal camp, it was a medium security institution, the real deal.

Ver's ten-month stint in prison had been an enormous wake-up call; what he'd previously thought of as a theoretical and philosophical battle with over-reaching government had suddenly become very real. As he told it, he'd been trying to make the world a better place by pushing libertarian ideals, and it had gotten him thrown in jail.

At first, he'd spent his time in prison studying, reading every libertarian book he could find. Both before prison and during, he'd taken to the works of Murray Rothbard, a major twentieth-century thinker who was a founder of the ideology of anarcho-capitalism and basically called for the elimination of the centralized state in favor of individual liberty. Rothbard believed that anything the government could do, the private sector could do better; more radically, he argued that the government was "robbery systematized and writ large."

He especially was against banks, and thought of the Federal Reserve as a "form of fraud."

Ver's arrest and imprisonment had also taught him a different valuable lesson; his views could get him in trouble, and the freedoms most people took for granted weren't as guaranteed as people thought.

As soon as Ver got out of prison, he'd moved his business and himself straight to Japan. By that point, the computer company he'd built before his imprisonment, Memory Dealers, Inc., an online retailer of computer memory chips, had made him a millionaire, and he'd had enough of living in the United States.

For nearly a decade, though his views had remained as radical as ever, he'd stayed pretty much silent, living abroad while beginning the process of giving up his U.S. citizenship. He didn't really want to be a citizen of anywhere: he, like Voorhees, didn't believe in borders and states. He'd been content being a silent citizen of the world.

And then he'd discovered Bitcoin.

Ver first heard of Bitcoin around 2010, listening to a radio show associated with the New Hampshire Free State movement called "Freetalk Live." At first, Ver hadn't paid much attention to it; but when Bitcoin had come up again a few months later on the same radio show, he'd decided to do some research.

The more he'd read about Bitcoin, the more he'd started to realize that its design and the technology behind it dovetailed beautifully with his beliefs; more than that, Ver had grown up reading and loving science fiction, and Bitcoin sounded exactly like the "cybercash" or "credits" that featured in so much of the genre. And since Ver was an entrepreneur in the computer sector, who had also spent years studying economic theory, he was in the perfect position to understand what Bitcoin was and where it could go.

He'd begun accumulating the digital currency at a rapid pace. Nobody was exactly sure how many bitcoin he'd bought, but there were plenty of rumors that his stash might have even been larger than the twins'. And along with his growing fortune, Ver had also found his voice again through Bitcoin, it was so exactly suited to his ideological beliefs.

From their very first meeting, Ver had begun proselytizing to Charlie. He'd sent him dozens of libertarian books and initiated many conversations questioning Charlie's faith in religion, government, and any other big organization that used force or fear to get its way. When Charlie would ask—"yes, but then who will build the roads?"—Ver would explain that everything in life had to be volunteered, that nothing should be forced, not even the roads. Economic and moral incentives would always be enough.

In retrospect, Charlie had to admit, it was no wonder that Ver and the twins did not get along. Although the twins had been let down by the legal system, they didn't want to tear it all down. The twins had grown up imbued with intense, old-world values: they were truly Men of Harvard. They had lost a fight—which only meant, to them, that they needed to fight smarter. When you lost a race in crew, you didn't react by trying to sink all the boats. You found a way to row harder.

Ver, on the other hand, believed the old-world structures were flawed—that the crew race was rigged from the beginning. The Establishment was built on lies and mythology—fantasies, like Charlie's "sky people," interpreted by rabbis pronouncing edicts that had very little to do with the real world. Although sometimes, Ver's libertarian views seemed equally distant from the real world.

"Reality over sky people?" Charlie said as a steaming tray of sautéed meat landed on the table between them. "Which reality? The one where we all live in some commune and volunteer to dig roads?"

Ver skillfully jabbed at the meat with a pair of chopsticks, then fed a piece to one of the Korean girls.

"I don't live in a commune, I live in a beautiful apartment. And my Porsche is parked outside. Volunteerism isn't hippy-dippy, it's the opposite. We just don't need Big Brother putting a gun in our mouth to get us to do what we should do on our own."

Charlie knew where that ideology led. Ver believed that taxes were essentially armed robbery. That serving in the military could be akin to forced murder. That anything you didn't choose to do on your own was the same as being coerced.

"Sometimes, you have to try to find a middle ground."

"The middle ground is where ideas go to die."

Ver didn't believe in compromise. It was part of what made him such a force in the Bitcoin world. From the minute he'd been turned on to Bitcoin, he'd been one of its biggest cheerleaders. But unlike the twins, he had no problem with the darker side of Bitcoin: he actually loved Silk Road. Ver didn't drink or do drugs, but he fully supported the rights of any individual to buy and sell whatever they wanted. And, Charlie believed, he also saw Bitcoin as the greatest way ever invented to bypass governmental organizations . . . like the DEA . . . or the IRS.

"Look," Charlie said, even though he knew he was taking himself out of the moment, forgetting that he was sitting next to a pair of beautiful women, and instead imagining he was back in the BitInstant office, "If Bitcoin is ever going to go mainstream, we have to build bridges, not burn them."

"You sound like Cameron. Or is it Tyler? You're all such statists."

Ver (and Voorhees too) were always mocking Charlie as a statist—someone who believed that a government, a state, was necessary. But the way Ver said it, the word now seemed more than just a simple tease. No doubt, he saw the twins as part of the Establishment, part of everything he loathed.

Charlie didn't think it was right to hold their privilege against them. He'd watched baseball all his life; he was a diehard Mets fan. So what if the twins had started out life on third base? It was still as hard as hell to make it to home.

"They're true believers, like you," he said.

Ver poked at another piece of grilled meat.

"In what? How much money they're going to make?"

As if that was such a bad thing. Charlie liked talking about the meaning of Bitcoin as much as anyone, but he considered himself an entrepreneur. At some level, weren't they all in this for the money?

In Silicon Valley, every pitch deck identified a problem and proposed a solution. All of them talked about changing the world, making life better for everyone. From Facebook to Apple to Uber, they were all trying to make the world a better place.

But did any of them really mean that? Charle had to wonder.

Charlie believed Ver did mean it; that Bitcoin, to him, was a weapon to re-make the world. In multiple interviews, Ver had said that "Bitcoin was the most important human invention since the internet." Even the twins had to respect that Roger Ver always meant what he said.

The night wound down, the dinner ended, and Ver dropped Charlie back at his hotel, leaving with both girls for another party. Charlie had to ask himself: The world Roger Ver wanted to make, was it going too far? Was that a world Charlie wanted to live in?

15

IN THE AIR

Bitcoin sounded just as good at thirty thousand feet.

Tyler stood in front of the whiteboard that had been set up against the glossy, mahogany wood-paneled wall leading to the dining area, his black marker hovering over the chart he had just drawn, a jagged Himalayan mountain range tracking the price of bitcoin from its inception to that very day—steep rises and stomach-turning drops—a line that overall, trended ever upward. A snail's pace at first, during those two years when nobody outside of a handful of cypherpunks, computer nerds, and math geeks congregating on alternative message boards had heard of the cryptocurrency, then launching higher just six months ago after a few more people like the twins themselves began to take notice. Then dipping slightly, before exploding skyward four weeks ago—thank you, Cyprus—hitting an incredible high of $266 a bitcoin. And then, in just the past twenty-four hours, crashing, diving, plummeting, down more than 60 percent, to a little over $120 a bitcoin.

"Yes, it's volatile," Tyler finished, putting the cap back on the marker. "But that's to be expected, as we're still in the very early stages here. There's still a lot of regulatory uncertainty, and there are so few people in the market, that it's extremely sensitive to day-to-day news. But that's exactly why we think there's so much opportunity. With high risk comes high reward. Bitcoin is only going to attract more and more attention. Cyprus was just a starting point. People are going to realize there are better places to store their wealth than government fiat currency. And because of Bitcoin's fixed supply, the more people buy into it, the more the price has to appreciate. Classic supply and demand."

Tyler looked at the small group gathered on the semicircular couch in front of him, which included his brother, of course, his head propped up next to one of the windows that lined the body of the plane. The shade had been drawn halfway, but behind Cameron, Tyler could still see wisps of clouds through the double glass. Closest to Tyler was a young man in a blue suit who'd introduced himself as an analyst; he was one of three supporting staff, two of whom were also situated around the couch, the third by the huge flat-screen TV that hung on the wall opposite the whiteboard. And then next to the young man was the owner of the private jet, Ron Burkle. One of the most successful businessmen in the country, he was a billionaire who'd built his fortune first by building and selling a supermarket chain, and then as the head of The Yucaipa Companies, LLC, a private equity outfit with billions in assets that included ownership stakes in Barneys New York, the Pittsburgh Penguins NHL hockey team, Morgans Hotel Group, and Soho House clubs.

"I'm not sure I buy it as a currency," Burkle said while writing notes on a pad on the table in front of him, next to lavish platters of sushi, caviar, charcuterie, cheeses, crudité, and assorted fruits that had been set down by one of the plane's uniformed crew. "It's a speculative play, a commodity. Like art. The value is entirely in the demand."

Tyler could see that his brother wanted to jump in, but they'd done enough of these presentations in the past few weeks that they both knew the script backward and forward.

"I agree," Tyler said. "In part, it is a store of value, one that can also be used as a medium of exchange. So just like gold, but better. Our thesis is that bitcoin will disrupt gold in the long term."

He could tell that Burkle was intrigued, but not convinced. That didn't surprise him; there was so much to take in all at once, it took time for even the smartest financial minds to wrap their heads around it. He appreciated that Burkle and his team were curious to learn more in the first place, and respected the fact that they were being diligent, asking questions, and coming at it with healthy skepticism. That's how any rational, disciplined investor would and should approach anything new, especially something as wildly novel as Bitcoin—and that's exactly why people like Burkle were so successful and wealthy.

Other than the soft rumble and the slight lilt of what he could only describe as an elegantly appointed flying living room, Tyler could barely tell they were in the air at all. He'd been in private jets before; but even the most lavish of them, including Gulfstreams and Bombardiers, were too cramped for all six feet five inches of him to stand up straight in the fuselage. And they certainly didn't have dining rooms, living rooms, and bedrooms with showers. Burkle's jet was more like a jumbo jet, a converted Boeing 757 that was almost as famous in the gossip magazines as the private equity guru's friends, who included Puff Daddy, Bill Clinton, and Leonardo DiCaprio.

Tyler hadn't expected to be making his presentation on Bitcoin at thirty thousand feet. But when he'd contacted Burkle's office as part of their "Bitcoin tour," Burkle had offered the cross-country lift.

"What about this Silk Road business? Who actually owns bitcoin and who's actually using it? Is it just gangsters and money-launderers?" Burkle asked.

This question was inevitable, it had come up in every meeting; Silk Road was certainly a stain that would be difficult to wipe away. But more and more, Tyler had become convinced that the dark web drug den was more hype than anything else.

"All of our studies show that Silk Road is actually a very small part of the Bitcoin economy. At present, less than five percent of Bitcoin transactions have anything to do with the site, and that's only getting smaller as the Bitcoin market grows."

And that market, Tyler had already explained, had just recently eclipsed the billion-dollar mark, on March 28, 2013; in fact it was Cameron who had placed a market buy order on Mt. Gox that had moved the bitcoin price up the few pennies necessary to climb above $92 and push the overall value of the Bitcoin market into the ten figures—the *Trois* Commas Club. That, of course, pointed out what was one of the bigger problems with Bitcoin in its infancy: there wasn't much liquidity, so even a smaller order could impact the market, making it prone to large price swings.

And the seismic drop of the past twenty-four hours was a perfect example of another problem that plagued the Bitcoin market; unlike with Cyprus, this particular crash didn't have anything to do with real-world news. It was entirely the result of a short-term problem at the Mt. Gox exchange; too much traffic and trading had overwhelmed the Mt. Gox's servers, and the exchange had shut down to deal with the issue, sending the entire market into a tailspin. That represented what Tyler was beginning to believe was the biggest obstacle facing Bitcoin's growth and its greater adoption. If Bitcoin was going to become mainstream, the exchange through which the majority of bitcoin was traded couldn't remain a former Magic: The Gathering exchange located in Japan, run by a Frenchman and his cats. The world of private equity and hedge funds was never going to take Bitcoin seriously until the Bitcoin economy grew up and moved away from the quirky landmarks of its origins.

Burkle's analysts were writing in their notepads, but Tyler could tell from the look on Burkle's face that he wasn't going to be sold on the cryptocurrency in the few hours they had him as a captive audience. Tyler doubted it was just Silk Road that was the problem; after all, Burkle didn't seem the type to be scared off by some dark scandalous alleyways in the overall Bitcoin cityscape. Though the jet they were flying on had been nicknamed Ron Air by Bill Clinton, the gossip columnists had another name for the flying tour bus that had been loaned to the former president for numerous junkets around the world: Air Fuck One. Tyler had no idea if any of the stories he'd read of the plane being filled with bevies of supermodels and celebrities, whisking them around from party destination to party destination, were true, and he didn't really care. So far, Burkle had been a consummate host and only regaled them with incredible stories from his professional life in private equity. He was a business genius and had built his empire by seeing value before anyone else. Even if he wasn't ready to buy bitcoin at that exact moment in time, bitcoin was now on his radar.

In addition to their Bitcoin tour, the other main focus of their grueling schedules these days had been a bit more challenging: trying to steer Charlie Shrem and BitInstant in the right direction, despite the challenge of Charlie's youth. Toward that goal, Tyler and his brother had landed a ton of meetings for the young CEO. They'd put him in front of venture investment firms in New York and potential banking partners, and indeed, together they'd achieved some meaningful victories. Specifically, their meeting with Obopay had yielded an important partnership: Obopay, a licensed money transmitter, had agreed to essentially rent their licenses to BitInstant so it could transmit money in accordance with state money transmission laws, which, for the first time, made Charlie's company legally compliant, something Charlie and his team had pretty much ignored up until that point. They'd also managed to get Charlie a meeting with a major U.S. bank that had agreed to begin the bank account opening process, another key development, because other banks were scared off by BitInstant and its uncertain legal status with financial regulators and tax officials.

Charlie had even taken the reins himself during the presentation at the major U.S. bank: standing in front of a similar whiteboard hanging on the wall of a glass-and-chrome boardroom, sweating his way through a blazer that looked like it had been mothballed the day after Charlie's high school graduation, Charlie had emphasized to the room full of bankers how serious he and BitInstant took compliance and legal licensing, how BitInstant had state-of-the-art internal controls. He'd continued in that vein, explaining how BitInstant performed its "KYC"—a banker acronym for "Know Your Customer"—as part of its compliance program, aiming to understand the identities of its customers and make sure they weren't criminals or money launderers. At one point, he'd even shouted: "The name of the game is three words—compliance, compliance, compliance!"

Overall he'd sounded like the boy wonder he was supposed to be, saying all the right things. And at that moment, Charlie had seemed to understand the direction BitInstant needed to go; he'd won over the bankers, just as he'd won over Obopay. He was still young, needed some polish and rounding out, but the raw material was there.

Tyler was beginning to feel more confident that their investment in BitInstant was the perfect entrance into the Bitcoin economy. Although Charlie's growing friendship with Roger Ver made Tyler and his brother nervous, and seemed a potential warning sign, as long as Charlie could continue to develop himself, mature, and keep himself from being drawn into one of those dark alleyways lurking on the Bitcoin map, he really was on the verge of doing something really special.

"Ron," Tyler said as he sat next to Cameron, then pulled his cell phone out of his pocket. He saw that the 757 had Wi-Fi—*of course it did, it had a dining room.* "I appreciate you hearing us out, and I know it's a lot to take in all at once. But in the interim, what's your email address?"

Burkle blinked once, then gave it to him.

"I'm going to send you five bitcoin. All I want you to do is hold on to them as a token of our gratitude, for your time. One day they will be worth more than the cost of fuel for this flight."

Burkle smiled.

"Do you have any idea how much fuel this bird burns?"

Tyler could tell by Burkle's expression that of all the arguments Tyler had made that afternoon, this simple act, sending the man five bitcoin by email to pay for what was obviously an insanely expensive flight, and the confidence it implied, had made the biggest impression.

As the airplane leveled off and one of the crew members invited the group toward the dining room for a gourmet lunch, Tyler tapped the screen on his phone and initiated the transfer.

Tyler hoped, prayed, and believed—those five bitcoin would one day be more than enough to pay for the fuel used during this cross-country flight.

P age one. Right on front. And they even spelled 'Winklevoss' right. I just might have to cancel my subscription to the *Journal* and focus all my attention on the *Times* from now on."

Tyler's head spun as he leaned over his father's shoulder to stare at the newspaper that was spread out on the maple wood table in the kitchen of their parents' Greenwich estate. He could hardly believe it. On the front page, halfway down the tower of newsprint, the bold headline in that familiar font streaking across Tyler's retinae, igniting his rods and cones:

NEVER MIND FACEBOOK; WINKLEVOSS TWINS
RULE IN DIGITAL MONEY

Just twelve hours after they'd disembarked from Burkle's private plane at Newark Liberty International Airport—it was too big to fly into Teterboro, where most private planes heading to New York landed—they'd come home to find their father opening the *New York Times* to an article announcing their place in Bitcoin history.

Actually, he hadn't even had to open the *Times*. The article was right there, on the damn front page.

"Page A1. You know what that means. People are actually going to read this."

Tyler's mother, Carol, came in behind him from the direction of the Sub-Zero refrigerator, carrying a tray of croissants and scones that none of them were going to touch for quite some time. Tyler was excited, and he could tell from the expressions on his parents' faces that they were too. Cameron's face was all smiles and near disbelief, his body half out of his chair on the other side of the table as he looked at the paper and his finger pointed to the second paragraph of the article.

"Your quote is great," Cameron said, and then read it out loud. "'We have elected to put our money and faith in a mathematical framework that is free of politics and human error.'"

"Now you finally sound like Men of Harvard," Tyler's father joked. "You got a great quote in too, Cameron. 'People say it's a Ponzi scheme, it's a bubble. People really don't want to take it seriously. At some point that narrative will shift to "virtual currencies are here to stay." We're in the early days.'"

"Nice," Tyler agreed. "The haters can take that and stuff it where it belongs."

Calling Bitcoin a Ponzi scheme, or equating it to the Dutch tulip bubble of the seventeenth century, were favorite criticisms of the virtual currency. They would never deny there were a lot of growing pains ahead: the Bitcoin market was volatile, still trying to recover from the crash caused by Mt. Gox going offline for twelve hours when it couldn't handle the overwhelming volume of transactions. But Cameron was making the point that Bitcoin wasn't just another fad like tulips, or Beanie Babies, or Tamagotchi pets. And a Ponzi scheme—Bitcoin was the opposite. Either everyone prospered, or everyone fell—together.

In a funny way, since Cyprus, Bitcoin was becoming too popular for its own good. And the fact that 80 percent of Bitcoin transactions still happened on the former Magic: The Gathering exchange was an embarrassment, almost as problematic as the fact that most people thought the primary use for bitcoin was to buy drugs or worse on Silk Road.

The twins had been written about many times before, when the movie had come out, and even before that, when the stories about their lawsuit with Facebook had reached a certain fever pitch. They'd also been covered in the tabloids a fair amount, even though they'd never courted the attention and had actively tried to avoid it. Regardless, gossip rags like the *New York Post*'s Page Six had a certain fascination with them.

But they'd never been written about on the *front page* of the *New York Times* before—the most revered and cerebral newspaper in the free world. And they'd never been treated so *fairly*.

The *Times*, the *WSJ*, the *Post*, the blogosphere, they'd all taken too many shots to count at Tyler and his brother over the years, mindlessly promoting and regurgitating the false one-note narrative of them being Waspy, blue blood, aristocratic rowers who had whined and sued their way into being bought off by Mark Zuckerberg. The media had spent years relentlessly pigeonholing and caricaturing them in search of juicy clickbait. And now, overnight, that narrative had been turned on its head.

"You know what?" Tyler said, skimming the article again. "There's only one mention of rowing. Just at the top, where they introduce us: Cameron and Tyler, Olympic rowers."

Tyler felt his mother's arm around his shoulders. She had always been supportive of whatever he and Cameron did, just like their father. And even though it was their father they would often go to for business advice, they got their fierce determination, their refusal to stay down, from their mother. She could be as tough as any cop's daughter had to be.

It was that determination and strength that had led to this front-page story. The piece wasn't an accident; Tyler and his brother had worked hard to convince Nathaniel Popper, one of the most brilliant business voices at the

New York Times, to write what would be his first Bitcoin story. They'd pitched him on the idea that they were the first legitimate investors to amass a large stake of bitcoin, when no venture funds in Silicon Valley would touch it with a ten-foot ethernet cable.

Popper was the *Times*'s currency guy, usually focusing on gold; he was the perfect journalist to write about gold 2.0. His article had blown up the minute it had hit the web. It had gotten so much attention, the editors had put it on the front page of the print edition the following morning—not just the front page of the business section, where most of Popper's stories usually lived. The article wasn't about just Bitcoin; it also announced the twins as the biggest known owners of the currency in the world, with them holding over 1 percent of all bitcoin in the entire market. Sure, Tyler fully admitted that there might be people out there with larger stakes; Satoshi—whoever he was—reportedly had close to a million bitcoin, but who really knew. Satoshi's bitcoin might as well have not even existed. The twins' stake, on the other hand, was not a philosophical paradox—it was in the palms of their hands, as much as any virtual currency could be. And now, with this article, they were the public face of Bitcoin.

"'Winklevoss Twins Rule in Digital Money,'" Tyler said. "I like the sound of that—"

He was interrupted by his cell phone, going off in his pocket. He didn't recognize the number, so he let it go to voice mail. Then he listened to the voice mail while Cameron and his parents watched.

"Is that Zuckerberg?" Cameron joked. Their mother nearly hit him with a scone.

"It's an invitation to speak at a conference in May."

"What kind of conference?" Cameron asked.

"Something called 'Bitcoin 2013.' It's being put on by the Bitcoin Foundation," Tyler responded.

Cameron whistled. This was the first time anyone had wanted to hear them speak about anything other than Facebook, and the losing fight against the boy king of the internet.

Tyler knew that the Bitcoin Foundation was a nonprofit corporation, established in 2012, to promote and protect the Bitcoin economy. At the time, it was the most prominent organization of its kind. Its board was a who's who of virtual currency. Its "chief scientist" was Gavin Andresen, who Satoshi himself had anointed as the lead developer of Bitcoin Core, the software client of the Bitcoin Network. Andresen had probably been closer to the mysterious Satoshi than anyone else in the world, until Satoshi had disappeared from the internet for good.

Bitcoin 2013 was only the second conference that the foundation had hosted, and it was going to bring together the smartest minds in the space, true luminaries, all the people behind the nascent but growing Bitcoin revolution.

"Biggest conference in the industry," Tyler continued. "And they want us to give the keynote speech."

Just the two of them, on a stage, in front of the world.

"Beats rowing off into the sunset," he said. And then he smiled.

16

THE KING OF BITCOIN

A nd just then, as the photographer was shooting away and the lights were flashing, I was up on the chair, making it rain!"

Without warning, Charlie leaped into a reenactment of the story he was in the midst of telling, right up onto the circular, maroon-colored leather banquette, nearly upending the liquor bottles on the gunmetal gray table in front of him, the pretty girls on either side of him diving out of the way just in time. Then Charlie had his hands up over his head and he was tossing two enormous wads of twenties into the air. Everyone in his corner of the two-story, postindustrial lounge cheered as the bills billowed down, a tropical storm of green paper caught in the dancing disco lights.

Charlie watched the bills floating around him, magnified a hundred times by the enormous mirrors that ran up all four walls, all the way to the balcony. The mirrors were surrounded by lights, the balcony circumnavigated by Edison bulbs, and almost everything seemed cloaked in glass, giving the whole place a steampunk feel; but the lasers and the DJ and the huge, glowing bar that took up most of the downstairs, the second bar upstairs, the catwalk-like stage running along one side, the gold sign outside, the lit-up menus that glowed like magical parchments at every table, all of it felt like a contemporary reinterpretation of the 1980s, when clubs reigned supreme. A *Bright Lights, Big*

City/Wall Street, lines-of-coke version of the 1980s, artwork hanging along one interior wall, black sketch-work on huge canvasses that would have been at home in Patrick Bateman's blood-splattered apartment.

Five thousand square feet of Midtown debauchery, right on Thirty-Ninth Street, and Charlie was there putting on the Charlie Show, like he'd been doing almost every night since the place opened. Because he wasn't just standing up on a couch in his corner of the club; he was standing up on a couch in his corner of *his* club, or at least, that was how everyone saw things. The fact that he was merely a small partner in EVR—pronounced "EVER," the city's hottest "gastro-lounge," a club Charlie's college friends had opened and the only one that accepted Bitcoin from customers—didn't matter to anyone. When Charlie was there—and he was there a lot—*he always made it rain.*

"The only good thing about cash is that you don't have to worry about cleaning it up after you toss it in the air. Nobody's ever been arrested for littering twenties."

Charlie grinned, lowering himself back down onto the couch, the two girls moving closer to make room for the rest of their party. Charlie's partner in EVR, Alex, was next to a woman on Charlie's right, but Charlie couldn't remember her name because he was already four Jamesons in. Another college friend, Mike, had his arm around the woman to Charlie's left, Angela something, who wrote for some magazine, which probably should have made Charlie more careful about what he said but actually had the opposite effect. For the first time in Charlie's life, people listened to him, and he had discovered that was a high on a par with whatever he could get from the consumables and smokables lining the shelves of the Bakery back at his office.

Damn, it was fun being king. And at the moment, that's how Charlie saw himself, one of the Kings of Bitcoin, a true crypto rock star. And it wasn't just him; the photo shoot he'd just described, of him throwing money up in the air to make it rain, had been for a full-page, color profile in *Bloomberg Business Week,* announcing Charlie as one of the newly minted Bitcoin millionaires— early adopters smart enough to get on the train before everyone else. And the *Business Week* piece was just one of dozens of articles introducing Charlie to a world where BitInstant was being touted as one of the most successful crypto-related startups.

The progress BitInstant had made in such a short time was incredible. The company had gone from processing a million dollars a month to doing almost that much in a single day. Charlie had calculated that at the moment, BitInstant was processing 35 percent of all bitcoin purchases. The demand for the service had been so intense, that the few times he'd had to temporarily shut the site down for server upgrades and maintenance, the downtime had caused an uproar among his customers. He'd received concerned emails from Tyler and Cameron, but Charlie had brushed it off; BitInstant had made him a celebrity in the Bitcoin world, and a microcelebrity in the outside world. This was Charlie's Moment, and he knew it.

In just a few short months since the twins had invested, Charlie had traveled the world, speaking to groups of Bitcoin fanboys in London, Paris, Tokyo, Berlin, and Tel Aviv. Bitcoin had opened up a life for him that he never knew existed, let alone that he could be a part of. It had made him a millionaire. And it had freed him from that brisket-soaked basement in Brooklyn—*literally*. Though in this, Bitcoin had had a bit of help, from a very unlikely source.

A soft hand touched Charlie's shoulder from behind the leather couch, and he turned just as an incredible-looking blond woman, way out of his league, leaned over and kissed him on his scruffy cheek. She was dressed like an EVR cocktail waitress, because that was her job, and was holding a tray of tequila shots, because shooting tequila at night was Charlie's favorite activity—but this wasn't some routine, sterile peck on the cheek because Charlie had ordered a round, or was a part owner, or was throwing twenties like confetti on New Year's Eve.

No, he and Courtney had been together for two months now. Charlie had fallen in love with her from the minute he'd first set eyes on her, just days after EVR had opened its doors. He'd asked Alex if she could always be his waitress, but even with this help, Charlie had been way too afraid to actually ask her out on a date. Despite his growing Bitcoin fame, he didn't know how to talk to girls like Courtney. The night he'd gone out with Cameron and Tyler after that first meeting in the Bakery, when he'd met the Bulgarian model, had ended with him on a couch in Cameron's apartment, alone, in vomit-soaked sneakers.

He couldn't have handled the same thing happening with Courtney. He'd fallen for her so hard, he'd spent more time thinking about her than about the overworked servers at BitInstant. Luckily for Charlie, his friends had taken charge of the situation by inviting them both to a staff happy hour and then collectively not showing up, leaving Charlie and Courtney alone, together.

Out of sheer social terror, Charlie had signaled for a Bacardi. And he hadn't stopped signaling until he'd consumed so much Bacardi that he'd thrown up all over Courtney. When he'd gone to the bathroom to clean himself up, he'd assumed she'd be racing for the door, but for some reason she'd stuck around. At that moment, Charlie had known she was the one.

It wasn't until their second date that he'd told her about "the Edict"—that he had a fundamentalist Jewish family that wouldn't accept her, moreover, that being with her could actually lead him to being thrown out of his entire community, as insane as that sounded. And it wasn't until another month later, when one of his sisters, overhearing him on the phone with Courtney, had squealed to his mother, that—everything at home had erupted. His mother crying and screaming, his dad actually ripping his shirt. After all of that came the ultimatum: the family or Courtney. Charlie hadn't had any trouble making up his mind. He was in love, and more importantly, he was ready to get out. What had started with Roger Ver's teasing about "sky people" had turned into a full-on, existential crisis, and Courtney had walked straight into that crisis with her tray of tequila.

He'd packed his belongings, climbed out of the basement, and made a break to EVR, moving in with his college friends, to an apartment several of them shared that was literally above the club. He was opening up a new tab in the bar of life.

"It's after one," Courtney whispered in his ear as she added the tray of shots to his table. "Don't you have a meeting tomorrow morning?"

"I always have a meeting tomorrow morning," Charlie said.

Then he reached for one of the shots. Sure, Courtney was probably right, adding tequila into the mix after 1:00 A.M. was never a great idea. But he wasn't concerned about the meeting, even though he wasn't exactly sure which meeting it was, or where, or with whom.

He had to go to a lot of meetings. He was, after all, CEO. And customer service. And chief compliance officer. He handled just about everything except the departments that Voorhees and Ira ran, or the deep computer stuff, which Gareth still took care of from his own bat cave in Wales, or wherever the hell Gareth lived.

With Voorhees and Ira, Charlie never had to worry; they were brilliant and professional, and had been instrumental in building BitInstant. In fact, they had developed some of the proprietary software that BitInstant was currently using, something that Ira had begun working on before BitInstant and that he and Voorhees had been letting Charlie use for free—a little fact that Charlie hadn't yet mentioned to the Winklevoss twins, because he didn't think it was that big a deal. Anyway, Voorhees and Ira were the glue keeping BitInstant together.

They weren't just part of his team, they were his friends, which these days to Charlie meant they were pretty much the only family he had. They were also both growing, just like he was.

Voorhees was becoming as big of a name in Bitcoin as Charlie. Even though he ran BitInstant's marketing, he was also working on a side project called SatoshiDice, a Bitcoin gambling website that was rapidly becoming a major draw in the Bitcoin community. The idea behind the game was simple: players sent bitcoin to an address that was either a winner or a loser. If "lucky," they'd receive a multiple of the bitcoin they had wagered. If "unlucky," they'd receive only a fraction. The game was instantly incredibly popular.

Of course, since it was a gambling site, its legality for American customers was unclear. To Voorhees, this was a frustration both business-wise and philosophically speaking. He, of course, didn't believe the government should be involved in regulating gambling, especially bitcoin gambling. The whole point of building SatoshiDice on the Bitcoin blockchain itself was to keep it far away from the hands of the U.S. government.

For Charlie's part, he couldn't even begin trying to understand the U.S.'s byzantine gambling laws. In fact, he had only just recently started giving himself a crash course on U.S. money transmission laws—the exact laws that governed BitInstant's business activities. He'd only done this after BitInstant's lawyers and the Winklevoss twins had convinced him that it was critical for him to understand and comply with U.S. laws and regulations, not just for BitInstant's sake, but for his own sake as well.

Since Charlie was both the chief compliance officer and CEO of BitInstant, laws and regulations were something he knew he should be taking seriously; but details had never been his strong suit. Still, he was trying. In fact, he'd learned enough to know that even his wearing three hats—CEO, chief compliance officer, customer service—was itself a conflict of interest. And only recently, this tightrope act had gotten complicated.

Someone with the handle BTCKing had been buying tons of bitcoin through the site with what appeared to be an endless supply of cash. As per the firm's rules, for security reasons, because large Bitcoin transactions could, on their own, be considered suspect, and BitInstant didn't have the resources to do deep-identity checks of their customers, BitInstant had capped regular customers' daily purchase limits at $1,000—but it had become clear BTCKing was trying to evade those controls; on one single day, he'd attempted to purchase $4,000 worth of bitcoin, using a technique called "structuring."

Although it didn't necessarily mean BTCKing was up to no good, it was an alarming attempt at circumventing BitInstant's controls. When Charlie had discovered what had happened, he'd immediately banned BTCKing from using BitInstant, personally sending him an email: "We have all your deposits on record, your picture from bank security cameras. Any attempt at a new transfer will result in criminal prosecution."

But after much thought, Charlie had relented. After all, the guy had only been trying to buy more bitcoin. What was so bad about being eager? Wasn't that good for everybody?

Charlie had eventually messaged the guy back, reaffirming that his current account and email address had been banned, but that he could open up a new account with a new email address if he wanted.

Charlie had no idea who BTCKing was. Most likely, he was a dealer or reseller, who bought bitcoin low and sold it to other people at a higher price. Charlie didn't really care, and furthermore, he didn't really believe it was any of his business. And why should he worry about some random guy he'd never met, and probably never would meet? BTCKing? Even the name was a joke—everyone knew who the new, real King of Bitcoin was.

In a few months, Charlie was going to be speaking at Bitcoin 2013, the same conference that the Winklevoss twins were keynoting. The twins might have been on page A1 of the *New York Times,* but Charlie had made it rain in front of a photographer in Bloomberg, and he was running the scene with his beautiful girlfriend at EVR.

Charlie was a crypto rock star on his way up, and like the price of Bitcoin, he was never going to come back down.

17

THE MORNING AFTER

What is wrong with you?! Seriously, that was the most embarrassing thing I've ever sat through."

Cameron was doing his best to keep his voice down as he ushered Charlie through a marble lobby and toward the revolving glass doors leading onto Lexington Avenue. Tyler was on the other side of Charlie, helping prop him up as they made their way out. Even with identical six-foot-five-inch bookends escorting him on either side, Charlie was barely vertical, staring at his feet as if they were part of someone else's body, struggling to put one foot in front of the other as he worked his way toward the lobby exit.

The three of them hit the revolving door like a vaudeville act: Tyler through first, dragging Charlie into the same spinning wedge with him because there was a good chance that Charlie, if left on his own, would smash right through one of the panes of glass. Then Cameron, a wedge later, so consumed with his rising frustration that his breath was steaming up the glass in front of him.

Once they were outside, Tyler led Charlie a few feet down the sidewalk toward Fifty-Ninth Street, then released the kid to prop himself up against the building on his own accord; the office lobby had given way to an oversized Gap, its plate glass windows teeming with mannequins in baggy sweats.

"Charlie," Cameron finally said as a passing group of suits moved far enough away that they hopefully couldn't hear. "Did you even sleep last night?"

Charlie finally looked up from his shoes. His eyes were wide, but still as bloodshot as they'd been since he'd arrived for the meeting on the seventeenth floor less than thirty minutes ago. His shirt was open three buttons—three goddamn buttons!—revealing a tangle of chest hair and the mottled skin of someone who had obviously spent the previous night in a club. Or maybe two. *Hat trick?* There were stains on his blazer, he reeked of alcohol, and if he'd slept at all, it had probably been on a floor.

"You look like you've been on a five-day bender," Tyler said.

"No, really, just a few drinks, some tequila . . . nothing to worry about. . . ." Charlie's voice trailed off into a mumble.

Cameron tried again to control his emotions. He was usually the more empathetic one, but at that moment, he was having trouble feeling anything less than anger toward their boy wonder CEO. "Train wreck" would have been a grievous understatement to describe the meeting they'd just attended.

"Do you know how hard it was to set that up?" Tyler asked. "John is one of the most powerful people in Fintech."

Fintech, a portmanteau of "Financial" and "Technology," was the fastest-growing sector of venture investing in New York. It essentially included any new technology that had the potential to push the financial world forward, or make it more efficient, such as online banking, robo advisers, statistical consulting, quantitative investing, and of course, blockchain technology. And Tyler was right, John Abercrom, whose office they'd just fled like a circus troupe that had just murdered a member of their audience, and his VC firm, was one of the most influential names in the industry. John and his partners had built a portfolio of investments in over a hundred major companies, many of which were some of the most prominent in the world of Fintech.

Through connections and hard legwork, Cameron and his brother had scored a meeting, only to unleash Charlie Shrem—in all his bloodshot and alcohol-drenched glory—on these titans of the industry.

Before the meeting, from their email exchanges, it had seemed like John and his partners really understood Bitcoin and were genuinely interested in hearing Charlie's pitch. But despite the warm audience, things had gone sideways from the moment Charlie had entered the room. Charlie had launched into his presentation like the Tasmanian devil. Swirling around in front of the whiteboard, he was literally all over the place. He'd been almost unintelligible, nonsensical. Speaking so fast, everyone in the room was getting whiplash. And all of it punctuated by jokes that fell completely flat; what might have landed in the wee hours of the morning at EVR hit like lead balloons in a boardroom on Lexington.

When the conversation had shifted to the specifics of BitInstant's model, Charlie had suddenly, bizarrely become defensive. The more technical things had gotten about BitInstant's operations, compliance, and financials, the more Charlie had shut the questioning down. It was as if he had no interest in talking about the nuts and bolts of his own company. He was too busy playing the CEO of Bitcoin to be the CEO of BitInstant. And before Cameron or Tyler knew it, the meeting was over.

"This can't happen again," Tyler said.

"Was it really that bad?" Charlie stammered.

"Worse. You weren't just unprepared. You looked like you were on coke. Completely schizo."

"Schizo? That's a good one. I like it."

"Charlie . . . I know you've got a lot of other responsibilities," Cameron said.

Like the nightclub, the cocktail waitress, the globetrotting.

Cameron had talked to Tyler about this a dozen times already; lately, Charlie had been so swept up in the hype machine it was hard to even keep tabs on the guy. He seemed to be everywhere except where he was supposed to be—which is to say either sleeping or at the BitInstant offices working. The site had experienced brownouts twice in the last two weeks, which terrified Cameron. How safe was their investment, if the site kept buckling? What else was about to give? And how had things started to go south so fast?

"But there is something you need to consider," Tyler paused, his voice lower, "the people who start companies aren't always the best people to run them."

Charlie seemed to suddenly sober up, at least enough to understand what Tyler was saying.

"Are you saying that someone *else* should be CEO?"

It was the first time either of the twins had floated the thought aloud.

Charlie had a ton of great ideas, a ton of energy, but did he have the consistency to run a real company? The type of company BitInstant was fast becoming? In a way, Voorhees and Ira weren't helping matters; they both being incredibly competent was only enabling Charlie, enhancing his worst attributes.

Charlie looked from Tyler to Cameron, craning his neck to match their eyes.

"Maybe Roger is right about you guys."

"What the hell does that mean?" Cameron said.

A pair of German tourists moved past, close enough for one of them, a young man with a shock of moussed yellow hair, to recognize the twins and point. The man's partner, a woman in a denim dress, pointed her cell phone at Cameron, took a quick picture, then kept walking. This type of thing happened almost every day.

"I mean," Charlie continued, "sometimes you guys can be such suits."

Cameron rolled his eyes. Sometimes suits were necessary. Certainly, they were appropriate at a meeting with one of the biggest names in Fintech.

"As we've told you before," Tyler said, still moderately controlled, "Roger isn't the best influence."

Although the twins had avoided meeting with Ver in person in San Jose, they'd been cc'd on numerous emails—and had eventually taken part in multiple hour-long phone conversations with Ver over the past few weeks, discussing BitInstant's future. It seemed the more successful the company got, the more friction they and the Tokyo libertarian had. Lately, a lot of the conversations had focused on Charlie's increasing absence from the office. No matter what, regardless of the topic or the set of facts and circumstances, Ver always defended Charlie, even when it meant doing so was to a fault. He'd probably find a way to defend Charlie about the nightmare of a meeting they'd just had too. Cameron could already hear Ver in his head, rationalizing how it was healthy for entrepreneurs to blow off steam.

"He's been supporting me since the beginning," Charlie said.

"It's no longer the beginning," Cameron shot back, "it's the now. The stakes are real, you can't be taking advice from an ex-con."

Charlie pressed his hands flat against the window behind him, leaving a sweat stain on the glass.

"He went to jail for selling pest control," Charlie said.

"Explosives," Cameron corrected. "He's the kind of guy who likes blowing things up."

"You don't know him. He really does want to change the world. Change the government."

"He wants to change the government because he hates the government. It's not some noble, philosophical cause. It's a personal grudge."

Was Charlie really trying to defend Roger's conviction? The same Charlie who was espousing the importance of compliance, inside the walls of a major U.S. bank, just weeks ago?

"You don't know him," Charlie sputtered.

"You're right," Cameron said. "And neither do you. Look, Charlie, you need to understand. These meetings—we're trying to mainstream Bitcoin. We don't want it to be some kind of circus novelty riding on fringe ideology. If this is going to be gold 2.0, it has to appeal to everyone. Investment banks aren't going to set up trading desks for an asset marketed by drug dealers that's supposed to kill governments."

Charlie rubbed his eyes.

"None of us are drug dealers."

"Right now, that's exactly what you look like. You need to clean up your act."

Cameron felt his breath coming more easily. Just getting it out into the open helped, like uncapping a bottle of soda. He could tell that Tyler hadn't finished with the CEO discussion, but for now, they had made their point. Hopefully, it had landed.

"That's what you guys are for," Charlie finally responded. "You're the keynote speakers."

Cameron had to give him that one. Cameron and Tyler were supposed to be the camera-ready ambassadors—which freed up Charlie to be a ringleader in the sideshow.

A part he seemed eager to play.

"Let's chalk this up to a learning experience," Cameron said, before his brother could end on a more pointed note. "At the conference, let's make sure to be on our best behavior."

The conference was still months away, but if Charlie hit Bitcoin 2013 like he'd rolled into the meeting they'd just escaped, there was no telling what trouble he'd cause. But then again, he'd said it himself: he wasn't giving the keynote, they were.

Charlie reached out to shake both their hands.

"You guys are right, of course. What I just did in there—that was inexcusable. And it won't happen again. Really, it was just a speed bump."

His palms were wet, and he was trembling, like the first time they'd met.

But as Cameron watched him walk away down Lexington Avenue, Charlie's little form was engaged in what could only be described as a strut.

18

BRIGHT LIGHTS

Almost two weeks later, the travesty of the Abercrom meeting fading into a bad memory, Tyler sat in a Starbucks, watching the crowds of tourists and Manhattanites moving along Eighth Street through the window. It was unusual for him to choose such a visible table where he'd be on display, but the place was crowded for 11:00 A.M. on a Tuesday; then again, it was Astor Place, one of the liveliest spots in the city, smack in the middle of the East Village and a stone's throw away from NYU. Tyler had chosen the table, but not the Starbucks itself. He searched the crowd outside for any sign of their quarry.

"There he is," Cameron said, pointing in the direction of a dapper man moving toward them through the traffic jam of coffee addicts.

Tall, hair flecked with silver, chiseled facial structure above a criminally square jaw, wearing what appeared to be a Savile Row suit and an ascot tied around his neck: the guy looked like he'd just stepped out of an F. Scott Fitzgerald novel. Certainly from a different era, and only as he got closer could Tyler make out the lines around his eyes, the cellular log of the psychic distance he'd traveled in his fifty-odd years.

"Lads," he said, taking the seat Cameron offered him, then smiling at the pastries and drinks spread out across the table. "Quite the buffet you've set up. I hope I didn't keep you waiting too long."

"Just got here ourselves," Tyler fibbed.

Matthew Mellon II was the sort of guy you didn't mind waiting around for. He descended from two of the most prominent financial families in the country: on his father's side, Judge Thomas Mellon had founded Mellon Bank in 1869, once one of the largest banks in the world, which in 2006 had merged with the Bank of New York, the oldest company in the United States, to become Bank of New York Mellon. On his mother's side, he was a direct descendent of Anthony Joseph Drexel, the founder of Drexel Burnham Lambert, a Wall Street investment bank created in 1935 that had gone bankrupt fifty-five years later, in 1990, following the indictment of its rainmaker Michael Milken, dubbed the Junk Bond King.

So Mellon had been born to banking royalty—and with that came all the ups and downs one would imagine. His father had killed himself when Matthew was in college at the Wharton School at the University of Pennsylvania. During his senior year, the younger Mellon had inherited $25 million at the age of twenty-one—and promptly bought himself a six-bedroom apartment off campus, a red Ferrari, and a black Porsche.

After graduating, he'd decided to cut his own path and had moved to Los Angeles. He'd chased careers in acting, modeling, and fashion before becoming an entrepreneur. Like his father, he suffered from bipolar disorder and had fought public battles with various addictions. Despite his struggles, he was one of the most charming, creative business thinkers in the country and, most importantly, one of the most open-minded. He'd cofounded Jimmy Choo, a high-fashion shoe company, with his ex-wife Tamara Mellon, whom he'd met at a Narcotics Anonymous meeting. In 2017, Jimmy Choo was bought for over a billion dollars by Michael Kors Holdings. Few people in the world understood the cross-section of the finance, fashion, entertainment, and politics better than Matthew Mellon II.

Mellon fit perfectly into Tyler and Cameron's ongoing Bitcoin tour. Although they usually met with institutions like hedge funds, proprietary trading firms, family offices, and other financial companies, they'd decided to expand their outreach leading up to the Bitcoin 2013 conference to anyone interesting enough, and interested enough, to take their calls.

It was a strategy that had landed them in front of some pretty spectacular people. Only days earlier, they'd dined with Richard Branson, the Virgin billionaire, at the Soho Beach House in Miami. At the dinner table, they'd used some of their bitcoin to prepurchase $250,000 tickets on Branson's Virgin Galactic, a suborbital rocket cruise. With only a few taps on their iPhones, Tyler and Cameron had become future astronauts, numbers 700 and 701.

Branson had already gotten involved in Bitcoin by investing in a company called Bitpay, which helped retailers and other merchants accept bitcoin as payment. After reading the front-page article in the *New York Times* about the twins' swan dive into bitcoin, the head of Branson's "astronaut relations" team had reached them through a mutual friend. He'd recognized the potential PR value of connecting with the twins and seeing if they might be interested in purchasing tickets to space with bitcoin through BitPay, which had led to that dinner. During dinner, Branson had explained that before they went on their suborbital journey, they would have to spend a week at astronaut school in the Mojave Desert—training for space, which hopefully wouldn't be quite as strenuous as training for the Olympics.

But Tyler knew that the sit-down with Mellon was different from many of the meetings that had come before. Mellon was not there to learn; he was there to confirm. His excitement and conviction reminded Tyler of how he and his brother had felt in the days leading up to their own headfirst plunge into the new economy.

"Here's the deal," Mellon said, once they'd exchanged pleasantries and a few stories about people they knew in common. "I've done a lot of reading since we connected over email, and I'm more than intrigued. I think you boys are onto something. I think you've found a rocket ship." He paused. "My problem is, I don't know how to get on." Mellon hadn't reached out because he needed their knowledge, or a crash course on Bitcoin; he needed their *access*—more specifically, a safe and secure way to buy himself a seat on their rocket ship, just like they'd bought theirs on Branson's.

Cameron and Tyler immediately agreed to help Matthew solve his Bitcoin problem. They also realized the significance of the request. If a man like Mellon—a scion of American banking royalty, literally a descendant of the people who created *the banking system* in the first place—had trouble getting access to Bitcoin, well then Bitcoin still had major kinks to work out.

Following coffee, the twins facilitated Mellon's request by promising to introduce him to Charlie—a risk after the unbearable meeting with RRE, but one they'd had no choice but to accept. Unlike the many business moguls they'd met on their road trip, Mellon was ready to buy, and buy big. And he—and everyone else who followed the twins into the pool—was about to do very well.

"My family and friends are going to think I've gone crazy," Mellon said, grinning. "And that's saying a lot."

"Crazy is a relative thing," Tyler said.

"You could just start small by buying a handful of coins," Cameron said. "Watch the market and build a position over time."

"That's not the way I approach things. I'm an all-or-nothing kind of guy."

It made sense, especially in the context of Bitcoin. It was like this bug—you either caught it, or you didn't. Once you were hooked, you were hooked for good. No matter how many people called it a Ponzi scheme or a tulip bubble, you weren't going to be swayed.

"Then buy as much bitcoin as you'd like," Tyler said.

"I want you to know that I'm pro–Wall Street, pro-business, pro-banking, pro-America," Mellon said. "And I think that's exactly where Bitcoin should live."

Mellon was a believer, but he was a believer cast in their image, not Ver's or Voorhees's. He knew that Bitcoin had to find its place within the financial framework that already existed. Facebook didn't bring down the internet, it had just pushed the internet in a direction that worked for Facebook.

As far as the twins were concerned, getting the Bitcoin story out there was only the first step in the journey. Getting people *into* Bitcoin was the next; it wasn't a coincidence that they were spending most of their time discussing Bitcoin in New York, which was ground zero of the world's financial system—where it all began. In 1792, twenty-four stockbrokers signed the Buttonwood Agreement under a buttonwood tree located outside 68 Wall Street, creating the New York Stock Exchange.

No matter what the ideologues believed, no matter how much they brayed about bringing down banks and governments, the twins knew that if Bitcoin was going to succeed, Wall Street was going to have to get involved.

After Mellon was off, blending into the foot traffic on Astor Place, Tyler turned back to his brother.

"Let's get Charlie on the phone," Tyler said.

Although they had reservations about having Charlie broker a deal for Mellon, the alternative was to send him to Mt. Gox, which posed a whole different set of risks that were potentially even worse than their boy wonder CEO. In any event, Charlie should be able to help Mellon buy a meaningful amount of bitcoin, just the same way he had helped them.

Cameron dialed the number, waited, made a face.

"What now?" Tyler asked.

"He's not there."

"What else is new," Tyler said, sarcastically.

"No, I mean I'm getting an international ring tone."

"What?"

"He's got to be out of the country."

"You've got to be kidding me."

The kid had left town without telling them? Their CEO?

"Where the hell is he? Where did he get the idea that this was okay? He has a business to run."

"I'll give you one guess."

19

THIS SIDE OF PARADISE

Charlie leaned forward over the Plexiglas balcony, staring out at the blinking lights of a city sprawl both modern and tropical, state-of-the-art skyscrapers mingling with squat, hacienda-style buildings with arched windows and tiled roofs. Everywhere he looked, there were cranes, the accoutrements of a burgeoning economy on its way up.

It had to be well after three in the morning, and yet the city was just coming alive. Part of Charlie wanted to get back down there, among the cars and the smog and the people, the energy of the packed discotheques, cafés, and restaurants that lined what was a bona fide Red Light District. And another part of him was content to just watch it all from the balcony of his shared, two-story penthouse. After all, why go down to the party, when the party so badly wanted to come to you?

The balcony extended all the way around the corner of the building, offering nearly 360-degree views of Panama City; from the Pacific Ocean and the famous canal, to the rolling greenery rising up on the other side of the old city behind. But the view *over* the balcony didn't hold a candle to the view *on* the balcony. He counted at least nine women—Panamanian, Colombian, Costa Rican, Mexican—mixed in among his friends. They were all stunning, and the combined effect of so many different flavors of perfume had turned into something palpable.

The girl next to Charlie was named Kitty and she seemed to be the leader of the group that had come home with them from the nightclub an hour before. A nightclub that didn't even have a name, lodged at the end of an alley not two blocks from their apartment. Before that, they had spent the better part of the night at the Veneto Casino. Its pink stucco exterior walls and huge, garish neon sign out front would have been right at home on Fremont Street in Las Vegas.

Charlie wasn't sure whose idea it was to move the traveling circus back to their place, and he definitely hadn't invited the girls—Courtney wasn't with him in Panama at the moment, but she was (and would always be) his everything. Somewhere inside, in the chef's kitchen on the first floor of the penthouse, their butler was making empanadas; yes, a butler had come with the apartment rental. The smell of frying meat and boiled egg wafted through the open double doors leading out to where Charlie and the rest were congregated.

Charlie didn't speak Spanish, so he couldn't exactly follow everything she was saying as she described the part of the city where the penthouse was located. But he'd read a guidebook during the flight from JFK, and he knew that the posh district—El Cangrejo—had actually been founded by Jewish immigrants more than a half century earlier. The city still bore many clues to its original inhabitants. In fact, earlier in the day, just a few blocks over, Charlie had walked past an enormous stone statue of Albert Einstein's head, squatting in the yard of what appeared to be an apartment building.

Since the 1950s, most of the Jews had moved out, and the neighborhood was now diverse, cosmopolitan, and so very much alive.

This sliver of Central America really was the Wild West: there didn't seem to be any laws at all, at least laws that you had to follow. Just about everything was negotiable. Not only was prostitution perfectly legal, but Panama's banking laws were also some of the most lax—or, one could say "innovative"—in the world. The city was rife with companies that would face much harsher scrutiny if they were located most anywhere else. Online poker companies, sports books, money-lending facilities, and now a growing number of bitcoin companies, large and small.

Charlie looked over to Ver, Erik Voorhees, and Ira, who were gathered around an open laptop, pretty much ignoring the girls. It was no surprise that Ver and Voorhees had gravitated to Panama. Its laws and mores dovetailed perfectly with their belief system. From the minute they'd stepped off the plane from New York, Voorhees had begun planning to make his stay in the Central American country permanent. Having a head of marketing living a thousand miles away, on a different continent, might not have been ideal—but in the age of Bitcoin, Charlie figured there was no real reason why they all had to be in the same physical location.

For his part, Charlie had left New York basically on a whim to come along with his friends. Since he'd gotten here, he'd avoided checking his email: he knew exactly what he'd find. Reluctantly, he moved away from the balcony and retrieved his own laptop out from under one of the lounge chairs between two tanned, bare ankles. He found a quiet spot close to where his roommates were sitting.

There they were: Cameron Winklevoss. Tyler Winklevoss. Cameron Winklevoss. Tyler Winklevoss. Multiple emails from both twins, all of them flagged as urgent.

Even their names somehow looked angry. As he started reading through their messages, he could picture them typing away, maybe in their new glass offices at Winklevoss Capital, maybe back home in Greenwich, maybe in their parents' house in the Hamptons. Sitting across from each other as they typed, their faces would be equally livid.

To be fair, he probably should have given them some warning he was leaving town, headed to Panama. But he knew that was only part of the problem. To them, it wouldn't just be that he was in Panama, it would also be that he was here with Voorhees and especially Ver.

Honestly, the invitation had come right when he needed it most. It wasn't just the pitiful meeting he'd attended after the night out of partying; he knew the twins had been justified in berating him about his behavior. It was the constant phone calls, emails, the continuous surge of suggestions that weren't really suggestions; sure, Tyler and Cameron were the primary investors in

BitInstant, but did that give them the right to micromanage Charlie, like he was some sort of twelve-year-old delinquent?

There was no doubt in his mind. If it were up to the twins, by now they would have replaced him as CEO with someone in a suit, or at least a blazer that fit properly.

"Look, Charlie," Ver said from his deck chair, as if he could read Charlie's worried thoughts. "I think I see them rowing through the canal. Any minute now they'll be scaling the side of the building to drag you back to New York."

"There's plenty of room for them to join us," Voorhees said. "I think there's a pull-out couch in the second-floor living room."

Charlie was still scanning their emails. "I think I might have pushed them over the edge this time. They're really pissed."

"Maybe this is a good thing," Ver said. "Maybe this is the stroke that sends them back to Greenwich."

Lately, things had been especially heated between the twins and not just Charlie but his associates too. Tyler and Cameron had started to view Voorhees and Ira as people who were being paid like full-time employees but only working part-time—building their own projects on the side—one of which was a Bitcoin gambling site. The twins believed BitInstant required full-time dedicated employees, not people with one foot in, one foot out. That was how they approached everything, and Charlie could understand it: you didn't make the Olympics by being a part-timer.

Ver, on the other hand, thought Erik's and Ira's side hustles were none of the twins' business—whatever they were building would only further the overall ecosystem and BitInstant along with it; but it was obvious, Ver's disagreement with the twins went much deeper than business. As Bitcoin had grown, Ver had become more and more vocal about his beliefs—you either agreed with them, or you were the enemy.

Charlie started to write a reply to one of the angry emails, then paused, because he wasn't sure there was anything he could write that would make things better, or calm Cameron and Tyler down. He knew they needed to try and work this out face-to-face. And that was part of the reason he had fled to Panama. He had known an especially difficult encounter with the twins was on the horizon.

"Can't you see where this is heading?" Ver said. "They just want to get you in bed with the bankers and regulators."

"They want Bitcoin to succeed," Charlie said. "They just have a different view of how we're going to get there."

"If you say so," Ver said. "Sometimes it's hard to know who are the barbarians, and who are guarding the gates."

Philosophical battles aside, the more successful BitInstant was becoming, the unhappier the twins were getting with how Charlie was running the company. They'd told him he needed to stop traveling, stop partying, be in New York tending to the business. But what they didn't appreciate was that BitInstant was his ticket out into the wide, wide world and all of its parties; he wasn't going to be chained to a desk in New York. Sure, the company had its issues, but it was still doing massive business. They just needed to let him continue doing what he was doing. No need to fix what was already working.

Charlie knew he needed to sit down with the twins and offer up a new strategy going forward. One thing that was important to discuss was BitInstant's relationship with the payment software that Voorhees and Ira had been developing, and which BitInstant was currently using to process its transactions. Something the twins didn't yet know but that Charlie needed to figure out a way to tell them was that, well, the software was actually not the intellectual property of BitInstant—but was instead owned, outright, by Voorhees and Ira, because they had developed it, apart from their duties at BitInstant. In light of that fact, maybe from the twins' point of view it wouldn't be ideal, but Charlie had come up with a plan to pay Voorhees and Ira with some of his BitInstant shares, so that BitInstant could continue to use their software—problem solved. All the twins had to do was sign off on it. Voorhees had even written up a business plan explaining everything, something he called the "United Front."

Once they were all in one room together, they could come to an understanding, a meeting of the minds, and together grow BitInstant into the behemoth they had all imagined from the beginning.

Ver had another idea of the way things should be. He felt BitInstant should relocate here, in Panama. "In Panama, they aren't locking anyone up for being adults and making adult decisions for themselves" was his refrain. It was a view shared increasingly by Voorhees and also expounded by another friend who had joined them in Panana City, a budding Bitcoin mogul named Trace Mayer, as much of an anarcho-capitalist as any of them. Mayer had been involved in crypto from the early days and believed, like Ver, that government wasn't necessary in finance, that financial incentives alone were enough to help guide and govern human nature toward positive outcomes.

The three of them had made some good points; the constant barrage of philosophy had maybe even caused a shift in Charlie's own thinking. For example, the continuing issue involving BTCKing, still one of the company's biggest customers: after initially banishing and admonishing the bitcoin reseller, Charlie had privately assured him he was welcome back. And since then, BTCKing had returned in full force. Over the past year he had done an enormous amount of volume; looking at his list of transactions, Charlie could see that the anonymous customer had turned over about $900,000 already, buying bitcoin at a steady clip—but strategizing his purchases in a way that seemed to obscure the volume of his trades. Gareth, usually silent on matters like this, had grown concerned from Wales, believing that such huge volumes from the reseller meant only one thing: BTCKing was buying bitcoin to sell to people wanting to shop on places like Silk Road.

"He has not broken any law and Silk Road itself is not illegal," Charlie had emailed Gareth. "We also don't have any rules against resellers. We make good profit from him."

Obviously, this email had not been enough to assuage Gareth's concerns. Right there on the balcony Charlie saw in his in-box another missive from his business partner, worrying that BTCKing was pushing the boundaries of what was legal.

"So many of his transactions smell like fraud or money laundering," Gareth's email read.

Sitting on the balcony, with the smell of empanadas in the air, Ver and Voorhees going on about how the world should work, the twins emailing him how the world actually *did* work, the imagery of barbarians at the gates and girls in miniskirts dancing in his head, Charlie reached down and shot off a single, succinct answer to Gareth.

"Cool."

And then he closed his laptop and tried to forget his problems, if only for a night. Running off to Panama felt good, and liberating, but he knew the feelings couldn't last. Soon he'd have to head back to New York, face the twins, and offer them Voorhees's United Front. He had to find a way to keep everyone happy.

Either that, or he'd be right back in Panama, looking for a permanent place to stay.

No matter what happened, one thing was for sure. There was one place where Charlie Shrem wasn't going to end up: back in his mother's basement.

20

THE UNITED FRONT

It wasn't a glass tiger cage surrounded by lawyers. Nobody was handcuffed to a watercooler, and this time around it was both of them entering the arena, not just Cameron. But as Tyler followed Charlie Shrem, Erik Voorhees, BitInstant's outside lawyer, and his brother into the conference room at BitInstant's headquarters, where multiple copies of the proposal labeled United Front were already laid out around a rectangular conference table, pages still warm from the printer—Tyler got the uncanny feeling that he was walking into an ambush. Someone was about to try to "fuck him in the ear."

Once the door was closed, Charlie moved to the front of the room and got the ball rolling. He didn't exactly apologize for running off to Panama, or the recent problems the site was again having, which he only paid lip service to, as if they were ultimately meaningless. And he didn't exactly address the growing issues with Obopay, which, just a few months in, was already threatening to end its agreement with BitInstant, putting the company's legal standing as a money transmitter in jeopardy. But he did acknowledge that it was time for an updated strategy, to put BitInstant on a new footing. To that end, he said, pointing to the United Front printout, he had a plan to officially merge Voorhees and Ira's payment software into the BitInstant company, and make them all one big happy family.

And from there, the meeting went right off the rails. To Tyler's surprise, it was his usually more laid-back brother who took the United Front document off the table, glanced at it—though they'd already read through the thing when Charlie had sent it to them, via email, days earlier—and then tossed it at Charlie, hitting him right in the chest.

"Are you kidding?" Cameron said. "Nobody in here is your family. In this room, in this office, Erik and Ira aren't your friends, they're your employees. This isn't a lifestyle business, it's a *business* business. There shouldn't be any discussion about their software being a part of BitInstant, because it's always been a part of BitInstant—our dollars paid for its development. But more importantly, this meeting has nothing to do with software. It's about you, and how you're running this company."

Tyler wanted to jump in right next to his brother but knew things were going to escalate too quickly if he did. Maybe Charlie really didn't realize it, but to the twins, this meeting had nothing to do with some software Voorhees and Ira had written, which in their minds BitInstant already owned; nor was it really about the unannounced jaunt to Panama, as unprofessional as that had been. To the twins, this was going to be a *corrective* meeting. They had been out there meeting with the biggest names in the financial world while Charlie partied, showed up to meetings bent out of shape, and sponged up whatever crazy bullshit Ver and Voorhees threw his way.

At this point, it was their money that kept the doors open and the lights on, not Roger Ver's. And that gave them the right—the duty—to try and keep Charlie in check and rein him in. Charlie had to understand: BitInstant wasn't his personal piggy bank, and it wasn't a bankroll for his journey of self-discovery.

Tyler signaled his brother to slow down and then asked for a minute alone with Charlie. Cameron took a seat by one of the windows overlooking Twenty-Third Street, boiling. He had a lot to be angry about. BitInstant had burned through a lot of their money in a very short time, and Charlie kept running around without a care, almost delusional. Now he was trying to change the stock structure to account for some software that his own employees had developed in BitInstant offices, on the company (and the twins') dime. As far as the twins were concerned, that software was part of what they'd funded.

Tyler moved Charlie to the back of the room; he knew that Voorhees and the rest could probably still hear him, but he didn't really care.

"As the CEO of BitInstant, you need to think about what's best for the company, not for your friends. You need to separate the two."

Tyler tried to speak calmly, precisely.

Charlie said, "Well, they're employees, but they're also family."

"No. Erik and Ira work for you. Roger Ver owns a percentage of the company. We own a bigger percentage of the company. And none of us are family. If we happen to all be friends as a result of working together then that's great, but friendship is not the goal, it's a by-product. We aren't on a bowling team together, we're in business together."

"It's the same thing."

"It's not. You need to create professional boundaries."

Charlie glanced toward Voorhees, who was pretending to chat with the lawyer, and Cameron, who was pretending to look out the window. Tyler put a hand on Charlie's arm.

"It's time for you and BitInstant to grow up."

"This is about Roger, isn't it."

"No, it's absolutely not about Roger, or Erik, or anyone else for that matter—it's about *you*. Look at the way you're running this place. You're your own chief compliance officer. You aren't protecting your licenses. You have no relationships with your banks. You're out at your club every night, out with the cocktail waitresses, out in goddam Panama. At what point are you going to check in with reality? After it's too late?"

Charlie's shoulders were hunched, but he was defiant.

"I'm out networking. It's important for me to be visible in the community."

"Charlie, you smoke and drink at the conferences until you can barely see straight. You think that's what Bitcoin needs right now? We're here trying to make people see it as something legit."

Charlie looked like he was about to say something, then stopped himself. Tyler could guess what the kid CEO was thinking: What would Roger Ver say?

"If you keep this up," Tyler said, louder than he wanted but he couldn't help himself, "you're going to end up like Roger."

"I'd be happy to end up like Roger," Charlie responded, almost under his breath. "I'd be happy to end up—"

"A felon."

Tyler rejoined the group but Charlie remained at the back of the room, in his own world.

Then Voorhees spoke. "This might be the right time for me to hand in my resignation. Rather than cause any more problems, Ira and I can leave."

Although Tyler and Cameron had previously discussed the possibility of losing Voorhees and Ira if they weren't willing to join BitInstant full-time, he didn't expect that to come to a head right here, right now, during this meeting.

On the other hand, it made sense. Voorhees never had both feet in to begin with, and these days he had good reason to have both feet out. He was smart, maybe too smart to be a marketing guy working for Charlie Shrem. But more importantly, his side project, SatoshiDice, was already gaining so much traction in the Bitcoin community that it represented a meaningful percentage of overall Bitcoin transactions. It didn't make sense for him to stick around as an employee when he was already the founder of his own fast-growing startup.

"Nobody needs to leave," Charlie sputtered, clearly dismayed by the turn of events. Then he turned to Tyler and Cameron: "Maybe Roger can buy you guys out."

Whether Charlie was picking a side, or just reacting with emotion, it was hard to tell.

"Roger isn't buying anybody out," Cameron said, angrily.

In fact, Ver had offered to buy them out at a valuation 10 percent higher than when they'd bought in; alternatively, Ver had offered to let *them* buy *him* out, at a two-million-dollar valuation. It was in keeping with Ver's personality to explore all options. But they were never going to make any deal with Ver.

"Guys," Charlie said, but Tyler was already heading toward the door.

Cameron followed his brother out. Charlie hurried behind, still talking, rambling about how things didn't need to go this far, that nobody needed to quit, that they could work this out. As he bargained, Charlie looked even smaller than usual, deflated. Maybe he'd really thought that things could be patched up with some handshakes and smiles.

"In rowing," Tyler said, "sometimes there's one guy in your boat who slows the whole thing down. He might mean well. He might be trying as hard, or even harder, than anyone else, but it doesn't matter, he's weighing everyone down. We call that guy an anchor."

And with that, the twins left the building.

On the street, Tyler and his brother began the two-minute walk back to their own offices. Neither of them spoke for the first minute. Tyler hadn't expected the meeting to end on such a note, but he wasn't entirely displeased. Maybe the harsh words, maybe the prospect of losing Erik and Ira, would be exactly what Charlie needed to knock sense into him and get him to start acting like a real CEO.

He felt the proverbial buzzing in his pocket. He expected some sort of missive from Charlie, maybe a last gasp attempt to keep the "family" intact. Instead he looked down to see an email from an unknown address. Curious, he opened it.

And then he stopped in the middle of a crosswalk.

Cameron continued walking a few paces forward before realizing that he had lost his brother.

"What are you doing? You're going to get yourself killed."

Tyler waved him over, then handed him the phone.

"What is this?"

"It's an invite. Something in San Francisco."

Cameron stared at the mysterious email on Tyler's phone.

The email was short, from someone they didn't know. Probably someone who worked for someone else. But that wasn't the only mysterious part. The invite was for May 16 in San Francisco at 6:00 P.M., the night before their keynote address at Bitcoin 2013. Other than the date, time, and location, there were no other details. The message read only:

Look for the Genesis Block at 631 Folsom . . . photo attached.

Tyler looked up from the phone.

"The Genesis Block," he said.

That was the name used in the community to describe the first block of the Bitcoin blockchain. It was mined by Satoshi himself back in 2009.

Charlie, BitInstant, the chaos of the meeting they'd just left, were suddenly put into perspective by that strange little email. Whether Erik and Ira really left the company or not, Tyler believed that they had succeeded in at least putting Charlie on notice. He would fix things and become the CEO he needed to be, or the twins would find a way to fix it themselves, without him.

But eclipsing those thoughts, the odd email reminded Tyler of that first moment in Ibiza, when he'd felt like they'd just peered down a rabbit hole toward something the rest of the world had somehow missed.

The honk of a taxicab coming around the corner broke through his contemplation, and he pulled his brother toward the curb.

"We're going to need to book an earlier flight to California."

21

BEHIND THE DOOR

M ay 16, 2013.

Six P.M. on the dot.

Rincon Hill, south of Market Street, San Francisco.

A mostly residential area of wildly priced condos. Their destination appeared to be a skyscraper with a nondescript lobby and a bored-looking concierge behind a desk, who had no idea what Cameron and Tyler were looking for. It wasn't until they were back out on the street, scanning the building's facade, that they found it—right out in the open for anybody walking by to see: a single door, with a small sign taped to it, which read THE GENESIS BLOCK.

"I wish Naval had given us a little bit of a clue about what we're walking into," Tyler whispered to Cameron.

The whispering was probably overkill, but something about the mysteriousness of the moment, the energy, made it feel right. Bitcoin 2013—which would begin the next day—had been hurtling toward them with much fanfare, publicity, and preinterviews. More than a thousand people would partake in the assault on the San Jose convention center, a rather large increase from the eighty attendees who had taken part the year before. Even some major news outlets would be there. Ever since Cyprus, which had sent the price of bitcoin skyrocketing, people were paying attention. But this—the Genesis Block—whatever it was, it was something else.

"A cryptic invite to a cryptic doorway. Makes sense, considering the theme."

It hadn't been hard to track down the originator of the email invite. By googling the name of the assistant who'd sent the invite, they'd found that it had come from Naval Ravikant, a serial angel investor and entrepreneur. Ravikant, a brilliant thinker with degrees in economics and computer science from Dartmouth, who had invested in numerous tech successes over the years.

The twins had met Ravikant a few months earlier at a tech dinner in New York hosted by Joe Lonsdale, a prodigy in his own right. Having interned at PayPal while still a student at Stanford, he'd gone on to work at Peter Thiel's hedge fund, Clarium Capital, and later had cofounded Palantir Technologies with Thiel and Alex Karp. Both Lonsdale and Thiel were chess geniuses known to battle it out with each other for hours on end. Thiel himself was, of course, a Valley legend, having founded PayPal, and was considered the "don" of the "PayPal Mafia"—a group of PayPal alums who'd gone on to start a slew of world-changing companies. The group included Elon Musk (Tesla, SpaceX), Reid Hoffman (LinkedIn), David Sacks (Yammer), Ken Howery (Founders Fund), Max Levchin (Yelp), and others. Thiel also happened to have been the first investor in Facebook; he turned a $500,000 check into a billion-dollar investment, a mind-blowing 13,000x return.

At the dinner, Naval had told the twins about the company he had cofounded in 2010, called AngelList, a meeting place for investors and entrepreneurs—something Business Insider had once called "Match.com for investors." Later, the twins had overheard Naval explaining Bitcoin (and explaining it well) to another guest at the dinner—Garry Kasparov, the Russian chess grandmaster and political activist.

That dinner was the first time the twins had ever heard anyone from the Silicon Valley "establishment" talk seriously about Bitcoin. After the conversation had ended, the twins and Naval had exchanged contact information. Other than that, they had no idea why Naval had reached out to them, or what they were doing in San Francisco the night before their keynote. They just felt it was wise to be there.

Tyler tried the knob and found that the door was unlocked. It opened into a surprisingly large space, like a loft apartment, except it wasn't really an apartment where someone actually lived, more of an artfully decorated "man cave." Tyler saw a regulation-size pool table, a round poker table, a pair of foosball tables, multiple flat-screen televisions, leather couches, a fully stocked bar, and steps leading up to a raised kitchen and pantry.

"We're not the first to show up," Cameron said.

Tyler had wanted to arrive thirty minutes late, but Cameron had argued that the only information they had was the hour and place, so they might as well follow the directions to the letter. And Cameron was apparently right, because there were already twenty people in the room, filling the couches and mingling around the bar. A few were gathered beneath one of the televisions, which displayed a Bitcoin price chart: Mt. Gox had suffered a recent brownout that had depressed the price, but Bitcoin had partially recovered and was sitting at around $120 a coin.

As Tyler stepped farther into the room, he realized that he recognized many of the other guests. With that recognition came a realization and a confirmation of his earlier feeling: this was a significant gathering.

Before he could tell his brother what he was thinking, Naval caught sight of them from one of the couches and walked over, bringing with him the co-host of the evening: Bill Lee. A handsome Taiwanese-American entrepreneur and investor, Lee had sold his first company for $265 million during the dot-com frenzy in the late 1990s. After that, he had exited to the Dominican Republic, where he'd bought a hotel and surfed for two years. Upon his return, Lee had promptly backed his best friend Elon Musk's new startups: Tesla and SpaceX. A few years later, he would marry Al Gore's youngest daughter. Lee was probably one of the most influential yet under-the-radar people in the Valley—virtually unknown to the outside world. Inside the Valley, he cut his own image—imbued with a style that strayed far from the khaki pants of the VCs on Sand Hill Road, or the hacker hoodies of the Facebook set. At the moment, he was wearing a distressed leather jacket over a white T-shirt, and a beaded necklace around his tan neck.

"Welcome to the party," Lee said, shaking hands with both twins. "Please help yourself to the bar and whatever you like in the kitchen. We'll get started in a few minutes."

As Lee stepped away to welcome more guests who had filed in behind the twins, they overheard someone saying, "He doesn't actually live here. He lives upstairs. He's got a penthouse that takes up most of the top of the building."

"I'm glad you guys made it," Naval said to the twins. "Now that you've been crowned the world's first 'bitcoin moguls,' I didn't think it would be right if you weren't here."

"So what's going on tonight?" Cameron asked.

"Bitcoiners Anonymous," Naval quipped, "a support group for the engineers and entrepreneurs suffering from a crypto addiction."

"So, you're the enablers?" Tyler asked.

"Precisely. We're the only people in Silicon Valley right now who care about crypto. I take it you guys haven't been spending much time in the Valley lately."

It was very true.

"The people in this room are mostly Silicon Valley outsiders anyway. They build the protocols and tools that power the internet, its plumbing. You could even call them the roadies of the internet."

Naval was right. While some of the faces here were known in deeper technology circles, and Tyler and Cameron recognized some of them, most were not the Silicon Valley "brands" that people across America knew, the billion-dollar unicorns who dominated the West Coast tech scene. They were, instead, the technical heavyweights, who spent their time working on the guts of the internet, focused on the deeper transport and network layers, not the surface, where sexy companies like Facebook and Google lived. They were the engineering equivalent of the back office, not the shiny front office types. They were often called "neckbeards"—they weren't exactly client-facing.

But when people talked about someone being the smartest person in the room—well, this was a room full of them. They were intensely interested in cryptography, protocols, and peer-to-peer networking, and coding in lower-level languages like C and C++. They were close to the bare metal, the 1s and 0s, bits and bytes, not the more user-friendly, abstracted layers.

Tyler certainly recognized brilliant billionaires among them, such as Max

Levchin, who had cofounded PayPal with Thiel. Levchin was credited with decimating fraud on the network in the early days, and was a leading member of the PayPal Mafia. Tyler also saw true protocol royalty in the form of Bram Cohen, who had built BitTorrent and essentially invented decentralized, peer-to-peer file sharing. Cohen was perhaps the greatest living protocol developer alive after Satoshi. Maybe, Tyler mused, he was Satoshi?

And then there were fellow early Bitcoiners like Paul Bohm, an information security expert who had written one of the earliest blogs explaining Bitcoin mining; Mike Belshe, one of the first engineers to work the SPDY protocol used by Google in its Chrome browser; Matt Pauker and Balaji Srinivasan, who had cofounded a Bitcoin mining company called 21e6 (the scientific notation for the number twenty-one million, the total number of bitcoin that would ever be created); Srinivasan was also on the way to becoming the CTO of a company called Coinbase, a cryptocurrency exchange on a rapid rise in the industry. There was Ryan Singer, who ran a Bitcoin exchange named Tradehill. And perhaps most notably there was Jed McCaleb, the founder of Mt. Gox itself. He had launched the original site as a Magic: The Gathering trading portal, had repurposed it as a Bitcoin exchange, and then sold the business to Mark Karpeles in 2011, keeping a minority stake before embarking on other crypto-related ventures.

Right in front of the twins was a security expert named Dan Kaminsky. He famously discovered a flaw in the Domain Name Security protocol that, until he helped fix, put every internet user at risk of being hacked. Cameron and Tyler had read a profile of him in *The New Yorker,* which chronicled his unsuccessful attempt at hacking Bitcoin itself. Kaminsky was arguably the greatest security expert in internet history, and the twins had been fascinated to read the story of how he'd locked himself in his parents' basement and spent weeks trying to penetrate the Bitcoin protocol, to no avail.

Kaminsky was the first person Tyler started talking to after he broke off from Naval. He noticed that Kaminsky was wearing three different brands of activity trackers on his wrists: a Fitbit, a Nike FuelBand, and a Jawbone UP. Tyler corralled the security expert by the pool table, where McCaleb and Levchin were geeking out on god knows what.

"Why all three?" Tyler asked. "Doesn't one do the job?"

Kaminsky shrugged.

"The second one is to tell if the first one is broken. The third is to tell if the other two are lying."

It was exactly how Tyler should have expected a security engineer to think—in terms of systems and their fault tolerance and integrity. Over the next ten minutes, he interrogated Kaminsky about his hacking efforts; at first, the security expert had expected to be able to penetrate such a complex piece of code easily—the fact that it was so complex, so long, meant there should have been many weak spots to exploit. But over the days spent in his parents' basement filled with computers, he kept coming up empty. Every time he thought he had found a bug or an exploit, he was met by a message in the code proclaiming "Attack removed." It was as if Satoshi had already thought of every attack vector and vulnerability ahead of time, which to Kaminsky, seemed impossible. Satoshi was always ahead, even if only by a few lines of code. That was why Kaminsky had trouble believing Satoshi could be one person. He felt sure the originator must have been a team of people to put together something so perfect, so secure. Either that, or he was a genius on a whole *different* level.

Tyler looked around the man cave.

"Would it be fair to guess that Satoshi could be right here in this room?"

Kaminsky didn't disagree.

Could it be Levchin, standing at the pool table nearby? The PayPal Mafia's goal from the beginning was to create a universal currency for the internet, but they'd fallen short, eventually selling to eBay. PayPal was by all accounts a huge financial win for Levchin and his colleagues, and a huge win for the user-friendly nature of payments on the internet, but even so, it was a payment network that ran on the existing banking rails. It hadn't made money into a protocol—the way Voice Over Internet Protocol (VOIP) had done with voice. PayPal still ran over the copper wires of the legacy banking system. They had changed the way people made payments. But they had not changed the world.

Bitcoin had essentially picked up where the PayPal Mafia had left off. Whereas PayPal was a new saddle on the same horse, Bitcoin was an automobile. It was the Holy Grail of virtual currency. Some PayPal alumns like Thiel were so disillusioned by their own early attempt at reaching that Holy Grail that it was like they couldn't bring themselves to get as excited about Bitcoin as Levchin; eventually, they all would see what he saw.

As Bill Lee rejoined them, taking the pool cue from Levchin and chalking the tip, the general conversation shifted to which country might adopt Bitcoin as its national currency first. It was a heady question—the idea that a government might embrace virtual currency to that degree, rather than seeing it as an enemy—and the speculation settled on Iceland, because after its recent financial collapse, the Icelandic people had become very suspicious of bankers, had even thrown many of them in jail. And Iceland was also cold, which made it a good place for Bitcoin mining. One of the biggest challenges for miners was keeping their computers from overheating as they did all that number crunching in search of the golden ticket.

Lee joked about moving his operations to Reykjavik, to get ahead of the curve. As the first money into Tesla and SpaceX, Lee was already so far ahead of the curve he was almost invisible. And his interests in space had only made him more convinced that Bitcoin was the future of money.

"Space is full of asteroids," he said as he lined up the cue for a shot on one of the pockets. "And asteroids are full of metals, precious metals—diamonds, titanium, especially gold. In fact, there's already a database that speculates how many billions of dollars in gold the closest asteroids contain. The technology is getting better every day, just ask Elon. Pretty soon, we'll be mining those asteroids. Gold in our universe isn't rare at all, it's actually plentiful, like sand on a beach. And we all know what that means."

"Precious metals won't be very precious anymore," Cameron said. "But Bitcoin will only increase in value."

Everyone in that room saw that clear as day. It might take another twenty years to play out, but it was inevitable. The people in that room, all experts and engineers, also clearly saw Cameron and Tyler as fellow early adopters. They were welcoming: it was the exact opposite of how they'd been treated by everyone else in Silicon Valley—a place where they couldn't even buy a drink for an entrepreneur at Oasis, because of who they were, because of their indelible connection to Mark Zuckerberg.

The group in this room was not the Valley establishment. They were the rebels, bona fide cypherpunks. Most of them were not "commercial" enough to even work at a company like Facebook. They didn't know how to play the game. But the game was about to change.

Tyler moved through the crowd, meeting and speaking with everyone he could. The conversations were all optimistic—everyone believed that adoption of Bitcoin was a when, not an if—that Bitcoin could truly become a world currency, and that blockchain technology would soon be ubiquitous.

At the same time, these engineers, technologists, and forward thinkers agreed that it was a critical time for crypto. Now that the world was watching, Bitcoin would need to hit "escape velocity" soon. Bitcoin was gold 2.0, and gold was money 1.0—but gold had a ten-thousand-year first-mover advantage. Bitcoin had superior qualities, but if adoption wasn't accelerated, the powers that be would try to kill it. Just as there were those plotting Bitcoin's success, like this motley crew with big ideas in a man cave on the evening before Bitcoin's biggest public conference yet, there were those who would see it as a threat. Wall Street, Visa, American Express, Western Union, governments, even Pay-Pal itself. The list went on and on. These organizations and businesses, which had the most to lose, had the most to gain if Bitcoin failed.

Tyler believed that the key to Bitcoin beating back those future enemies was to grow fast, fast enough so that by the time the banks and governments woke up, it would be too late for them to try and kill it—they would have no choice but to work with it. For that to happen, the decentralized genie had to get out of the bottle before it got capped. Once this happened, every government would instead fight to become a crypto capital.

As the evening ended, and Naval walked with Tyler and his brother toward the door, he told them that just by being part of Bitcoin at such an early stage, the twins were helping tremendously with the cause; for Bitcoin to grow quickly, it now needed to reach the mainstream. It needed the right people to be out there saying the right things. The world was listening.

It was exactly what he and Cameron had been trying to explain to Charlie the past few months. The world was listening, and the voices they needed to hear weren't those of anarcho-libertarians in Panama. With Voorhees gone—he'd kept true to his word and resigned shortly after the meeting, actually moving to Panama full-time—and with their help, Tyler still wanted to believe that Charlie Shrem could also be one of those voices. But in truth, it was hard to imagine Charlie Shrem in this room of engineers and futurists, spinning through the man cave like a circus sideshow.

"I'm just glad you let us be a part of this," Tyler said to Naval as they reached the door.

It was more than just patter; Naval adding them to the invite list hadn't been as simple an act as typing their names on a spreadsheet.

In fact, their addition had raised conflict with at least one Silicon Valley bigwig that they knew of: Chamath Palihapitiya. He had been Facebook's vice president for user growth until 2011 and remained an ally of Mark Zuckerberg's. In the twins' mind, he was an outspoken, often boastful, overdressed suit in the Valley, quick to parrot groupthink buzzwords and clichés like "disrupt," "data driven," "tipping point," and—a personal favorite—"meaningful solutions to meaningful problems." At Facebook, Palihapitiya's claim to fame had been growing the social network's user base—which during Facebook's boom was like taking credit for making sure the sun came up in the morning.

From what the twins had heard, upon finding out that Naval intended to invite them, Palihapitiya, an invite himself, had tried to convince Naval to rescind the twins' invitation. When Naval had told him he wouldn't, Palihapitiya had refused to attend.

In Tyler's mind, that was Palihapitiya's loss, and deep down, he was glad Palihapitiya had opted out of the Genesis Block. He was glad that, in fact, nobody from Facebook, the biggest unicorn of the past decade and supposedly one of the most forward-looking Silicon Valley companies, was there.

"It means a lot," Tyler added, "to be a part of something as important as this."

"I always root for the underdogs," Naval said, with a grin.

22

BITCOIN 2013

———•

<p>urple curtains framed the main stage of the San Jose McEnery Convention Center. The crowd assembled represented everything Bitcoin: developers in shorts, hoodies, and sneakers, sporting laminated lanyards and name tags, fresh from a day spent setting up their respective portable booths, which were now spread across the gargantuan convention center like interlocked cells of a honeycomb. Bitcoin miners, constantly checking their phones to monitor the basements and garages and insulated lairs where their hardware waged constant battle to unlock those elusive block rewards, the perpetual race that Satoshi had set in motion years earlier. The libertarians, with their T-shirts painted with colorful, antigovernment slogans. The cryptographers, with their long hair and overgrown beards. And then the financial press, with tape recorders, lights, and cameras, all aimed toward the stage, ready to capture the moment, in case it really was *the moment*, that fulcrum moment in the history of Bitcoin that everyone in that industrial hangar of a room believed was inevitable, was coming, and *soon*.</p>

"First they ignore you," Cameron bellowed from the center of the stage, his pulse rocketing beneath the glare of the spotlights hanging from the ceiling and the attention of all those eyes.

"Then they laugh at you."

"Then they fight you," his brother added, next to him on the stage, his voice reverberating through the massive speakers set throughout the room.

"Then you win," Cameron exclaimed.

As a ripple of applause moved across the audience of close to a thousand people, Cameron's nerves finally settled down. This was not a hostile crowd. These people were part of the same movement, and though many of them may not have known what to think about the choice of the twins as headliners, it was obvious from the minute Cameron walked onstage, they were willing to give the Winklevii a chance.

Beginning their speech with a quote from Gandhi might be ambitious, but his famous words had a perennial appeal to this Silicon Valley crowd. They could have been the mantra of almost any company in Silicon Valley; but in their speech, Cameron and Tyler were actually going back farther than the Twitters and Facebooks to make their point.

"Cars," Cameron continued. "Once viewed as unreliable, especially when compared to horses. Faddish, not fit for wide adoption, limited in their range and utility."

To further make the point, Cameron and his brother presented a couple of quotes, including one from the president of the Michigan Savings Bank, circa 1903: "The horse is here to stay, but the automobile is only a novelty—a fad." The idea that the automobile could have been laughed at when it was first invented seemed ridiculous, but as Cameron pointed out, most major innovations that ended up truly changing the world had been met with a similar initial response.

Amazon had been thought by many to likely fail. These doubters believed consumers would be unwilling to use their credit cards online, or shop without a "crucial personal element." The internet itself, Cameron explained, and its potential impact on the world had been doubted early on. In 1998, Paul Krugman, the famed Nobel Prize–winning economist and *New York Times* columnist, infamously said that "by 2005 or so, it will become clear that the internet's impact on the economy has been no greater than the fax machine's."

Now that Bitcoin was making headlines and part of the global lexicon, it was no longer being ignored; instead, the laughing part was in full gear and the fighting had begun. Bitcoin was either lampooned as a joke, or lambasted as "dangerous." Skeptics compared it to proverbial bubbles, whether Dutch tulips in the 1600s, the dot-coms of the late 1990s, or the housing market in 2008. But Cameron and his brother didn't believe any of these analogies applied. Bitcoin wasn't some perishable flower masquerading as a store of value, or a company whose stock price was out of whack with its economic output, or a highly leveraged second home. Bitcoin was a network, and if there was one thing they understood, it was the power of networks. The more people that bought in, the more valuable it became—Metcalfe's law, plain and simple. And networks didn't grow at a slow and steady pace; they experienced viral growth.

"It's not a bubble, it's a *rush*."

When the real fight came, and came fiercely, as it would, how would Bitcoin win?

Cameron was convinced that the people who were most likely to fight Bitcoin were those who had the most to lose by its adoption. Which meant all the middlemen, rent seekers, and toll collectors of the legacy financial world—the banks, money transmitters, money remitters, credit card companies, and governments.

Cameron and Tyler also knew that government regulation would come; and unlike many in the room, they believed that it was important to embrace and help shape that eventuality. Because over the past year, through their experience of buying bitcoin, pitching Bitcoin, and investing in one of the rising stars of Bitcoin, they had come to the following realization: the biggest danger the Bitcoin community faced was itself.

Mt. Gox, failing again and again, caused tremendous instability in the market. Silk Road stained everything it touched. The radical philosophers, who were important in Bitcoin's beginnings, were now so at odds with the campaign to bring Bitcoin mainstream. All of it was the Bitcoin community getting in its own way. Not because of some external threat or fight, which would arrive soon enough.

Regulation would come. *And should come.* Before that, Cameron warned the audience, the community needed to be "buttoned up and have all our ducks in a row."

"Perhaps right now, the biggest irony of Bitcoin is that Bitcoin, the math-based currency, is being held back by man. We can all change this."

Bitcoin needed to learn how to stop fighting itself.

For the speech, Cameron and his brother had left their suits at home. Cameron was in all-black, down to his sneakers, his brother in a patterned shirt, his sleeves unbuttoned and rolled up; nobody knew better than they that there was a time and a place to look like Valley entrepreneurs, creative, relaxed, like you were making up the rules as you went along. And there was a time and a place to look like you understood that some rules mattered, that there needed to be structure.

There was a time and a place for the suits, and this was something the Bitcoin world would need to learn to understand, because it might help decide whether Bitcoin went the way of the automobile, or the tulip.

It was a hell of a high, coming off that stage to raucous applause, pushing through a crack in the billowing purple curtains and following Tyler down a narrow catwalk that led to the speakers' lounge. Cameron shook so many hands along the way, mostly people he didn't know—conference organizers, handlers, even the sound and lighting guys—that he barely had time to catch his breath before he reached the open doorway a step behind his brother, and found himself in the green room, where a buffet was set up along the back wall: water bottles, pastries, and Bitcoin-related promotional paraphernalia like hats, T-shirts, and pens. In this room he saw the CEOs of every significant Bitcoin-related company in the world, the heads of Mycelium, ZipZap, Open-Coin, Coinbase, Ripple Labs, CoinLab, Coinsetter—just about any company that had "coin" on its business cards.

It wasn't until he'd reached the buffet and retrieved one of the water bottles, imprinted with the Bitcoin symbol on the label, that he caught sight of his own investment in the flesh, in the far corner, standing under a blank TV screen, which undoubtedly had just televised their speech. Charlie Shrem was in animated conversation, his hands flying up and down, his body rocking on the balls of his feet.

Across from him was Roger Ver.

Cameron gave his brother a tap, then nodded toward the pair.

"Here we go again," Cameron said.

"Give you three guesses what they're talking about," Tyler replied.

"Explosives," Cameron said. "Drugs. Armed rebellion."

The truth was, since the contentious reckoning they'd had in New York, as far as they could tell, Charlie had been on his best behavior. Though he was still traveling too much, living above a nightclub, and not spending enough time in the BitInstant offices to suit their wishes, the loss of Erik and Ira seemed to have pushed him to get his act together. He'd been saying all the right things about where his company was going and how it was going to get there. He had at least managed to keep the lights on at BitInstant.

But obviously, he hadn't taken their advice about Ver, who seemed to have cast a spell over their young CEO, a spell that didn't look like it was going to lift anytime soon. Even from a distance, Cameron could see why.

You had to hand it to him, Ver was charismatic. Although the twins had still managed to avoid spending any face-to-face time with their "investment partner," there was no doubt, in their mind, that he was the kind of guy who was either going to be an eccentric billionaire, or a crazy transient, with no in-between. To those who latched on to his words with religious fervor, he was Bitcoin Jesus, the Messiah. Less because he'd gotten in so early, or made so many investments in the space, but because he had a magnetism about him that pulled at those wanting to believe, those craving a different world, a different system.

But Ver's crypto cult revolved around some truly extreme beliefs. Ver hadn't spoken at the conference yet, but he'd just given an interview to Coindesk, a Bitcoin-related blog that had recently sprung up to cover the burgeoning industry. Ver's answers had sounded off alarm bells in Cameron's head. When Ver had been asked if his prosecution, the one that had landed him in jail as a young man, had influenced his decision to get into Bitcoin, he'd responded:

"My political views before my run-in with the law were more abstract and philosophical . . . [they] became much more real. The thing that has me most excited about Bitcoin is all the ways it will strip government control away."

Ver had gone on to describe Bitcoin as "this incredibly powerful tool that's not going to [just] free Americans, it's going to free every country on the planet . . . I've been shouting from the rooftops."

The idea that Americans needed to be liberated seemed bizarre to the

Winklevoss brothers, and the idea of Bitcoin stripping away the U.S. government's power seemed potentially dangerous. Cameron definitely agreed that one of the wonderful things about Bitcoin was that it brought economic liberty to places where people lived under tyranny, but ascribing this need for freedom to citizens of an open society like the United States—that seemed to him to be pushing things in a frightening direction.

But Ver hadn't stopped there.

"I'm in favor of regulation," he'd told the Coindesk reporter. "I'm not in favor of regulation at the point of a gun. That's a really important difference. When the regulators from Washington, D.C., make a law they're not *asking* you to do that. They're *telling* you to do that. The difference between asking someone and telling someone to do something is fundamental. It's the same as the difference between making love and being raped."

Making love and being raped. It wasn't just an inflammatory comment, it was also tantamount to anarchism. Ver's logic could easily apply to taxation, or really any law at all. And Cameron believed that was exactly what Ver meant. Ver seemed to believe that laws backed up by the power of government were analogous to rape. Ver was saying that Bitcoin was a way around laws, any laws.

Whereas Cameron and his brother had just given a speech suggesting that the way for Bitcoin to win the fight was to preempt it and stop the battle before it began by working with regulators and lawmakers where needed, Ver had thrown down the battle-ax and declared war.

And now there he was, across the green room, planting seeds as usual in Charlie's head and watering them; and like a sponge, Charlie was soaking it all up.

"Should we join them?" Cameron asked. "We're the ones paying for the armed rebellion, after all."

Tyler pointed in the other direction, toward a group of assorted other Bitcoin power players.

"Not tonight. Let's enjoy the moment."

Cameron threw one last glance toward Charlie, who had both hands up in the air, in the midst of telling some over-the-top story, and Ver, who was grinning like the Cheshire cat.

"We started the evening with Gandhi. Let's not end it with Che Guevara."

———

By the time Cameron had navigated through the mazelike convention center and finally arrived at the BitInstant booth—really, just an oversize poster painted with the BitInstant name and logo hanging above a desk inside a makeshift cubicle created by intersecting black curtains strung along with what appeared to be chrome towel-rods—Charlie was already at full *Charlie*. He was beaming and glowing like a cherub set on fire, and Cameron could immediately see why.

A microphone.

A camera.

A pretty reporter in a low-cut top.

Charlie was seated in a director's chair, feet dangling in the air, soles searching for the ground. He was a few yards from the rest of the BitInstant team and was sporting a black BitInstant T-shirt, black blazer, and dark jeans. And he was halfway into an interview with the anchor of a show called *Prime Interest* on the international television station RT. Originally known as Russia Today, RT was a network funded by the Russian government. At that point, all Cameron knew about it was that it had some surprisingly good programming content, at least in the financial sector. Cameron could tell, even from five feet away, that the reporter was loving Charlie—and Charlie was loving Charlie. He was charming and talkative, a great interview—a little man with a big mug and even bigger maw, built for the camera. But Cameron could also tell that Charlie's *reality* was becoming slightly unhinged, disorganized. The kid was playing to the camera, and as lovable as that made him, it was disconcerting.

To be fair, the Convention Center, halfway into Saturday—the speaking sessions in full swing and the humongous trade show crowded with people—was Charlie's playground. In this arena, he *was* a celebrity. On the walk over, Cameron had actually passed vendors hawking T-shirts with Charlie's face on them. BitInstant was one of the most talked about companies in the place, and most of the people at this conference could recognize Charlie by sight.

Charlie was being interviewed on RT to announce the Winklevoss twins' investment in BitInstant, news that had been kept controlled until it had finally leaked out leading up to the conference. And as Cameron listened, Charlie launched into the news in truly bizarre fashion, telling the reporter that he himself had been the one who met the twins in Ibiza—"I gave them my lounge chair!"—and how Azar had coaxed them: "You gotta meet this Charlie guy, boy genius blah blah blah, and it was love at first sight."

Cameron had to laugh. It was a sheer combination of "what the fuck" and "you have to hand it to him." It wasn't just the fact that Charlie was not letting the facts get in the way of a good story; it was that Charlie actually believed what he was saying.

Charlie told the reporter how he was in his basement when the twins came over and encouraged him to build BitInstant, saying: "Charlie, you've got to make this thing"—and now here he was, at the top of his game, and BitInstant was about to move into a brand-new, swanky SoHo office.

SoHo office? Cameron shook his head. The BitInstant offices were still in the Flatiron District, and they were anything but swanky.

Was Charlie losing his mind?

Eventually Charlie shifted from his creation myth to the present-day business: "We have money-transmitting licenses in over thirty states. And federal licenses."

But then, as the reporter pressed, Charlie suddenly seemed to lose himself again. And right in front of Cameron's eyes, in one sentence, his young CEO displayed the conflicting allegiances inside of him.

"We want this Bitcoin thing to overturn everything—but at the same time we have to be compliant."

That simple sentence seemed to encapsulate everything Cameron and his brother were concerned about. The pull of Ver on Charlie in one direction, versus the way Cameron and Tyler wanted him to take the company. Cameron wished that Tyler had joined him in the stroll over to BitInstant, but at the moment, his brother was meeting with fellow VCs at one of the booths across the hall.

Charlie always tried to say the right things: "You have to know every single customer no matter what . . . if they are spending a dollar or a thousand dollars," but then went off script again. Cameron could clearly see where Charlie was really struggling with what he believed:

"With money laundering, they treat you like a criminal right away, and that's not fair. . . . You should be able to say to a customer if you trust us, we'll trust you . . . we are trying to overturn it from treating you like a criminal to I'll scratch your back you scratch mine. . . ."

What the hell did that even mean? But then Charlie seemed to find his footing, going back to something he'd said during his own speaking session, a freewheeling, fun, off-the-cuff talk that had the audience applauding and laughing. "Bitcoin is cash with wings . . . take something local and do it globally."

"And that's going to overturn the financial infrastructure," Charlie added.

Another minute of talking and the interview was over. The reporter thanked Charlie and began packing up her gear, giving Cameron the opportunity to pull Charlie aside.

"That was . . . interesting," Cameron started. Charlie hopped out of his chair and suddenly gave Cameron an awkward baby bear cub hug.

"This is so amazing, your speech was awesome, isn't this place nuts?"

The words were dribbling out of him like water from a broken faucet. In that moment, Cameron didn't have the heart to say what he was thinking. It wasn't just that Charlie was young or that he had too much energy or too many distractions, or as Tyler now firmly believed, he just wasn't made to be a CEO. Charlie was clearly struggling, internally, trying to figure out who he was in this new world. He was being pulled almost visibly in multiple directions. Cameron, being more empathetic than his brother, felt for the kid; he'd played devil's advocate to his brother multiple times, arguing on Charlie's behalf. But in the end, he knew Tyler was right.

To Cameron, it was clear: if Charlie Shrem, *"boy genius, blah, blah, blah"* didn't figure himself out soon, he was headed for a fall.

Let yourself get pulled in two directions long enough, and sooner or later, you'll be ripped in half.

By 1:00 A.M., Cameron was having too much fun to spend any more time worrying about Charlie. And to be fair, as the day progressed—as the conference shifted from the trade floor and the speaking sessions to the outdoor casino someone had set up on one of the convention center's many patios, to the cocktail parties at the nearby Hilton and Marriott, to the local restaurants, where the Bitcoin revelers mingled with a raucous crowd in San Jose Sharks hockey jerseys, out celebrating the fact that their team had just won a big playoff game—it was easy to forget about all of their philosophical differences. For that moment, however brief it may have been, they were all united and celebrating the thing they all loved.

"This is how you know a partnership is going to work," Charlie said as he wobbled between Cameron and his brother, the three of them making their way down a cement-walled, fluorescent-lit hallway that led through the interior of the convention center. "I never hire anyone I haven't drunk or smoked with, and I think that should apply to the people who invest with me as well."

Cameron laughed, though it did occur to him that Roger Ver didn't smoke or drink. He let the thought slide. After the RT interview, he'd spent much of the day watching Charlie in action. The kid was obviously in his element. BitInstant was a big deal; many people in the Bitcoin community who he'd spoken to during the day estimated that 70 percent of the trades on Mt. Gox now came through BitInstant. Although CNBC had put the number at closer to 30 percent, Cameron believed that most people at the conference had bought their first bitcoin through Charlie. He had, after all, made buying bitcoin easy; you could walk into most convenience stores, hand the cashier cash, and receive your bitcoin in thirty minutes.

The T-shirts with his face on them were just the tip of the iceberg. Although Cameron and Tyler found themselves mobbed after their keynote, and while there were plenty of people who wanted to take a selfie with them or shake their hands, Charlie couldn't go five feet in the convention center without drawing a crowd. And as Cameron had seen firsthand, the kid couldn't get enough of the attention. At one point, when two developers approached Charlie to introduce themselves, Charlie reached behind himself into his back pockets, then flung both of his hands forward, dangling two of his business cards from the fingertips of his outstretched arms, as if he were performing a magic trick. It was a move he'd clearly been practicing.

All afternoon, he'd ping-ponged from one group of admirers to the next. But what really got Charlie going was every camera or microphone in his vicinity. He simply couldn't turn down an interview, no matter who was asking the questions. At first, Cameron had tried to steer him toward the more professional outlets—the CNBCs, the CNNs—but soon he'd realized there was no point. Charlie would talk to anyone. This was a kid who had been ignored in high school. Now, suddenly, everyone was paying attention to him. Everyone wanted a piece of Charlie and the Bitcoin factory.

And by the end of the cocktail parties, as they'd segued into a boisterous dinner of steak, fish, and fireballs, so many goddamn fireballs that the tunnel-like hallway they were now walking through smelled like it ran beneath a lake filled with whiskey, Cameron felt it was right to let the kid have his moment. He'd built something cool, and he deserved the accolades. It was up to them to try and keep steering him in the right direction; but that was something that could wait until tomorrow.

"You sure this leads to the right place?" Charlie said as his hand fumbled in the pocket of his dark jeans. "If this tunnel leads back to my mother's basement I'm going to kill myself."

Cameron laughed. He was sure that Tyler knew where they were going. His brother had studied a map of the convention center the day before. Tyler was always prepared. Cutting through the convention center via the loading dock had been his idea. If they'd gone around the front, the walk from the nearby restaurant would have taken an extra ten minutes, and neither of them thought Charlie would be able to stay on his feet that long.

Courtney, Charlie's girlfriend, had been at the restaurant as well and was going to meet them at their destination a little later. Cameron didn't really know much about her other than that Charlie was clearly smitten with her, and that she was about a foot taller than he was. He hadn't decided yet if she was good or bad for Charlie. At the end of the day, maybe her being around would keep him in New York more often, but it probably wouldn't keep him out of the club.

Voorhees had been at the restaurant they were coming from too, and for a brief moment, Roger Ver. Cameron had spent a lot of time at the convention talking to Voorhees. Awkward at first, but they quickly got past the tension and were able to speak like former colleagues. Although Voorhees held many of the same beliefs as Ver, he was a pleasant guy to be around, and his disagreements, no matter how firm, always had a smooth tone to them. He was arguably Charlie's best friend, but he didn't seem to cultivate the same Svengali relationship with the CEO as Ver did.

At dinner, they'd all played SatoshiDice as a drinking game—using their phones to wager bitcoin, taking shots if the money they wagered returned twice the bitcoin. No doubt, Voorhees was going to make pretty good money when he unloaded his new company, which he'd probably end up doing soon, because online gaming lived in such a murky legal limbo. No matter how much he might disagree with the way the world was run, at heart Voorhees was a realist, not a martyr.

Maybe that was the big difference between Voorhees and Ver.

Cameron hadn't talked to Ver at the conference. Though the guy was never anything but polite to the twins (to their face, at least), Cameron got the sense that he was avoiding them. At one point, Cameron mentioned to Voorhees that he'd read Ver's recent interview on Coindesk, remarking that it was some pretty radical stuff. Voorhees had only smiled and nodded, as if to say *that's just Roger being Roger.* If Tyler had been in the conversation, he might have started arguing with him. But Cameron knew it wouldn't do any good. Voorhees would have defended Ver, and Ver was a fundamentalist. Hell, he believed taxation was rape, that the military was a bunch of murderers. Nobody was going to change his mind.

"Here we go," Tyler said, pointing to a pair of double doors at the end of the hall.

They could hear electronic music reverberating down the hallway, interspersed with voices and the unmistakable sound of dozens of keyboards clacking. Cameron could already picture the scene behind the doors: a large conference room with groups of people split into twos and threes, hovering around computers lined up next to one another on long tables. Boxes of pizza stacked high in a corner, maybe cases or kegs of beer along a wall, the music coming from an iPhone connected to a boom box. And "mentors" strolling from group to group, computer engineers, advisers, and founders, helping the teams along as they chased their ideas late into the night.

Cameron was proud of what he was picturing, because, in large part, he and his brother had made it happen. Winklevoss Capital was sponsoring this night of the Hackathon, paying for the room, the pizza, and the beer. The two-day event had begun that morning at 9:00 A.M. Teams of hackers—computer programmers, entrepreneurs, and technologically savvy creatives—who wanted to participate had gathered in this room for a short speech. Then a panel of five Bitcoin investors had discussed the sorts of ideas they were looking to back. After that, the teams had broken off and started "hacking." They had until Sunday to build anything that qualified as a Bitcoin application. They'd then be judged by the panel and have the chance to win prizes. They might even impress a judge, or someone else, enough with what they built to attract an investment.

Some of the hackers in the room would be elite programmers, others just tourists and civilians, but the idea that they were all working on Bitcoin businesses, a camaraderie of young, motivated people—it made Cameron think that anything in the space was possible. It was how he pictured Silicon Valley garages two decades ago; but this time, the Valley had missed the boat.

Charlie stopped in the hallway, still ten feet from the double doors. He opened his fingers, and Cameron saw an expertly rolled joint, as thick and long as something you'd see in a rap video.

"Really?" Tyler said as Charlie pulled a lighter out of his jacket pocket.

"It's medicinal." Charlie laughed, putting the joint in his mouth. "Okay, maybe not medicinal, but my doctor says it's healthier than the whiskey."

He leaned back against the wall and put the lighter to the tip. The paper at the end of the joint glowed orange, then a little blue.

"You guys gave a great speech," he said. "You're bringing a lot of credibility to the industry. The Harvard thing. What did they call you in the movie? Men of Harvard?"

"What did your doctor say about smoking that on top of six whiskeys?" Cameron asked.

"No, seriously. You're making us all look good. And look, I know I can be a little crazy, I mean, I can get a bit overexcited. But you're right, we've got to be serious. I know that. And I might make mistakes, but I'm going to do whatever it takes to make sure we win."

"Just remember to keep your head on straight. And don't do anything stupid."

Cameron looked at Charlie, holding up the wall.

"Of course not." Charlie's eyes glazed over.

"Stay tethered. One day, we're going to wake up, and it won't just be a thousand people in a convention center talking about Bitcoin, it will be everyone," Cameron said.

As Tyler and Cameron started to walk toward the keyboards typing away, Charlie pushed himself off the wall to follow them. His eyelids were halfway over his eyes, but his eyes were flashing, alive, on fire. Cameron could guess what Charlie was thinking.

Imagine it—the whole world talking about Bitcoin. And Charlie right in the middle of it, all five-foot-five of him, ready for his close-up.

"Your lips to the sky people's ears," Charlie said.

23

GOING MAINSTREAM

"I t isn't A1, but it's above the fold," Tyler shouted through the open door of his glass walled office at Winklevoss Capital, his voice carrying across to Cameron's own identical glass-walled office across the hall. "Business section, front page. Everyone on Wall Street is going to be reading this in about twenty minutes."

Six weeks after the high of Bitcoin 2013, they were back in New York. It was well before seven in the morning and the streets of the Flatiron District hadn't awakened around them yet. The sound of garbage trucks and street-cleaning vehicles seeped in through the windows onto the newly painted five thousand square feet of office space. Tyler's copy of the *New York Times* print edition was spread out on his desk. He knew his brother had his own copy open to the same page, the highly vaunted Business Section. They waited until they were both ready to read the article so that they'd be getting the information at exactly the same time. They knew their dad and mom were at their home in the Hamptons doing the same.

This time, at least, Popper's headline avoided using the word "Facebook":

WINKLEVOSS TWINS PLAN
FIRST FUND FOR BITCOIN

Tyler knew this was an even more significant announcement than the one that had alerted the world to their massive bitcoin stash. As the article explained, Tyler and his brother had just filed a registration statement for the "Winklevoss Bitcoin Trust" with the U.S. Securities and Exchange Commission (SEC) to create a Bitcoin ETF, an exchange-traded fund, that would allow anyone to purchase bitcoin as easily as they could buy a stock.

"They use the word 'audacious,'" Tyler said.

"I love it when they use SAT vocabulary words. Reminds me of mom and her flash cards: 'The Winklevoss twins are Audacious. What makes them Audacious?'"

If the ETF was approved by regulators, it would make it as simple for anyone to buy bitcoin as it was for them to buy a share of Apple or even Facebook. It would bypass the shadowy process that existed at the moment, like having to go to shady exchanges like Mt. Gox, or, let's face it, BitInstant, which was not any more reliable under Charlie's stewardship than it had been before San Jose.

At the moment, buying shares in an ETF was typically the way investors got exposure to commodities and precious metals like gold. The first gold ETF had in fact launched back in 2004, under the ticker symbol GLD. It was an enormous success. By making it easy for people to invest in the metal, it had ushered in unprecedented amounts of liquidity and investor interest, totally transforming the gold market. You no longer needed to go through the trouble of buying a bar of gold, storing it in your safe at home, and worrying if the plumber was going to rob you when you weren't there. With GLD, all you had to do was call your stockbroker or, better yet, go online to E-Trade, Charles Schwab, or Fidelity, and type these three letters in before pressing the buy button. That's how simple the Winklevoss twins wanted to make buying bitcoin. Except for the twin's ETF, the ticker symbol would be four letters instead of three: COIN.

Tyler knew that if COIN ever got through the regulatory hurdles and was approved, it would be a game changer. They would have succeeded in bringing bitcoin to the masses. As the *New York Times* also pointed out, it was a direct effort to "remove the stigma hovering over Bitcoin" and put it right into the laps of regulators.

The ETF filing wasn't just going to send a signal to the legacy banking community that Bitcoin was on its way into the mainstream; the filing would also etch a permanent line down the middle of the Bitcoin world, between people like the twins, who knew that Bitcoin's future had to include regulation, and those who believed Bitcoin was meant to exist apart from Wall Street, the SEC, or any other regulator or government. The Winklevoss Bitcoin Trust was a preemptive strike, meant to end the war before it began.

People were going to notice, both inside and outside of the Bitcoin world. And they were going to react.

"Holy shit," Cameron yelled from his office. "Forget the paper, look online. This is insane."

Less than an hour after it had been announced, COIN was going viral.

"We're trending number two on Yahoo. Guess what's number three?"

Tyler hit his keyboard, then laughed out loud.

Number three on the Yahoo list, right after their ETF, was a new movie, due to hit the theaters that Independence Day weekend: *The Lone Ranger,* starring Johnny Depp and Armie Hammer, the latter having played the Winklevoss twins in *The Social Network,* the movie about their battle with Zuckerberg.

"Says here they spent seventy-five million dollars in marketing and advertising," Cameron said.

"It shows. Every cab, bus, and train in Manhattan is covered with the movie poster. Even the fountain soda cups in Subway have Tonto and one of the Winklevii on them," Tyler said.

"That's insane, we spent zero dollars, and our ETF is beating them by a country mile in Trending."

How was a financial product—a financial acronym like ETF—something many Americans had never even heard of—melting the internet?

Tyler had no idea how the SEC was going to react to the COIN proposal. Most likely, they would move cautiously, at a snail's pace, which is to say, the speed of government. Making a virtual currency available to everyone, like a stock, would make Bitcoin as accessible as gold, which was a multi-trillion-dollar market. It would also mean that every bank and wire house on Wall Street would have to adapt, start a bitcoin trading desk, hire virtual currency analysts and compliance officers, and maybe even start their own virtual currency funds. Change like that was going to take time, it wasn't going to happen overnight.

But the twins had taken the first step. And for them, the timing couldn't have been better.

The glow of Bitcoin 2013 had faded. Charlie's promise to buckle down, put his blinders on, and be the corporate leader BitInstant needed, hadn't stuck. He had snapped back into his old ways, traveling all over the place to promote what could only be described as his personal brand, while BitInstant was plagued by myriad issues, including delays of service and the threat of losing its relationship with Obopay. After speaking to their lawyers, Tyler wasn't even sure that BitInstant was still compliant with U.S. money transmission laws, and it was growing more and more clear that if Charlie didn't get ahold of things, the company wasn't going to last much longer.

Worse yet, the company wasn't profitable. In fact, it had eaten through most of the twins' investment, including a last-minute $500,000 bridge loan they'd given Charlie a few months ago. Giving Charlie $500k, on top of everything else they'd already invested, now seemed to be the definition of "good money chasing after bad." But Charlie had begged for the money, telling them at the time that it was needed immediately in order to secure the company's account at Mt. Gox after BitInstant's bank had let them down. The twins had reluctantly wired him the money. It had seemed like the best of two terrible options—the other being the immediate death of BitInstant.

The $500k loan was meant to be temporary, for a few weeks at most. However, after a few weeks, when they'd asked Charlie to wire back the money, he had been evasive, telling them that the company didn't have it at the moment but would have it soon. It had gotten to the point where it was pretty obvious that Charlie was again outright dodging their calls, texts, and emails.

Cameron had hoped that Charlie was going to be able to grow past the resignations of Erik and Ira, but it now appeared like the reverse had happened. Even when Charlie was in New York, he wasn't at BitInstant; he was the CEO of his corner table at EVR, entertaining his legions of Bitcoin fanboys.

Whatever confidence they'd had in Charlie was dwindling by the day. Filing the ETF felt like a rebirth. If Charlie couldn't change, they would have to move beyond BitInstant for good; and even if he somehow could change, well, there was a good chance it was already too late.

■　■　■

From: "Charlie 'Charles' Shrem" <<#><#>@<#><#><#>.com >
Subject: Our Call
Date: July 9, 2013 at 4:43:11 PM EDT
To: Cameron Winklevoss, Tyler Winklevoss

Guys,

I just wanted everyone to know that I heard what you were saying on the call and I take it very seriously. Things ARE changing dramatically to fix problems on all fronts and put us in a position for growth as quickly as possible.

I've made a lot of mistakes, the ones that you guys called me out on as well as others that I'm seeing now and taking steps to fix.

Here are the immediate steps:

- I will be in the office every day from 9-6 Monday through Friday unless it's essential BitInstant business (like bank visits)

- I won't leave NY for the next month—I'll be focused and at the office

- I won't talk to any press or reporters in person, over the phone or via email

- My time will be focused on fixing immediate problems (sourcing technology leadership and other star team members to fill the gaps and get things done)

- I will provide regular updates about the status of things (good and bad)

We're generating an internal audit report to figure out exactly what we need to fix and how. You'll have that at the end of the week—it will be exhaustive with problems, solutions and a roadmap.

Thanks,
Charlie

Charlie hunched forward over his computer keyboard in BitInstant's new offices, blocks from its original headquarters. It wasn't SoHo, but it wasn't

Brooklyn either; the place had enough room for thirty employees, natural light streaming through multiple windows, and the electricity worked—for the moment. Two weeks into their new digs, even Charlie, the ultimate optimist, was wondering how long they'd be able to continue to afford to keep the lights on.

"You think it will be enough?" Courtney asked, from over his shoulder.

Her shift at EVR wouldn't begin for another hour, and it wasn't uncommon for her to stop by Charlie's office before work. Over the past three days, Charlie had basically been living at BitInstant. He'd only gone back to the apartment above EVR to shower and to get away for a minute from the electronic hell he was now facing on a day-to-day basis at work.

It had all come to a head over the Fourth of July weekend, during a frantic conference call with his team of lawyers. All of those things that had kept him busy since Bitcoin 2013—servers getting overloaded with traffic, website issues, bugs in the codebase—paled in comparison to what his lawyers were telling him now: Obopay was officially gone as a partner, and BitInstant could no longer continue operating until it addressed its licensing issues. Though the current money transmission laws had not been designed for the Bitcoin economy, and *might* not apply, which meant not having licenses *might* be okay, Charlie's lawyers had cautioned him otherwise. They believed it was too dangerous for BitInstant to continue doing business now that Obopay was no longer providing them with licensing.

Charlie felt certain this was not an insurmountable problem. Given time, he could find a new licensing partner. Or perhaps he and BitInstant could go out and get licenses in each state themselves.

But first, he also had a more personal issue.

"I think I'm being as honest as I can be. I'm here and ready to work."

No more partying, no more late nights, no more travel. *Focus.* That's what he was promising the twins, and that's what he was going to provide. If they only gave him the time, he could fix BitInstant.

Of course, he'd have to listen to the lawyers and shut the site down for now as he dealt with the licensing issues. It wasn't something he was going to mention in the email he was writing; he knew how poorly that would go over. Telling them that the site had to be shut down, even temporarily, was going to set them off. He didn't want that to happen.

Charlie wasn't naive enough to believe that this email was anything more than a stopgap. But right now, he desperately needed any time he could get. Even a Band-Aid would do. The twins had been breathing down his neck, so he had to respond with *something*.

They were probably already in a less-than-agreeable mood. When the twins had first filed their ETF just days earlier, Charlie had been thrilled by the amount of positive attention it had been getting. But that morning, as he'd looked through the new round of articles, he'd noticed that the tone of the follow-up pieces was decidedly different. The optimism and excitement had suddenly morphed into something else: a digital cacophony of ridicule, contempt, and abuse. The mostly positive reception, evidenced by the original *New York Times* article, had been overwhelmed by a fresh round of negativity coming from the Silicon Valley establishment.

Charlie had browsed through the articles, stopping on the ones that seemed most prominent. First, there was Michael Moritz, the famed head of Sequoia Capital, one of the biggest and most famous VC firms in Silicon Valley and an early backer of Google. Speaking sarcastically to CNET, Moritz had said, "You know when the Winklevosses get into the business, it's serious."

Felix Salmon, a financial journalist, writing for Reuters:

To be clear: this thing is a really, really silly idea, from a pair of brothers whose main ambition, these days, is to be the biggest helminths in the bitcoinverse. The Winklevii, muscling in to the financial-innovation game, are being much more selfish about the whole thing. They're going to fail; I just hope they don't cause too much harm to others in doing so.

Bill Borden, a senior vice president at UBS:

When I read the headlines my initial reaction was to chuckle . . . while I find developments in the Bitcoin story to be intriguing, I doubt that the Winklevoss ETF would be how I would play it should I ever decide to buy Bitcoin.

Reginald Browne, a managing director of Cantor Fitzgerald, widely known as the godfather of ETFs:

The Bitcoin ETF idea is so far-fetched that SEC approval, if it comes, could take years. I think it's a riot.

And for the encore, economist and *New York Times* columnist Paul Krugman had written an op-ed titled "Bitcoin Is Evil," after previously calling it the "Antisocial Network."

The pundits had all shown themselves to be either against the Winklevoss twins, Bitcoin, or both. In retrospect, the negativity wasn't surprising. Big ideas were scary, little ones were not. The ETF was a big idea, a challenge to the status quo. Even the Silicon Valley elites like Moritz had a failure of imagination when it came to anything outside of the framework they knew.

With the ETF, the twins were challenging the legacy banking world right where it lived. No matter how well the twins dressed it up, it was still all about Bitcoin, a barely four-year-old digital currency.

Charlie knew exactly what the legacy banking world really thought of Bitcoin. BitInstant was hanging by a thread—despite huge demand, loyal customers, fanatical fans—precisely because the legacy banking world wasn't ready to embrace the digital coin.

That's what Charlie needed the twins to understand. He, and they, were fighting the same fight. Sure, maybe he hadn't been the best soldier. Though he'd tried to put on a good face after the resignations of Voorhees and Ira, the loss of his brain trust had knocked the wind out of him. He knew that his friends had done fine since they'd left. Voorhees was eclipsing all of them; he'd recently sold his side project, SatoshiDice, for a whopping 126,315 bitcoin, which at the time of the sale, was valued at around eleven and a half million dollars.

But without Voorhees and Ira, BitInstant hadn't felt like home. Even Ver seemed to have moved his focus to other investments, and Charlie couldn't really blame him. It had been Charlie's idea to go with the twins in the first place, and if BitInstant didn't get through its current problems, it would be on Charlie's head alone.

Reading over his email one last time, Charlie knew that ultimately his pleas, no matter how heartfelt, would not be enough; he would need to produce. But he did truly believe that all he really needed was more time. Everyone knew that Bitcoin was volatile. One day, it could dip toward a soul-crushing abyss. The next day, it could soar just as high. Like entrepreneurship itself, the twists and turns of the price were not for the faint of heart. Catch it on the way down, you could lose your shirt. But if you could handle the abyss long enough, if you could hang on through the dark times, maybe you'd get the chance to catch it again, on the way back up.

Charlie gave Courtney his most confident smile, then hit send.

ACT THREE

All human wisdom is contained in these two words: "Wait" and "Hope"!

—ALEXANDRE DUMAS,
The Count of Monte Cristo

24

A PIRATE'S TALE

San Francisco.
    October 1, 2013.
    3:15 in the afternoon.

Diamond Street, quiet, tree-lined, winding through a mostly residential neighborhood, sloping toward a small business district. The Glen Park branch of the San Francisco Public Library, a granite cube with oversize windows. A warm, orange-lit interior. Hardwood floors, paneled ceilings. Up the stairs to the second floor, rear corner, tucked into the science fiction section of the library, a small, brightly lit desk by the window.

A twenty-nine-year-old kid with shaggy hair lowered himself into the seat behind the desk, placing his backpack by his feet. Good-looking in that California way—though he was originally from Texas—relaxed, though a little bleary eyed, the kid retrieved his Samsung 700Z laptop computer from the backpack, placed it on the desk, and opened the screen.

Seconds later, he initiated a Tor connection. An anonymous browser that was originally developed by the U.S. Navy to keep its ships' communications safe, Tor was now a mostly free service used by people all over the world who wanted to keep their internet activity private. Once the kid's connection was established, piggybacking over the library's free Wi-Fi, he opened an encrypted portal to a website that could be found only by those who knew where to look, in the area of the internet known as the dark web, deep beneath the outer layers of the "onion." Only browsers like Tor, an acronym for the "Onion Router," could carefully peel it away and find sites like this.

Entering his password, the kid's sneakers bounced against the hardwood floor beneath the desk. He was tired. He'd spent many late nights working on the website, which was no surprise, considering it was massively successful, with hundreds of thousands of visitors per year. In fact, the kid was, despite his humble appearance, an unlikely mogul; the volume of exchanges that had passed through his website was valued not in the millions, but over a *billion*. His personal net worth was already close to thirty million. But although the site ran well, in the digital, well-oiled-machine kind of way, nothing about managing a monster like that was easy. It required constant maintenance and oversight, and even though the kid didn't have an office of his own, his laptop was like a traveling C-suite. Instead of some corporate cube in a tower in the Financial District, or the atmosphere-controlled cabin of a private jet, he had a corner of the public library, or a coffee shop, or a tiny bedroom in his shared apartment just a few blocks away.

He'd left the apartment just twenty-eight minutes before, at 2:47 P.M., planning to spend the afternoon at Bello, perhaps his favorite of the coffee shops with free Wi-Fi that dotted Glen Park like an overwhelming case of chicken pox. But he'd found Bello too crowded with customers for his liking. So instead, as he sometimes did, he'd strolled another ten yards to the library, choosing the solitude of the science fiction section over the elbow-to-elbow mosh pit of the coffee shop.

Now he was ready to work. And almost as soon as he entered his password into the site, that work found him, in the guise of a chat notification from one of his many employees, who operated under the handle "Cirrus." The kid had never met Cirrus in person, but he'd emailed with the employee many times a month, sometimes even daily, and paid him $1,000 a week to manage many of the site's forums and answer user requests.

As soon as the kid got the chat window open, Cirrus was there, business in hand.

"Hi, are you there?"

The kid rubbed his eyes, glanced around himself at the empty second floor of the library, then typed:

"Hey."

"How are you doing?" Cirrus asked.

"I'm okay. You?"

As usual, the chitchat ended there, because how friendly could two people be who had never met face-to-face, and who, out of necessity, would never have a relationship beyond blinking cursors facing each other over a heavily encrypted, anonymous online connection.

"Good, can you check one of the flagged messages for me?" Cirrus wrote back.

It was the sort of uninspiring, admin work that came up almost daily, usually something that could be handled and put to bed in minutes. All he needed to do was use his password to log into the back end of his site, and most likely hit a few keys to fix the tiny, technical issue. Nothing particularly urgent, but when you ran a website that had moved over a billion dollars in product over the few years of its existence, bringing in millions in profit, it was never a good idea to let any problem, no matter how small, fester.

"Sure," the kid wrote back. "Let me log in."

As he navigated to the correct page, entered his unique password, and began searching for the flagged message, he was so engrossed with the task at hand that he didn't notice the two people coming up the stairs from the first floor of the library until they were practically right behind him, and their shadows flashed across his laptop's screen. The kid glanced back and saw a man and woman, well dressed, obviously affluent, the sort of modern-day yuppies you saw all over San Francisco, especially in neighborhoods like Glen Park. The man was tall and thin, and probably worked at one of the tens of thousands of internet startups that had sprung up all over the city, the farthest outward ring of the hurricane whose epicenter was down in Silicon Valley. The woman was obviously his lover, because as soon as they'd reached the second floor, they'd started bickering in the way that only two people who had seen each other naked could argue: viciously and too loud.

When they reached a spot behind the kid, the woman's voice hit an entirely new octave of fury, and now their lover's quarrel was impossible to ignore. Annoyed, the kid actually rose from his chair to see if he needed to get involved—and that was when it happened.

The man leaped forward and grabbed the kid's laptop with both hands, then slid it across the desk to the woman, who had lunged to the other side. The woman yanked the laptop off the desk—careful to keep it open—and then handed it to a third man, who had suddenly appeared from behind one of the nearby bookshelves.

As the kid watched, his face frozen in shock, the third man jammed a USB memory stick into the laptop. He then retrieved a BlackBerry from his coat pocket and began snapping photos of the open laptop screen. From three feet away, the kid could easily see the screen—the open chat window showing his conversation with Cirrus in one corner, the backdoor page of his website in the center, where he'd been navigating to the flagged message.

But before the kid could say or do anything, the lovers were on either side of him, and the man was yanking the kid's arms behind his back. Something ice cold and terrifyingly hard touched the skin of his wrists, and then there was an unforgiving metallic click—and suddenly he was handcuffed, arms tight behind his back, his shoulders burning at the pressure. Then the man was leading him through the library down the stairs while the woman was reading him his rights. Just like on the TV shows.

The realization that he was under arrest hit him, followed by a nail in the pit of his stomach as he also realized that his laptop computer—still open, its glow illuminating the face of the third man, who was most likely not some local cop, not even a resident of Glen Park or San Francisco or even California but a trained FBI agent, probably an expert in computer forensics—contained enough information, now completely unencrypted, to have him locked up.

For the rest of his life.

25

THE DAY AFTER

M oney laundering." Cameron was reading off his computer as Tyler hovered behind him. "Computer hacking, conspiracy to traffic narcotics, and procuring murder."

Tyler leaned over his shoulder to stare at the screen.

"Procuring *murder*?"

"Apparently he tried to hire two hit men who turned out to be undercover FBI agents. Assassins for hire . . ."

"That's so dark."

Cameron leaned back from the computer, then looked out over the bustling office that was now Winklevoss Capital. So many people, and almost all of them under the age of thirty, recent grads from Harvard, Yale, Columbia, NYU, Berkeley, Stanford, and so on. All of them eager to be there, gravitating toward the twins as they worked to turn Bitcoin into something respectable. And up until today, fighting that fight had meant Silk Road was hanging around their neck every day like a drug-addled albatross. And now suddenly, just like that, it was gone: cooked, just like Ross Ulbricht, the twenty-nine-year-old who had been IDed as the mogul behind the biggest illegal drug bazaar in history.

"Dread Pirate Roberts is going to jail."

Dread Pirate Roberts was the online name Ulbricht had given himself, after the Cary Elwes character in the movie *The Princess Bride*. In the movie, he's a mythic character who, it turned out, is actually multiple pirates, the name being handed down from generation to generation.

Ulbricht would later claim that he hadn't created Silk Road, that, like Westley the farm boy in the movie, he'd inherited the title from someone else. In fact, one of the potential names that the blogosphere theorized as the possible true creator of Silk Road was Mark Karpeles, the Mt. Gox CEO. But the FBI disagreed, and it seemed as if they had gathered enough evidence to convict Ulbricht. With all the charges against him, he was looking at facing the rest of his life behind bars. The FBI was claiming that by running a website over which a billion dollars of drugs was bought and sold, Ulbricht had become one of the biggest drug kingpins in history. Although Ulbricht could argue that by running a website, he was merely a software provider, which didn't make him responsible for what was sold on that site—Amazon, eBay, and plenty of other sites had seen illegal items sold on them many times over—it would be, in the end, a hard argument to win in front of a jury. For one thing, it was unlikely that any jury did not include at least one person who cared for or knew someone whose life was ravaged by an opioid addiction. Pills like oxycodone seamlessly changed hands in bulk over Silk Road every day. Dread Pirate Roberts knew exactly what his marketplace was selling and had continually argued in his own writings that he was proud of the niche Silk Road filled. In fact, he wasn't just the site's operator, if the feds were to be believed, but he had also tried to hire hit men over the site—he was one of its *customers*.

No matter what the results of the eventual trial might be, the site was finished, and the news was going to reverberate through the Bitcoin economy.

"It's already dropping," Tyler said as he reached past Cameron to the mouse next to his computer. "It's dropping fast."

The price of a single bitcoin had started the morning at around $145 a coin, but since the news of Ulbricht's arrest, the price had begun to spiral downward. Now it was approaching $110 per coin. That meant the economy had shed more than $700 million in value in just a matter of hours. The twins themselves had lost millions of dollars on paper; but Cameron kept his mind on the bigger picture.

The twins' own research had shown that Silk Road did not dominate the Bitcoin market, as some breathless observers in the press had proclaimed. Silk Road was in truth a small fraction of the Bitcoin economy, even though it was the fodder for many juicy headlines. The brothers' thesis was any drop in the price of bitcoin due to the Silk Road closure was sure to correct. And, of course, as far as the twins were concerned, the death of Silk Road was very good news for Bitcoin's future legitimacy.

"There's only one thing to do," Cameron said.

"Buy!"

Cameron opened his computer and started to type furiously. Even though it was risky, he always kept cash—dry powder—on Mt. Gox and some newer exchanges that had popped up in anticipation of buying opportunities such as this one.

His phone began to ring.

"It's Charlie again."

Over the past few weeks, Charlie Shrem had been calling them both nonstop, but he'd been particularly persistent with Cameron, who had always had more of a soft spot for him, sometimes leaving Cameron three messages in a day.

It was only days after he and Tyler had received the email from Charlie promising a new start (and failing to mention any clouds on the horizon) that BitInstant had suddenly shut down. The loss of BitInstant's licenses, which designated the company as a legal money transmitter, had been insurmountable, and Charlie had done the only thing he could, shuttering BitInstant's doors. But he had kept the twins in the dark until the last moment, and that's what they couldn't forgive. He had posted some nonsense online, that it was just a temporary suspension of business to revamp and refit, that BitInstant would soon return better than before. But Cameron knew that Charlie's message to customers was as untrue as his previous email had been. BitInstant wasn't coming back.

To actually revamp, he'd need new money transmission licenses, he'd need a new banking partner, and most of all, he'd need cash, lots of it, because he'd burned through everything the twins had given him, including the $500,000 bridge "loan" that had still never been paid back.

Cameron and Tyler had begun the process of mentally separating themselves from Charlie. If he treated his partners that way, withholding the shutdown of the site, what else wasn't he telling them and how else was he behaving? Failure was okay, it was part of the game they signed up for and the odds they chose to play. One in twenty startup investments succeeded, according to the numbers. But Charlie's behavior, in their minds, bordered on bad faith and a dereliction of duty—he had checked out, run the other way instead of diving headlong into fixing BitInstant. Traveling more, partying more, drinking and smoking day and night. Instead of warning the twins that bad news was coming, he had kept looking for a lifeline, asking them to chase bad money with good.

No doubt, that's why he had been calling now. But the spigot was dry: they were finally ready to write BitInstant off as a learning experience and walk away.

Cameron would likely have ignored this call too, but with the news of Silk Road still open on his computer, he decided to give Charlie a few minutes—if only to feed his own curiosity. After all, Charlie was close to Ver, and Cameron wanted to know what Ver thought about the death of Silk Road.

"He thinks it's a travesty," Charlie said. He sounded out of breath, like he was running in place. "He thinks Ulbricht is being railroaded."

Cameron should have suspected as much. Of course Ver was going to join the other ultraradical libertarians on the internet and try to turn Ulbricht into a martyr. In fact years later, in March of 2016, after Ulbricht's sentencing and imprisonment for *double life in prison plus forty years,* Ver would go even further in an open letter to the former "Dread Pirate Roberts":

> *I suspect you will go down in history in a similar spot to Harriet Tubman for helping slaves escape their slave masters. By creating the Silk Road you have helped millions of peaceful drug users escape their violent oppressors in the form of the police, DEA, FBI, and judges who lock peaceful people in prison like yourself. . . .*

"I don't know what's scarier, Ver's views, or the fact that you consider him a mentor," Cameron said.

As often, his brother took a harder line with Charlie. "And look where he's gotten you. BitInstant is closed because you never really gave a damn about licensing and you were too busy buying into Ver's bullshit."

"I believe in compliance," Charlie said over the phone. "Guys, we can fix this!"

"We aren't interested in your circus anymore," Tyler continued. "We're interested in minimizing the damage at this point. Starting with our five hundred thousand dollars."

There was a pause on the other end of the line. Cameron wasn't sure how Charlie thought this conversation was going to go, but it was obvious he'd put the money out of his mind long ago.

"It's . . . tied up, it's not possible."

"Tied up? What do you mean? That loan was earmarked for working capital, not operating expenses."

"Three out of every ten people who own bitcoin bought it through me," Charlie said, trying to divert the conversation. "BitInstant can come back. We just need a new license. We still have thousands of people who want to buy through us."

"Nobody is going to give you a license. This isn't a game anymore. It's fine to sit in Panama and gripe about the evil government, but in the U.S., if you don't play by the rules, you end up in handcuffs. That's the way this works. And that's the way it's supposed to work."

The conference room phone started lighting up. Cameron put Charlie on hold and answered it.

It was their chief of staff, Beth Kurteson. Beth was a midwestern transplant who had come to New York City from Illinois for college and then later Columbia Business School for her master's in business administration. She was the first person the twins had ever hired. She was smart, hardworking, and had extremely high integrity and emotional IQ. She had quickly become one of the twins' most trusted and relied-upon team members.

"I've got the *WSJ* on three. Bloomberg on four. The *Financial Times* on five."

Cameron felt his cheeks growing cold. Could they all be calling to ask about Silk Road? That didn't seem likely; the twins had no connection to the site.

"Put us into the *Journal*," Cameron finally said. "Might as well start at the top."

The reporter didn't waste much time with pleasantries. "Guys, do you have any comment about the subpoena?"

The question was completely out of left field. Cameron pressed the mute button, looking at Tyler.

"What the hell is he talking about?"

Tyler unmuted the line.

"What subpoena?" he asked into the phone. "Who's being subpoenaed?"

There was a brief pause on the other end of the line.

"You are."

Cameron's heart pounded in his chest as he stared at the conference room phone, lit up like the Christmas tree in Rockefeller Center. He had completely forgotten that Charlie was still on hold on his cell phone lying on the table.

Cameron and Tyler Winklevoss had just been subpoenaed by the superintendent of the New York State Department of Financial Services, New York State's bank and insurance regulator.

Their dance with Charlies Shrem might be over, but the battle for Bitcoin had just begun.

26

THE FALL

JFK International Airport.

A little after 7:00 P.M. on a cold and gray Sunday night in January.

A light dusting of snow coated the curves of an Icelandair Boeing 737, engines still warm from the landing twenty minutes earlier and the typically long taxiing to the gate.

A horde of passengers slowly moving up the Jetway toward Customs and Immigration.

"It's called a liminal state," Charlie said as he led Courtney at the back of the moving crowd. "It's when you've exited one of society's structures, but you haven't yet entered another. *Liminality*. I read about it in college."

Courtney squeezed his hand as she walked, a backpack slung over her right shoulder. Charlie trailed a carry-on with one wonky wheel, the sort of bag that had seen one too many overhead compartments.

"It sounds like the kind of thing you come up with when you're stoned," Courtney said. "Although, to be fair, when are you not stoned?"

Charlie laughed, returning the squeeze back to her hand as they followed the crowd. Charlie noticed that most of the group was doing more shambling than walking; it wasn't only because they had all just spent seven hours in an aluminum tube filled with recycled oxygen, it was also the time difference.

Checking his watch, he calculated that it was two in the morning in Amsterdam; not that he would have been in bed if he'd remained another night in that permissive city. He'd spent most of the two-day e-commerce conference hitting the "coffee shops" that dotted the city's historic Red Light District, taking advantage of the Netherlands' progressive marijuana laws. Even so, he'd knocked his speech out of the park; he could still hear the applause that had come from the audience of hundreds of European Bitcoin enthusiasts.

And Amsterdam had just been one stop on what he'd begun to think of as his Comeback Tour: a multiweek, globe-trotting excursion, filled with speaking gigs, meet-ups, and sit-downs. Everyone wanted to talk about Bitcoin. Contrary to conventional wisdom, the price had skyrocketed since Silk Road had gone down, actually reaching $1,000 a coin within one month of Ross Ulbricht's arrest. The tenfold rise was incredible to fathom: the Winklevoss twins alone were now sitting on $200 million in Bitcoin. And though BitInstant might have been down—temporarily closed, momentarily shuttered—Charlie certainly wasn't; he was still one of the main faces of Bitcoin. Even if the twins weren't taking his calls, even if they were really trying to move past him, even if his site was technically down, he would return, bigger and brasher than ever. He might have stumbled, but he was the real deal, a real OG, and still just as popular as ever, as evidenced by the reception from the Amsterdam fanboys.

"Truly," he said, pulling Courtney closer to him as they moved, "it's a thing. I think it was from Anthropology 101. Society is made up of structures. That's how we cope with all of the things we can't control—life, death, illness, love, the fucking weather. We make structures and we live in them. But when we cross out of those structures, we enter a weird, strange, odd state."

"A liminal state," Courtney repeated. Only a few people separated them from the double doors now; they were nearly out of the Jetway and into Customs and Immigration.

"Yeah. And when you're in a liminal state, everything just feels *off*. Like your feet aren't entirely on the ground."

His carry-on caught on a seam in the Jetway floor, and he had to give it a yank to keep the wheels going forward. Courtney laughed again, pulling him along.

"And you think the walk to Customs at JFK is a liminal state?"

"Isn't it? Look at all these people. Coming off a plane, which is about as unnatural and inhuman as any place can be. And we haven't entered the next structure yet, we're not in New York, but we're not in Europe. We're in this place that doesn't really exist on a map. We've gone liminal."

They stepped into the vast room they were well used to by now, full of various lines of travelers waiting to exit the liminal statelessness of the airport. They chose what appeared to be the shortest line—leading to a window managed by a bored-looking agent with a ring of curly blond hair and narrow eyes. Beyond the agent, Charlie could see a second set of double doors that led out into the airport proper, into the morass of JFK.

"Until we go through those doors." He pointed. "Then we're in New York. We're back in our lives, our structures, and we can feel normal again."

"So maybe we should enjoy the right now. Embrace the liminal."

He leaned over and kissed Courtney—and then the line was moving, faster than usual, because it was a Sunday, and maybe because it was late enough that the Customs agent didn't want to spend any more time dealing with tired passengers than they wanted to spend with him. Ten minutes, maybe fifteen, and Charlie and Courtney were at the front of the line, and the man waved them forward.

Their turn.

As Charlie reached the window where the man sat, those narrow eyes barely looked up; just a hand held out, a wave of fingers, the universal sign for "passport please." Charlie had gone through this routine so many times in the past months, it had truly become rote. He handed over his and Courtney's passports, then leaned back against his carry-on, waiting for the man to check his computer, issue the stamp, and get them on their way.

But to Charlie's surprise, the man did none of those things. Instead, he just sat there, looking at Charlie's passport.

"Is there some sort of problem?" Charlie asked.

The man didn't answer. Then Charlie felt Courtney's fingernails digging into his palm.

"Charlie."

He turned—and saw another man in uniform approaching from behind Courtney, and he realized it wasn't a Customs uniform, it was something else, something he didn't recognize. More like a suit, but with a badge attached to the lapel.

And handcuffs, hanging from his belt.

Charlie turned back toward the Customs window—and saw another uniform approaching from the other side. Before he could register what was going on, he was boxed in.

The man in front of him stepped past Courtney and looked him square in the eyes.

"Are you Charlie Shrem?"

Charlie looked from him to Courtney, real fear on her face. Then he turned back to the man.

"You've got my passport," he said uselessly to the man behind the desk.

"We need to ask you a few questions."

And suddenly they had him by the arm and were leading him out of the line. Courtney was still next to him, rushing to keep up, and the second man moved alongside her. Charlie could see that she was shaking, that there were tears forming in the corners of her eyes, and he wanted to tell her not to worry, that this was obviously some sort of mistake. But he was too terrified to think of any words. As they moved he could also see people watching from all sides, some he recognized from their flight from Amsterdam, some from different planes. All those eyes, watching as he was led through the Customs area, an atmosphere of silent attention that felt so strange, so—

Then suddenly they'd reached a door at the back of the Customs area, a door Charlie must have walked by many times before but had certainly never noticed. Charlie was alone—where had they taken Courtney?—in a room with a long metal table in the center. The door was shut behind him with a metallic click.

"Where are we?" Charlie finally gasped.

"A secondary screening room," the man still holding his arm said. "My name is Officer Gary Alford. I'm a special agent for the IRS."

And suddenly, in one swift motion that pair of handcuffs came off of the man's belt and flashed toward Charlie's wrists.

"Wait," Charlie said, panic tearing through him. "What's happening?"

"Mr. Shrem, you're under arrest."

The words hit Charlie like bullets and he actually swooned, his knees buckling, but the man was holding him up by his arm. His wrists burned where the cold metal of the handcuffs touched him.

"For what?"

Before the man could answer, the door clicked open and more officers poured into the room, in twos and threes. There must have been fifteen of them. Some of the badges he recognized, others looked foreign. He saw NYPD, FBI, DEA. JFK Security, customs agents, more IRS.

Jesus Christ.

"This is a combined arrest," Officer Alford said. "Multiple agencies have been involved for some time."

Involved. Charlie realized, this wasn't just happening now—this *had* been happening for a while, maybe weeks, months—years? His arrest was the culmination of an investigation involving what appeared to be dozens of people. They had been following him. God only knew for how long. *But what had he done?* What could this be about? Aside from smoking a little pot here and there, what crimes had he committed?

"We're going to move out now," the officer said, not a request, a statement, and Charlie was being moved again. Out the door and down more hallways, a parade of law enforcement trailing behind him. For a moment, he could hear Courtney crying somewhere down the hall. Then they took him through another door—and into a much smaller room, what was really a concrete cell. The door shut behind him—and for a brief moment he was all alone.

He stood there, staring at the concrete walls, trying to focus, trying to think. But his mind was moving too fast; everything had suddenly become blurry.

And then the officers and agents were back, all of them, and he was being carted down the hallways again. This time he wasn't brought to a room, he was led outside, to a waiting caravan of black SUVs.

"Where's Courtney?" he said as he was shoved into the back of one of the oversize vehicles.

"Don't worry, you'll see her when we get there."

And then the SUV was moving. Flashing sirens, buildings racing by on either side. Charlie didn't know how long he was in the car before it came to a sudden stop, and he was then being led out through an underground entrance.

"Welcome to the DEA booking center," someone said, in his direction.

And then, thank god, he saw Courtney again, jumping up from a wooden bench next to the main booking desk. But two officers quickly moved between them, keeping them apart.

"Call my lawyer," Charlie shouted, and Courtney nodded. Charlie was certain he needed a lawyer—and he was pretty sure he had a lawyer.

When Courtney was gone, they sat him down at the desk and started peppering him with questions. One agent after another, asking him what BitInstant did, where the money came from, even how Bitcoin worked. It was like he was back at the conference in Amsterdam—except no stage, no mic, and now all the questions were coming from men wearing badges and guns. Charlie had seen enough TV to know you didn't answer questions, no matter how innocent you thought you were. He just shook his head.

When it became obvious that he would say nothing, the agents began the booking process. Fingerprints, photographs. They took his wallet, his belt, his shoelaces. His ring, imprinted with part of his Bitcoin private key. And the next thing he knew, he was being pushed into a real jail cell. Not a screening room or a cement holding cell, but a real jail, like with bars on the walls. There was a bunk bed next to a metal toilet right out in the open. Then he heard someone laughing from the bottom bunk.

He wasn't alone. There was someone in the cell with him.

"You better wear your socks to sleep," the other inmate said. "It gets cold. Real cold. You don't want to get sick and die in here."

"Why are you in here?" Charlie responded, instantly regretting the question, because he had no idea if it was something you were allowed to ask in prison, if it was the sort of thing that got you killed.

"My celly pissed the toilet seat in my crib so I jumped him. I guess they figured I needed some 'me' time." When Charlie didn't say anything, he laughed. "Don't worry, little man, I'm cool. Just keep the seat clean when you go, and we'll have no problems."

Charlie stood there—the bars behind him, the bunk bed and the inmate and the toilet ahead—and closed his eyes.

"Charlie, do you know anyone by the name of Bobby Faiella?"

It was eight hours later, and Charlie was still in that jail cell. He was standing up close to the bars, and Courtney was on the other side, trying to keep it together—and mostly succeeding. She hadn't been home yet, hadn't showered or unpacked or changed her clothes, but she'd redone her makeup, combed her hair, and gotten some of the red out of her eyes. He knew she'd been crying most of the night—but then again, so had he, quiet as he could in the top bunk, until around 3:00 A.M., when they'd taken the other inmate out and left him in alone. Now it was the next morning, and he was no less confused than he had been when those handcuffs had first hit his wrists.

"Bobby Faiella? Never heard of him. Who is he?"

Courtney had reached Charlie's lawyer. His lawyer had immediately conferred with the various agencies bringing the charges against Charlie. He was on his way to the holding center to bring Charlie up to speed, and then take him in front of the judge who would decide his bail situation. In the meantime, Courtney was trying to fill Charlie in on what she knew.

Bobby Faiella. Charlie wracked his brain but couldn't think of anyone he knew with that name. All night, aside from fighting his emotions, he'd been trying to figure out what the IRS, DEA, and FBI had on him, what he could possibly be facing. And he'd come up with almost nothing. If he had to guess, he thought maybe it had something to do with licensing. But he'd closed BitInstant as soon as the lawyers had told him to. Was this the type of government conspiracy that Roger Ver had been talking about all along? Was Charlie getting *Rogered*?

"I really can't think of anyone named Bobby."

"Online he called himself something like—B-T-C-King."

Charlie's mouth opened—then closed.

"Shit," he said finally.

And in that moment, suddenly he knew. He fucking *knew.*

"It's Silk Road."

Silk Road had been taken down four months ago, but that didn't mean the government was finished with it. They would be going after all the leads, all the intelligence, that the bust had produced, for years to come. And now it appeared that Charlie was suddenly, somehow, one of those leads.

BTCKing. Charlie's mind raced backward, trying to figure out what, exactly, he'd done. What stupid things he'd maybe written in emails, or said to friends. Could you really be arrested for emails? Could you go to jail for jokes you made to friends? What had Charlie actually *done*? Helped someone to buy bitcoin? Could that be a crime?

"What are the charges?"

"One count of conspiracy to commit money laundering. One count of failure to file a suspicious activity report. And one count of operating an unlicensed money transmitter."

Charlie blinked, hard. Failure to file a suspicious activity report—okay, he could see that. He'd known about BTCKing moving close to a million dollars in bitcoin, buying and presumably reselling, and despite suspecting that those coins might be going to Silk Road, he had never filed a suspicious activity report with the Financial Crimes Enforcement Network, a bureau of the U.S. Treasury. Charlie was BitInstant's compliance officer, which meant he was responsible for creating and filing a SAR. If he'd only listened to the twins— hired a compliance officer, not tried to do everything—but it was obviously way too late for thoughts like that.

But money laundering? What did that even mean? How had he laundered anybody's money? The only money he could think of that he had laundered was a few dollars that he had from time to time forgotten to take out of his pants before they went through the wash. And he didn't think he had ever run an unlicensed money transmitter—had he?

"Charlie," Courtney said, quietly. "Your lawyer says you could be facing twenty-five years."

Charlie pressed his face against the bars. This couldn't be happening. The numbers hit him hard.

"Twenty-five years, Charlie," she repeated. "What are we going to do?"

We. Hearing her say that made him feel good, even standing behind those bars. Because it meant it was both of them now. If Charlie went to prison— could he really go to prison?—for selling bitcoin?—Courtney was still going to be there for him.

"I don't know," he finally said. They were maybe the most honest words he'd ever spoken.

Two hours later, Charlie finally got his moment in front of a judge. Sitting next to his lawyer on a wooden bench, his wrists still sore and aching from the handcuffs that had just been removed, and staring at his shoes, which were still missing the laces, he listened as the prosecutor made his case.

The government argued that he shouldn't be let out on bail—because they believed he was a flight risk with means. In fact, they even played a video for the judge from an online interview in which Charlie told some podcaster with a microphone and a camera that he had a house in Singapore. The prosecutor further added that Charlie had a private jet and millions of dollars in bitcoin, a fortune hidden all over the world. Like Bloomberg had reported, he was a Bitcoin multimillionaire, a Bitcoin King.

It was a joke, of course. He didn't have a house in Singapore. He didn't have a private jet. He had some money—but all of it was now going to go to his lawyer. He was a face of Bitcoin, an OG—but unlike the Winklevoss twins, or Roger Ver, or Erik Voorhees, he hadn't been loading up on bitcoin personally. He'd been so busy traveling the world and telling everyone about Bitcoin, he hadn't stopped to accumulate hardly any, he'd never really had the means to begin. In fact, after legal fees, his net worth wasn't going to be in the seven figures, it wasn't going to be in the six figures—he'd be lucky if it was in the five.

Hell, very soon he'd probably be left with close to nothing.

In the end, the prosecutor did not get everything he wanted. Charlie's lawyer argued for house arrest and an ankle bracelet—and the judge ended up granting it.

But before the judge would allow him out of the courtroom—out of jail—with that ankle bracelet, Charlie had to have a place to go, under the care of a responsible guardian. His apartment over EVR—a nightclub—was off-limits, and he couldn't be on his own, or alone with Courtney without a viable means of support. Which meant there was only one place he could go.

And Charlie sagged onto the bench.

When his lawyer came back into the courtroom, Charlie was still on that bench. His lawyer didn't wait to give him the news.

"So I spoke to your parents."

Although Charlie hadn't spoken to either his mom or dad since he'd left home to be with Courtney, they'd followed the news—they didn't need Charlie's lawyer to inform them of what had happened. Charlie's arrest was front-page material. It was everywhere, front and center. The *New York Times*. The *New York Post*. CNBC. Even the BBC.

The papers were calling it the first Bitcoin arrest. Although Silk Road had functioned on a Bitcoin economy, Dread Pirate Roberts wasn't arrested because his site dealt in Bitcoin; the Bitcoin was beside the point. He'd have faced the same charges if it had accepted any currency. Charlie Shrem, boy genius, one of the faces of the new digital economy, was now the first person to be arrested expressly for dealing in Bitcoin. The press was having a field day.

"But there's a problem," Charlie's lawyer said.

Of course there was a problem, Charlie thought to himself. *I've been arrested!*

"Here's the situation. The judge is offering you bail at one million dollars. To meet that, your parents will have to put up their house as collateral. After which, you would be released—to live with them, under house arrest."

An unpleasant situation all around, considering their fractured relationship and the fact that his parents had made it clear that he would need to apologize and live under their rules while in their house—but what could he do.

"You don't have a choice."

And Charlie realized—his lawyer was right. He couldn't stay in jail; it would take months, maybe a year before he went to trial. He needed to get out of there, to try and figure out how to beat this thing, to change the narrative. *The first person arrested for Bitcoin.* What his parents were asking was horribly unfair.

But he had no choice.

He would tell Courtney the truth, and lie to his parents. Courtney could go back to Pennsylvania, to her own mother's house, wait it out until the trial.

Charlie could fake the religion: he'd done it before for years before he even realized he was faking.

"It's the right thing to do," the lawyer was saying. "We'll get you out of here, and then we can work on building your defense. We'll beat this."

But Charlie was barely listening. Because as bad as temporarily losing Courtney was going to be, as bad as dealing with his parents and pretending to believe in the sky people again was going to feel—the worst part was: he was heading back to that basement.

And this time, he'd be wearing an ankle bracelet—courtesy of Uncle Sam—that would go off like a fire alarm if he so much as stuck a foot outside his front door.

27

ACROSS TOWN

Less than thirty blocks away, Tyler Winklevoss sank into the black leather of a Cadillac Escalade SUV backseat, trying to shed the nervous energy pirouetting through his body. Through the window, he could see the nondescript entrance to their office building; the SUV was sitting right by the curb, engine running. There was a good hour before he and Cameron's sworn testimony at the Virtual Currency Hearings was set to begin. The public hearing was being held by the New York Department of Financial Services, the regulator that had subpoenaed him, Cameron, and twenty-two other Bitcoin heavyweights. Given the midmorning traffic between the Flatiron and Tribeca, the trip would probably take thirty minutes. Enough time to calm himself and mentally prepare.

Out on the sidewalk, Cameron was stretching his legs before joining Tyler in the back of the car. Although they weren't in rowing singlets and they were nowhere near water, Tyler felt the same sensations—anticipation mixed with a little fear—that he'd usually felt before a big rowing event. Maybe not quite the level of the Olympics, but something close, perhaps Henley or the Head of the Charles.

When Cameron finally entered the SUV and sat in the bucket seat across from him, Tyler gave his brother the same look he'd given Cameron a thousand times before, oars above the water.

"You ready?"

"Pretty sure. It's hard to be certain when you don't know if you're heading toward a gunfight or a square dance."

"No doubt it's going to be a little bit of both."

After getting over their initial dismay at being subpoenaed by the government for the first time in their lives—and finding out about it from the press—Tyler and his brother had quickly discovered that the move had not been meant as an accusation of wrongdoing or criminal activities; in fact, the request for documentation and later for them to testify in front of the superintendent was a real opportunity; the twins had been chosen as representatives of the new virtual economy to help the Department of Financial Services understand Bitcoin and virtual currency, and help shape what sort of regulations were necessary, now that Bitcoin was becoming an unavoidable part of New York City's financial landscape.

In a way, the subpoena was actually an honor that had been bestowed on the twins. As *Forbes* magazine had headlined, EVERY IMPORTANT PERSON IN BITCOIN JUST GOT SUBPOENAED BY NEW YORK'S FINANCIAL REGULATOR. Among the people and companies subpoenaed were venture capitalists Marc Andreessen and Ben Horowitz, along with the founders of Coinbase, Bitpay, CoinLab, Coinsetter, Dwolla, Payward, ZipZap, Boost VC, and even Peter Theil's Founders Fund—pretty much a who's who of everyone who had made a major investment in or ran a major company in the Bitcoin space.

At the same time, there was reason to believe that the event would be confrontational. Ben Lawsky, the head of the NYSDFS, the man who had signed the subpoenas, had been quoted as calling Bitcoin "a virtual Wild West for narco-traffickers and other criminals." The point of the session was not just to gather information, but also to use that information to rein in the Bitcoin economy. In his statement, Lawsky continued: "We believe that—for a number of reasons—putting in place appropriate regulatory safeguards for virtual currencies will be beneficial to the long-term strength of the virtual currency industry."

On the one hand, it was exactly what the twins had been pushing for. That being said, regulation had to get it right. It had to be tough enough to snuff out the darker elements of Bitcoin, while at the same time not so draconian that it killed the innovation itself.

As Tyler and his brother prepared for what would undoubtedly be an intense day—hunkered down at the headquarters at Winklevoss Capital writing their testimony and gaming potential questions and answers—they'd tried, and hopefully succeeded, to come up with what they believed to be the sort of healthy regulation that would make sense.

The SUV fully loaded with Winklevii, the driver began to pull away from the curb when there was a loud knock on the window next to Tyler. He looked up and saw Beth standing next to the car. She appeared out of breath, like she'd just sprinted down the stairs from their offices instead of taking the elevator. Tyler rolled down the window.

"Charlie Shrem," Beth managed to get out as she was catching her breath. "He was arrested last night at JFK. He was just arraigned."

Tyler's stomach dropped. His first thought was he hoped it was for something minor—but then again, did they keep you overnight for smoking pot on an airplane?

Beth told him the charges: money laundering, failing to file suspicious activity reports, operating an unlicensed money transmitter.

Fuck. This wasn't just Charlie. This was BitInstant. This was—

"Silk Road," Tyler said. "This has to be related to Silk Road. What the fuck did that kid do!?"

The money laundering charge on first blush seemed insane, probably something tacked on, and the "unlicensed money transmitter" could be the sort of thing Charlie might have unwittingly stepped into by being a mostly absentee CEO—but the suspicious activity reports had to be related to someone using BitInstant to purchase bitcoin for illegal activity—and the most obvious possibility was buying drugs on Silk Road. Once Silk Road had been taken down, it was open season, more like a turkey shoot, on the people who had been using it for illicit purposes—and the feds had probably dedicated a whole unit to trying to track them down. If Charlie had been stupid enough to knowingly let someone use BitInstant for that purpose—he was going to go down.

"We need to put out a statement," Tyler said. "Right away."

Here they were, literally on their way to testify in front of Superintendent Lawsky and the New York regulators to urge them to regulate Bitcoin in a reasonable way, and the CEO of the Bitcoin company they had first invested in had just been arrested for exactly what the regulators feared most about this new virtual currency.

Working with their outside counsel, Tyler Meade—a former prosecutor who had served as a legal adviser for the twins during the Facebook saga—they quickly put together what they needed to say:

> *When we invested in BitInstant in the fall of 2012, its management made a commitment to us that they would abide by all applicable laws—including money laundering laws—and we expected nothing less. Although BitInstant is not named in today's indictment of Charlie Shrem, we are obviously deeply concerned about his arrest. We were passive investors in BitInstant and will do everything we can to help law enforcement officials. We fully support any and all governmental efforts to ensure that money laundering requirements are enforced, and look forward to clearer regulation being implemented on the purchase and sale of bitcoins.*

If the charges were accurate, then Charlie had duped them. Tyler and Cameron had done everything they could to try and make BitInstant a serious player in not just the Bitcoin world but also the financial world. They had put Charlie in front of prestigious investors, banks, and other potential partners, had made sure the company was licensed, and had tried to make Charlie into the CEO that BitInstant needed. And when that hadn't worked, they had demanded that he straighten up—and obviously, all of it had failed.

Tyler knew the arrest would hit the Bitcoin community hard. Charlie was one of its biggest names and one of its thought leaders, even a founding member of the Bitcoin Foundation, a nonprofit organization headed by many of the biggest names in the cyber economy, aimed at building up the reputation of Bitcoin and helping raise its profile in the world at large. He guessed that many Bitcoiners would support Charlie—some, for the wrong reasons.

"Roger Ver has already given a statement to *Forbes*," said Beth through the car window, echoing Tyler's thoughts as he looked at his phone:

> People own their own bodies, and have the absolute right to put any-thing they want into it. People like the FBI, and DEA agents who want to lock people in cages for buying, selling, or using drugs are the ones committing evil, and they need to stop. I look forward to the day when they see the error of their ways, and stop committing evil acts in the name of "law enforcement."

Tyler felt these same beliefs had seduced Charlie into handcuffs. These two opposing statements perfectly illustrated the divide in the Bitcoin community. The libertarians and anarchists saw Bitcoin as a weapon in their war against regulated society. The entrepreneurs and VCs increasingly gravitating toward cryptocurrency wanted Bitcoin to be part of that society, a new, programmable money for the modern world.

Beth headed back toward the office to get their statement out on the news-wire. The connection to Charlie and the crimes he'd been charged with were unpleasant, but Tyler and Cameron had done nothing wrong beyond invest-ing in the wrong company. Investing in the wrong person. They had made a mistake, but that didn't change where they were going, or what they had to do to get there.

"Let's roll," Tyler said.

It was not an overstatement to say that they were on their way to fight for the life of Bitcoin. Without the blessing of the regulators, Bitcoin would never rise above the dark cloud of these early days, and the entire virtual currency industry might be doomed.

"The timing of this couldn't be worse," Cameron muttered as the SUV pulled away from the curb.

"I don't know," Tyler said. "One could argue that the timing couldn't be better."

Maybe Cameron didn't see it yet, but in Tyler's mind—the anchor had just been thrown out of the boat.

28

MEN OF HARVARD

Ninety Church Street.

A massive federal office building, a charmless monstrosity of limestone, taking up the entire block between Church Street and West Broadway. A multiuse government facility that contained the New York State Health Department, the New York Public Service Commission, a Central Post Office, and the space where the Virtual Currency Hearings were to be held.

The Fourth Floor Boardroom, 11:30 A.M.

If there was ever a time for suits, this was it. Cameron sat at the long witness desk—essentially a plank of wood cluttered with notepads, laptops, and a tangled jungle of old school microphones. Tyler was to his left, and to his right were the three other witnesses who had joined them for the headlining session of the first day of testimony. Directly next to Cameron sat Fred Wilson, a seasoned venture capitalist veteran who had moved into the cyber currency space in a big way, with the countenance of someone who had seen a number of technology waves, including the first dot-com boom and bust. Next to Wilson, the up-and-comer venture capitalist Jeremy Liew, a partner at Lightspeed Venture. And at the end of the bench, Barry Silbert, the founder and CEO of the startup SecondMarket.

Behind Cameron was a peanut gallery made up mostly of press, along with a handful of Bitcoin tourists who'd managed to find room in the crowded hall, everyone seated on a sea of folding chairs stretching all the way to the back of the room. Cameron knew there were many more people watching: the public hearing was being simulcasted to over 130 countries.

But the audience, as big as it might have been, was not central in Cameron's thoughts. In front of him, across the vast, utterly serious boardroom, raised high above the witnesses and audience on a dais like some sort of medieval judgment panel, sat the shooting gallery of regulators. These would be the people asking the questions—and in this place, they had real power. Cameron and his brother would be answering under oath—anything they said could be used against them—if they were found to have perjured themselves here, they could be sent to prison. Hey, right next door to Charlie.

In the center of the dais, of course, was Superintendent Lawsky, embraced by a row of flags—the flag of the United States, of New York State, and god only knew what else. Lawsky was in his early forties. He possessed a visage that harkened back to a different era when civil service was dominated by Kennedys and intelligent, piercing dark eyes. Next to him sat an assortment of fellow departmental personnel, but it was obvious that Lawsky would be running the show. Almost as soon as the room came to order, muffling the clatter of keyboards, scraping chair legs, and running audio equipment, Lawsky introduced the session, made short work of the swearing in, and then dove into the matter at hand.

Lawsky quickly turned to the reason he had gathered the brightest stars in the new economy to his boardroom:

"The goal is to put forward a proposed regulatory framework for virtual currency firms operating in the state of New York. We'd be the first state in the nation. And clearly when it comes to virtual currencies, let's admit it, regulators are in new and somewhat uncharted waters."

So far so good. Cameron had hoped that these hearings would strike a collaborative tone, and he was encouraged that Lawsky understood what he didn't understand. But Lawsky quickly moved on to address the eight-hundred-pound gorilla in the room that Cameron had known was coming.

"The legal action that we saw yesterday underscores how critically important it is, that we put in place guardrails for this industry to help root out money laundering and other misconduct."

The boy genius, who could have been sitting here right in this room, sandwiched between the twins, extolling the virtues of Bitcoin, was instead sitting in his mother's basement under house arrest.

"I mean frankly," Lawsky continued, "if we want innovation to happen, and we also want to root out money laundering, and we try to get that balance right—we also want to give businesses certainty."

Perhaps Tyler was right—the timing of Charlie's fall had put a spotlight on the very need for the hearings themselves, the need for the government to start stepping in, not just to protect Bitcoin customers or the general public, but also to protect people like Charlie from themselves.

From the very first question Lawsky asked of the panel of witnesses, it was clear he felt the same way.

"The arrest we saw yesterday put a bit of a cloud hanging over the industry right now," he began, "and my question for each of you is—how do you react to yesterday: is it that any technology can have bad people who are going to allegedly use it in bad ways? Drug dealers use cell phones, it doesn't mean we condemn the cell phone. Terrorists use computers. Although, there are arguments that virtual currency is more susceptible—what we don't want is a world where Bitcoin is a haven for those committing illicit activities."

Lawsky had taken the words right out of Cameron's thoughts. Technology did not prescribe to an ideology, it was agnostic. Just because it was co-opted by bad actors, or people like Ver with a certain belief system, didn't mean it was itself a bad actor or had a clear ideological cast. Bitcoin was a technology; technologies were neither good nor bad.

Barry Silbert took the question first, giving a succinct answer:

"If those accused are convicted, it seems like the system is working. Bad guys are going to do bad things and they will use whatever technology is available to them."

Liew, next to him, agreed and elaborated, in a light Aussie accent:

"I'd echo—it's the existing framework of regulation and law enforcement working well."

But then he made a point that put Charlie's arrest in perspective—and placed it on a timeline of the Bitcoin industry that coincided with Cameron and his brother's experiences.

"I also point out," Liew said, "that we've seen over time a change in the character of the people involved in Bitcoin. When it first started out, it was an academic novelty—over time it attracted different people for different reasons. Decentralized, open-sourced—that attracted a first set of people. . . . A lot of those people were libertarians and radical. . . . The second character that attracted a second wave was anonymity—people who thought they could conceal their behavior behind Bitcoin. In the last year and a half a set of people were attracted to two other aspects—first, it's freeish, dramatically reducing transaction costs. And it's programmable. This changed the nature of the Bitcoin population."

And, Liew added, this was a very good thing for those, like him, who wanted to invest in the new economy.

"The market of radical libertarians is not very big. The market of criminals is not very big. But offering free transaction costs—you have a market of everyone in the world."

It was a VC's answer to the question. The big money wasn't interested in backing something dirty or illegal—not for moral reasons, but because those things weren't good for business. It was what the twins had been saying all along.

Wilson, in his answer to Lawsky's question, broke it down even more, describing what he called the Five Phases of Bitcoin.

"First, development of the open source community . . . a geeky, nerdy, crypto-libertarian thing, 2009 to 2010. Second—a vice phase. Silk Road, drug trafficking. Gun running. 2010 to 2011. Third phase, speculation, trading— we are getting to the end of that now—2013, 2014. Next phase is the transactional phase—real merchants accepting bitcoin. And the final phase is the phase of programmable money—when money can move via a programmable infrastructure."

Programmable money. The phrase sounded space age, sci-fi, to Cameron, but he knew it was truly the next step in the nearly instant economy that Bitcoin allowed; basically, it referred to programmed transactions between banks or individuals that could be self-validating and perfectly efficient; smart contracts that could be set in place to occur automatically, without any middlemen or oversight. For instance, self-driving cars and autonomous agents of the future would exchange value back and forth, perhaps while changing lanes in real time, paying for faster rates of travel—but they wouldn't be doing it via wires, ACH, or credits cards, which were too slow and costly; they would have to use crypto. Machines couldn't open accounts at Wells Fargo, but they could plug into protocols exchanging bitcoin. At their heart, cryptocurrencies were built for machines—which made them the perfect currencies for the future.

"The vice phase is in the rearview mirror," he added. "The majority of Bitcoin is not vice."

It was finally the twins' turn to answer. Even though the question was asked to the entire panel, it might as well have been directed to them and only them; everyone in the room knew that they had been the ones to invest in Charlie, and everyone in the room, on the live stream across the world, was waiting to see what they said.

Tyler leaned over to be closer to the microphone in front of him. As the more serious, analytical of the twins, they had decided he would speak first. Cameron could feel the entire room glued to Tyler, the whole world watching as Tyler opened his mouth and began to speak.

"I think yesterday was a speed bump."

Those few words, Charlie's own words from after the disastrous meeting with the Fintech venture capitalist, captured the essence of what Charlie had become. If Charlie was listening to the hearings, wherever he was, probably with a government-issued bracelet around his ankle—he would no doubt be sobered by the cold reality of Tyler's answer. Cameron couldn't have agreed more. They believed that Charlie, by his actions, had betrayed their trust. The Winklevoss twins had been betrayed before—and it wasn't something they were built to take lightly.

"Like with the closure of Silk Road," Tyler continued. "And the subsequent price increase of ten times, it indicates that the demand for Bitcoin is far from just illegitimate activity."

Later in the hearing Cameron described the early days of Bitcoin in his own words.

"When we first saw Bitcoin about a year and a half ago, I don't think anyone would deny that it was a bit of a Wild Wild West, because there was no regulation, there was no framework to evaluate the assets, to evaluate companies, determine who was compliant, who was not. And a Wild West attracts cowboys."

Like Tyler, he had now relegated Charlie to the past—a relic of that Wild West, a tragic figure from Bitcoin's frontier history.

"I don't think anybody here would disagree with the fact that a sheriff would be a good thing," Cameron said.

People like Roger Ver may have given up on *the system* a long time ago, but the twins had not. To some people, they probably *were* the system, but that wasn't the full story. They had their own reasons to be disappointed in courts, judges, lawyers, Harvard presidents, Harvard classmates, mediators, men in suits, men like Superintendent Lawsky; they had been let down by them all. But they were resilient, you had to give them that.

They had been taught by their parents to never stop fighting. It didn't matter how many times life knocked you down, all that mattered was that you got back up. Anyone who had lost a sibling knew something about resilience. Despite their appearance, despite what people thought of their privileged background—time and again, they had been knocked down. Life hadn't always been easy; but they still believed in the general fairness of people. They had experienced other lessons in the wider world: they knew it wasn't *the event* that was the defining moment, it was how you handled the *aftermath*.

From an early age, Cameron could remember his father—who he knew was out there listening to them—reading him and Tyler a speech given by Teddy Roosevelt—himself a member of the Porcellian final club and a true Man of Harvard:

It is not the critic who counts; not the man who points out how the strong man stumbles, or where the doer of deeds could have done them better. The credit belongs to the man who is actually in the arena, whose face is marred by dust and sweat and blood; who strives valiantly; who errs, who comes short again and again, because there is no effort without error and shortcoming; but who does actually strive to do the deeds; who knows great enthusiasms, the great devotions; who spends himself in a worthy cause; who at the best knows in the end the triumph of high achievement, and who at the worst, if he fails, at least fails while daring greatly, so that his place shall never be with those cold and timid souls who neither know victory nor defeat.

Cameron looked around the room, at the regulators on their high dais, the Bitcoiners on the witness stand, and everyone else, watching from the gallery. And then he looked at his brother.

Who at the best knows in the end the triumph of high achievement. Who at the worst, if he fails, at least fails while daring greatly. . . .

"Bitcoin is freedom," Tyler was saying to the assembled. "It's very American."

At that moment, Cameron thought that maybe, just maybe, some of the regulators realized that the world that the twins were fighting for was the same world that they were fighting for too.

29

JUDGMENT DAY

It was a strange sensation, being surrounded by people and yet knowing you were completely alone.

Charlie guessed it was what it felt like to die of some gruesome disease, in a bed in a hospital with your family and friends next to you, helpless to do anything but watch as you took your final breaths.

He knew he was being macabre, but it was hard not to be dramatic in such a place: it was obviously built for drama. A dusty, aging, wood-adorned courtroom in the bowels of a New York judicial building. Charlie could only imagine how many degenerates—murderers, arsonists, rapists, bankers—had been sitting exactly where he was sitting, on an uncomfortable chair next to his lawyer in the defendant's galley. Over to his right, about five yards away, he could see the prosecuting team. Serrin Turner, the assistant U.S. Attorney who had been the front man on the case since before Charlie had agreed to settle, and Turner's various assistants. Fitting, since Turner had also led the prosecution against Silk Road that had sent Ross Ulbricht to prison for life. Next to them, Preet Bharara himself, the U.S. Attorney for the Southern District, the famous prosecutor who had taken down too many white-collar criminals and Wall Street bankers to count. And somewhere behind them, the IRS agent who had first arrested Charlie at JFK, Gary Alford, there to witness the results of all his hard work.

And directly ahead, on the bench, was Judge Rakoff, a kindly-looking man in glasses.

Charlie tried not to stare directly at the judge; Charlie was barely holding it together, and if he matched eyes with the man, he knew he was liable to burst out in tears. He also avoided turning around. Behind him, the overcrowded pews of the courtroom were crowded. Walking in with his lawyer, the ankle bracelet humming against his ankle, he had seen that every seat was filled.

On one side was his family—not just his immediate family, but seemingly the entire Orthodox Syrian-Jewish community of Brooklyn had also come out to see the show. Just two rows back, his mother, father, and sisters, and behind them, he'd seen his rabbi, his next-door neighbor, his childhood eye doctor, and his orthodontist. There to—support him? Condemn him? Bear witness?

On the other side of the room were Courtney and her parents. Even in the packed room, he could still hear her sobbing. And the rest of that side of the gallery was filled out with other secular supporters, mostly from the world of Bitcoin. People who had worked at BitInstant, colleagues from the various conferences he'd attended, fans. Maybe "secular" wasn't the right word—many of his Bitcoin supporters were as religious in their own way, as fundamentalist in their beliefs as the Orthodox black hats on the opposite side of the aisle.

Charlie knew the audience didn't matter. They may have been gathered by his bedside, but they couldn't affect what was about to happen. You were born alone, you died alone.

And you were sentenced alone.

Charlie's lawyer touched his arm, signaling that things were about to begin. The look in his lawyer's eyes was supposed to be encouraging; they had gone over the possibilities again and again in the days leading up to this moment, and they had both agreed that actual jail time was unlikely. After all, the court's case had come down to a handful of stupid emails. Even though Charlie had admitted he had been an idiot and allowed a reseller to buy bitcoin to use on Silk Road for illegal drugs, he wasn't a money launderer or a drug dealer himself. You could almost say he'd done the opposite of money laundering; he had foolishly dirtied money, rather than made it clean.

He'd committed a crime, but he didn't believe he deserved to rot in some jail cell. He had pled guilty because he knew that he was in the wrong, and because it was too risky and expensive to fight the charges in court, but he didn't deserve to be sent away to some hole.

After a brief introduction, his lawyer got the chance to speak first. As he and Charlie had discussed, he was asking for a probationary term—something they felt fit the crime.

"He's only a twenty-five-year-old person," went his lawyer's argument. "So I don't know that he gets to be a Greek tragic hero, but he hurt himself tremendously, tremendously. Because he had it made. He found a way. He has mixed feelings about his small, Brooklyn neighborhood, but he was out, and he was attached to this wonderful idea, and all he had to do was guard it with his life, and he didn't. . . . I don't think we need a jail sentence to send a message to Charlie Shrem that what he did is bad and wrong and illegal."

It sounded right to Charlie, and a quick glance toward the judge told him that he was at least listening, but then the prosecutor rose for his response.

"The defendant was essentially facilitating drug trafficking," Turner started, and Charlie's stomach churned. It sounded so vile and wrong—and yet, he knew, at least technically, it was absolutely correct.

"He was moving drug buy money. I know it doesn't look like the usual drug-trafficking case. . . . It's online, rather than on the street. These are digital drug deals, but he's moving drug money nonetheless."

Correct—but still, Charlie believed, unfair. Because what he was doing—helping people get bitcoin—was, at its heart, something good, something that he believed was making the world a better place. Offering a form of freedom.

Or was that just Roger Ver and some of Erik Voorhees in his mind again? He didn't know anymore what to think.

Finally, the judge gave Charlie a chance to speak for himself.

Trembling, he tried to put what he was thinking into words. He knew he was rambling; he was scared, but his family, his whole upbringing really, was behind him, watching.

"I screwed up really bad, Your Honor. My attorney and Mr. Turner were correct in saying that I was given a responsibility and I failed myself and my community, my family, and the Bitcoin community as a whole."

He could hear a rustle of noise behind him, but he plowed forward, his thoughts coming faster, maybe even a little too fast.

"You know, you see the movie *Spiderman* when you are younger and one of the only quotes that you kind of remember from that is with great power comes great responsibility, and I always would watch that and said what does that mean—when you have great power, where does that come from."

He was riffing now but he didn't stop himself. Here was his chance to speak, after a year of pure hell. Trapped in that basement by the ankle bracelet and the bail money—bail which his parents continually threatened to pull, especially when they caught him speaking to Courtney.

"When you're in a powerful position, when you're in a position of power, it's a lot harder to stay responsible to yourself and stay morally responsible. It's a lot easier when there's nothing riding on you. And I failed that. I was very young. I was twenty-two and I was the CEO and I was the compliance officer. . . . It was just me and my partner running this out of our basement."

His lawyer shifted in the seat next to him, and Charlie knew he had to get control, reel himself in, but he wasn't done. He had an audience and somewhere there had to be a microphone and god damn it, he was going to speak.

"I broke the law and I broke it badly, and I'm really sorry for doing that, and I'm sorry for failing you and failing this country, but I cherish so much and I want to change the world and I'm trying to . . . I was a kid and I want to be that person that is remembered for even doing one little thing to change the world. . . ."

He looked right at the judge. He was saying everything he needed to say.

"Bitcoin is what I love and all I have. It's my whole life. It's what I'm on this Earth to do, is to help the world see a financial system that does not discriminate and provide for corruption, and I think that Bitcoin will do to money what email did to the postal service. It allowed everyone to be equal. People in Africa, the Middle East, Asia, will have the same opportunities now with Bitcoin, and because of this now, because you can move money instantly and information on a peer-to-peer system. And I think that's really important. And if Your Honor grants me that, I'd love to be back out there healing the world and making sure people don't do stupid things like I did."

Charlie paused—it sunk in that the whole room was staring at him. The judge, his lawyer, the prosecution, his family, the Bitcoiners present. He swallowed, then slowly lowered himself to his seat.

"And again, I'm sorry." He coughed.

There was another pause, as the judge peered down at him.

And then, finally, it was time. After a brief statement, telling Charlie that indeed he was brilliant, maybe too smart for his own good, thinking too far ahead, not paying attention to what was in front of him; that he was young enough that he would go on and assuredly do great things—then, the judge made his decree.

"The court thinks that the appropriate sentence is two years. Accordingly, the defendant will be sentenced to two years in prison."

And suddenly, the courtroom seemed to recede down a long tunnel, and Charlie was shrinking into somewhere very small. He could hear his mother crying on one side and Courtney crying on the other, and then shouts of defiance from some Bitcoin supporters, and then his lawyer was whispering something to him, how he'd only serve 85 percent of the sentence, how for part of it they would send him to a halfway house, where he could get a job, something simple like washing dishes in a restaurant. How he would be okay, he would make it, when he got out he would still be a young man, in his twenties. How he didn't need to be scared.

And Charlie looked at him, and then he was back out of the tunnel, he was himself again, because he realized that for the first time since his arrest, he didn't feel scared. He felt—relieved.

For nearly a year he'd been locked in his basement, drinking and smoking and being dragged to temple every Saturday, strapping on tefillin every Thursday. Sneaking phone calls to Courtney when he could to keep his sanity. Hell, he'd even Skyped into a Bitcoin conference or two, railing and raving at his computer screen with a Bluetooth microphone hanging from his ear that the court-ordered bracelet was heavy on his ankle. When he'd watched the videos afterward, he'd been shocked at how insane he'd looked. But that period in his life was over now.

He was going to prison. After that, he'd wash some dishes or mow lawns or whatever it took.

He'd get back on his feet and then he'd get back into Bitcoin. Because what he'd just told the judge, they weren't just words, they weren't just him pleading for his life. They were from his soul. Maybe that's why he felt so good right now. Bitcoin was his life. He was going to prison—*for selling Bitcoin*. Well, at the end of the day, he could handle that. And then he would begin again.

Behind him, his parents had reached the wooden rail that separated the audience from where he was sitting. They were trying to reach him: crying, calling his name. But he didn't look their way. Instead, he turned to his lawyer.

"Can we please make everyone leave the room? Except Courtney."

His lawyer signaled to the marshalls and they agreed to the request. The uniformed officers had to actually physically lead Charlie's mother and father away. Soon, it was just Charlie in the defendant's pit, Courtney holding him.

"It's going to be okay," he said while she cried. "We're going to be okay."

And the best part was he knew it was true. And then he hugged her—and the tears filled his eyes.

30

LAUNCHED

I t was the last week of August, the middle of the afternoon, and Cameron was wading through a postapocalyptic moonscape. His sneakered feet raised clouds of fiery dust as he moved over the sun-hardened playa. He was wearing cargo shorts and little else; the air was so hot he could see it through his sunglasses—really, oversize goggles that would have been appropriate for either welding or skiing—the oxygen, nitrogen, and carbon molecules shimmering in swirls around his head. The temperature was somewhere between ninety and infinity, yet Cameron didn't care; he hadn't stopped smiling since the tiny, single-engine Cessna puddle jumper had dumped him and his brother on the makeshift landing strip at the far reaches of the impromptu desert city. The scene around him may have been postapocalyptic, but it was the friendliest apocalypse he could have imagined.

"It's spectacular, isn't it," Tyler said as he stepped off of a dirt-crusted bicycle and joined Cameron on the playa. He was wearing shorts too, and some sort of *Mad Max*–inspired vest, with his goggles up on his head.

Tyler could have been talking about any number of things. The desert itself, 300,000 acres of flat playa and lava beds in the northern part of Nevada, surrounded by mountains and hills. Or he could have been referencing "Black Rock City," the pop-up community that had sprung up—as it did every year at the end of August—around where they were standing, a work of art and planning and genius, laid out like a large clock, with twelve smaller clocks inside, concentric circles, each one with an equally smaller radius than the previous one, like a Russian nesting doll. Or he could have meant the thousands of camps sprouting right out of the desert floor, covering every conceivable clock position in between the edge of the largest clock and that of the smallest one, starting from 2:00 P.M. and moving clockwise all the way around to 10:00 P.M.—camps that ran from spartan tents, domes, and yurts, to elaborate, fantastical constructs that housed dozens of people. Or he could have been speaking about the art installations and sculptures springing up next to the camps—some of them camps themselves—things like pyramids or crashed UFOs or giant carcasses of retired jumbo airliners. Geometric constructs, statues, temples, polyhedrons. Or the art cars that slowly rolled around the desert clock, hundreds of Pac-Man–like organisms moving through the organized maze of camps, mutant vehicles ranging from mobile boom boxes, pirate ships, and sharks, to steam trains, hotrods, dragons, and fire-breathing octopuses. At night, some camps were lit by strings of lights or panels of LEDs, some strafed the night with flashing strobes and laser beams, while some glowed fluorescent and others possessed fire-breathing torches and fire pits. Altogether, they transformed this barren, inhospitable desert flat into a Technicolor phantasmagoria.

Or he could have been talking about The Man himself, rising up in the center of it all, towering like a humanoid skyscraper, forty feet tall, made entirely of wood, with kindling stacked by each massive foot. Eventually, The Man would be set on fire toward the end of the one-week festival, a tradition that gave this place its name and symbolized one of the main principles of the gathering: "Radical self-expression." To many of the seventy thousand people populating the desert around Cameron, known as "Burners," it was an annual pilgrimage or raison d'être that bordered on being religious.

And nearby to the Burning Man was the Temple, a spiritual structure that housed the "Soul" of the Man. A cathartic wooden sanctum, where people left photos and notes and inscribed messages written to themselves, to loved ones, or sometimes to no particular person at all, just anyone passing by. They contained advice, wisdom, joy, happiness, gratitude, inspiration, heartbreak, heartache, loss, trauma, pain; the entire range of deep inner emotions and experiences that cut to the core of what it meant to be a human, experiencing life on this earth with all of its vicissitudes. The Temple was one of the only places on the playa that was quiet. A place where you could hear your own thoughts in between the delicate sound of whispers, faint sobs, and human embrace. And perhaps your own tears. An emotional journey, at times overwhelming, that left you with an intense sense of gratitude and inner peace. When the Temple burned on the last day of the festival, it unlocked all of its emotional content in a release, a rebirth, so powerful, so spiritual, that it helped assuage the grief and begin the healing process, closing a chapter to begin anew.

Cameron wasn't exactly sure what had brought Tyler and him to Burning Man that summer; a friend's invite, an escape from East Coast humidity, pure curiosity—but he was glad they'd come. No matter who you were when you headed to that desert, the atmosphere could change you; even if the change was momentary, it was something worth experiencing.

They were staying in the "Lost Lounge," a conglomerate of canvas, tent-like cubes stacked together, a sort of makeshift desert motel. Inside, in different cubes, there was a DJ booth, a shared kitchen, dance areas, and simple places to hang out and do whatever you felt like doing.

Located at eight o'clock on the innermost of the twelve clocks—known as Airstrip—the Lost Lounge was a fifteen-minute walk, or shorter bike ride, from where they were strolling now: the other side of the Esplanade, the vast, dusty center or face of all the clocks, where the Man himself stood, right in the middle, the shaft that anchored the imaginary clock hands of this sprawling desert sundial known as Black Rock City. For the moment, Cameron was content to wander along the edge of the Esplanade and Airstrip, stopping every once in a while to venture down the radial streets and alleys that cut across all of the clocks at fifteen- and thirty-minute intervals and explore some of the thousands of camps that covered this desert timepiece. Having nothing to do, and nowhere to be, was a large part of Burning Man's charm.

As they walked they passed groups of other Burners doing the same thing, men and women of all ages, anywhere from late teens into their seventies, dressed—and in some cases undressed—in costumes to fit the scenery.

Leather, feathers, goggles, straps, chains, boots, gloves, hats—the sort of fashion show you'd expect to see moments before the end of the world.

As Cameron continued clockwise around the Esplanade, he caught sight of another group coming toward them. A half dozen young people, mostly shirtless, in shorts, covered in dust. As they passed, one of the Burners in the group suddenly stopped and looked at Cameron and his brother.

"Excuse me, I don't mean to interject," he said, a little formally. "But are you the Winklevoss twins?"

A question they'd heard so many times, it had become almost background noise. The Burner had a boyish face, curly dark hair, cherubic cheeks. Cameron didn't think he recognized the guy, but he seemed to be about Cameron and Tyler's age, maybe a little younger, but then again, in playa garb, covered in dirt, Cameron might not have recognized Tyler if he wasn't standing right next to him.

"We sure are," Cameron said.

"Um, wow. Cool. I'm Dustin Moskovitz."

If Cameron didn't know the face, he certainly knew the name. Moskovitz had cofounded Facebook with Mark Zuckerberg, and had been his number two until he'd left the company in 2008 to start his own business, Asana, a software-service company that helped teams work more efficiently. *Forbes* had named Moskovitz the youngest self-made billionaire in history, because he was eight days younger than Mark Zuckerberg and owned more than 2 percent of Facebook.

They had attended Harvard together but had traveled in very different circles. Cameron had never met Moskovitz and wouldn't have been able to pick him out of a lineup. That said, Moskovitz had been personally named as a defendant in their lawsuit and had no doubt followed its progress, like much of the world, as it wound its way through the legal system for years. Cameron knew Moskovitz and Zuckerberg were close, and that there was a good chance he viewed him and Tyler as adversaries, maybe even mortal enemies. Maybe Moskovitz had been merely a bystander, swept up in the legal tornado, and not a party to any of duplicitous actions of Zuckerberg. Nonetheless, it was likely that he shared Zuckerberg's version of the Facebook origin story rather than their own.

Cameron stood there, the dust swirling between him, Tyler, and Facebook's former number two. He stared at Moskovitz, Moskovitz stared at him. And then, suddenly, Moskovitz stepped forward and hugged him.

It was a Burning Man moment. Here "radical inclusion" reigned supreme. This moment might have gone completely differently if it had happened in the real world, outside this desert realm, in New York or Silicon Valley. Would the world outside this world even allow it? Or would some force, someone, or something get in the way? No one would ever know, because it had happened here, and in this way. And for at least the brief moment of time that it took to hug it out on the playa, the past was the past—the water of discord was under the bridge.

After they'd separated, Moskovitz shook both their hands and invited the twins to a grilled cheese party at his camp the next day. As it turned out, Cameron was too busy working through his feelings to remember where the camp was located. But maybe that was for the best; as he later discovered, Zuckerberg had flown into Burning Man on a helicopter to help serve the grilled cheeses. If Cameron and Tyler had attended, who knows what would have happened? Was it even possible that they might have also hugged it out with Zuckerberg? On the playa, among the dust of the earth and the sea of humanity, among all that spirituality, love, and gratitude, could even the Winklevii and Zuckerberg have let bygones be bygones over grilled cheeses?

Well, it was a nice idea.

Cameron opened his eyes to find himself sitting behind his desk in his glass office in New York, as far from the Black Rock City desert and Burning Man and the never-ending playa as he could be. Sometimes it was hard to know why a specific memory bubbled up when it did; that hug on the Esplanade seemed like such distant history. And yet it had been simmering in the back of his mind for some time. Maybe it was because he and Tyler had founded a startup, their first since Harvard Connection/ConnectU almost a decade ago.

The idea was called Gemini—a fully regulated, fully compliant, virtual currency exchange headquartered in New York.

Once Silk Road had gone down, Mt. Gox had become Bitcoin's biggest liability. And then, two weeks after Charlie's arrest and the NYDFS Virtual Currency Hearings, where the twins had spoken in front of Lawsky and the regulators, Mt. Gox had collapsed. Karpeles, in a last-ditch effort, had frantically approached the twins to see if they would fund an emergency bailout of Mt. Gox. But it had already been too late—800,000 bitcoin had been looted from customers' accounts by sophisticated hackers—a loss worth over $450 million at the time.

After the fall of Mt. Gox, the twins had become convinced that Bitcoin desperately needed a new wave of entrepreneurs and companies that could sweep away the broken pieces of that first wave—the Charlies, the Karpeleses. If there was no safe and secure place for people to buy, sell, and store virtual currency, the innovation would soon fail. Even before Mt. Gox's collapse, Cameron and Tyler had been searching for entrepreneurs who were building the next generation of exchanges—but they hadn't been able to find anyone who they believed was taking the right approach.

The twins believed that for an exchange to be successful, it needed four fundamental pillars seared into its DNA: licensing, compliance, security, and technology. Some entrepreneurs they talked to had the technology part right but didn't emphasize compliance enough, while others were not focused enough on the security. There was always a corner being cut or a dangerous compromise being made. No one was embracing all four principals equally, and eventually the twins had decided that they would have to take matters into their own hands.

On January 23, 2015, Cameron had announced their plans to the world:

Today, my brother, Tyler, and I are proud to announce Gemini: a next-generation bitcoin exchange. What exactly do we mean by "next generation"? We mean a fully regulated, fully compliant, New York–based bitcoin exchange for both individuals and institutions alike. Why? Because it's about time. . . .

Cameron knew it was ambitious, another big bet on a par with their original purchase of 1 percent of the new currency and their still unrealized ETF.

He and Tyler had been assembling the Gemini team for more than a year. Their goal was simple: bring together the nation's top security experts, technologists, and financial engineers to build a world-class cryptocurrency platform from the ground up with a security-first mentality. A fully regulated exchange in the heart of the old-world financial realm: New York. One that asked for permission, rather than forgiveness. They weren't trying to hack their way around regulation; they were going to help build it. In light of how ambitious the venture was, they had named their new venture, well partially, after one of NASA's early space programs: Gemini. The comparison to NASA's second spaceflight project, which was meant to be a bridge from the Mercury program, which had put men into orbit, and Apollo, which put them on the moon, made sense to Cameron: if it succeeded, Gemini would be a bridge to the future of money.

But they hadn't been thinking only of rocket ships when they'd chosen the name. *Gemini* was also the Latin word for "twins." As such—and as they'd explained in their announcement—"it inherently explored the concept of duality." The old, legacy world of money melding with a future filled with virtual currency, both intersecting on the Gemini platform.

Eight months after their announcement, on October 5, 2015, Gemini had opened its doors to the world.

Their goal was not just to build a billion-dollar company—a "Unicorn," in Silicon Valley parlance—their goal was to build something more. A company that would last for a hundred years—what they called "Centurion." Cameron and Tyler were playing the long game. Gemini, they often joked, was trying to be the fastest tortoise in the race.

Cameron and Tyler were not just Gemini's founders, but they were also its investors, through Winklevoss Capital. They didn't just have their skin in the game—they were all in, down to the bones.

Sitting in his office, Cameron wondered if the recurring memory of that moment at Burning Man had something to do with the fact that he and his brother were finally entrepreneurs once more. The first time since college, since they'd approached Mark Zuckerberg with their idea.

Did he keep coming back to that moment when he'd come face-to-face with Facebook's number two, because he and Tyler had finally reached the point where they could move on from where they'd started? Had their second act finally eclipsed their first?

Cameron realized his brother was at the door of his office. He guessed that if Tyler knew what he was thinking, he'd have told him that he was reading into things too much. Cameron has always been the dreamier one. To Tyler, real life didn't have first, second, or even third acts. Life was a ride down a river in a boat.

"You see it?" Tyler said, almost offhand, like it was the most meaningless question in the world.

Cameron glanced past his brother, through the open door. Winklevoss Capital, now also home to Gemini, was bustling. They were hiring so fast to keep up with Gemini's growth and with Bitcoin's that Cameron recognized only half of the people who populated the desks in the open area, a sea of monitors, software engineers, operational personnel, customer support representatives, and more. Although their ETF was still a dream, Gemini was humming along, and over the past year, the price of bitcoin had been enjoying a steady rise since January.

"See what?" Cameron asked.

"Look at your computer."

Cameron shifted in his seat, then faced the screen on his desk. His eyes moved to the ever-present ticker at the bottom, and then he paused. If he hadn't known better, he might have thought it was a mistake—a zero where something else should have been, a glitch of pixels on the screen.

Bitcoin had just hit $10,000 a coin. Cameron knew there were many reasons that had led to this incredible rise: regulation around cryptocurrencies had gotten clearer, and most people didn't believe that governments around the world were going to outlaw the new forms of money. More and better entrepreneurs had moved into the space, built more infrastructure, making it easy to buy, sell, and store bitcoin. There was a greater level of education—people had started to see that Silk Road wasn't Bitcoin, that there was so much more to the technology.

In effect, it was akin to how the internet had started off as a niche, hard-to-use thing—and then had just proliferated over time, as infrastructure and user-friendly applications emerged, and as more entrepreneurs flooded into the space. And so bitcoin had risen, and risen and risen—and was now at $10,000.

The calculation wasn't hard for Cameron to do in his head. As of that moment, the entire market cap of bitcoin had reached over $200 billion. Beginning in 2011, they had acquired 1 percent of that market. And since they'd started buying the virtual currency, they hadn't sold a single bitcoin.

Cameron looked at his brother, then smiled.

"I'm six foot five, two hundred and twenty pounds, and have a billion dollars' worth of Bitcoin," he said. "Oh, and there's two of me."

His brother was ready with a line of his own:

"A million dollars isn't cool. You know what's cool? A billion dollars . . . in bitcoin."

Cameron and Tyler Winklevoss had just officially become the world's first known Bitcoin billionaires.

31

FROM DUMAS TO BALZAC

January 4, 2018.

1 Hacker Way, Menlo Park, California.

A state-of-the-art campus in the heart of Silicon Valley, the headquarters of one of the biggest companies on earth.

One might imagine a brightly lit corner of a vast, open floor of cubicles.

A boyish man edging toward his midthirties. An expressionless face beneath a mop of slightly curly, auburn hair, caught in the glow of a laptop computer. A gray hoodie, flip-flops, shorts.

A vast room, inside the headquarters that he had built on top of an idea that began as a revolution and morphed into something else, something worth many billions of dollars, something huge and omnipresent and, as of late, controversial, maybe enduring another mere "speed bump" in its never-ending quest for total, worldwide adoption and domination, or maybe, finally fraying at the edges.

His back to the vast room, the man, still boyish, though he was married and the father of two, might have begun to type.

As with every year at approximately this time, there was a mission statement to write: looking back on how far he'd come since the year prior, telling the world what he had planned for the year ahead. Why he was writing such a thing was not a question that anybody would ask. As the CEO of the juggernaut that had connected the world, changed how it interacted, he was one of the most powerful people on the planet. His words mattered.

"Every year I take on a personal challenge to learn something new," his statement began. "I've visited every U.S. state, run 365 miles, built an AI for my home, read twenty-five books, and learned Mandarin. . . ."

It was an enviable bucket list. As he continued typing, he moved from accomplishments to history—how he'd begun chasing these experiences in 2009, when the economy was faltering, before his company was profitable. Because things suddenly felt similar today:

"The world feels anxious and divided. . . ."

It wasn't just the world that felt disjointed; many felt his company was feeding that anxiety. Mistakes had been made, lines had been crossed. Fake news spewed and targeted to millions of unwitting eyes. Election interference that seemed so profuse, it just might have altered history. Egregious amounts of user data packaged, given away, hacked. A business model built on the commodification of private lives . . .

"This may not seem like a personal challenge on its face, but I think I'll learn more by focusing intensely on these issues than I would by doing something completely separate. These issues touch on questions of history, civics, political philosophy, media, government, and of course technology. . . ."

Somewhere in that vast room, one of the many dozens of computers in one of the many dozens of work spaces may very well have been open to a screen showing the current price of bitcoin. At the moment, the virtual currency sat at a little over $16,000 a coin. Incredible by any measure—considering that in 2009, the early days that he had just referred to in his letter, Bitcoin had just been starting its journey worth well below a penny a coin.

No doubt he knew that history—because that was how he approached everything. He studied, he learned, he *consumed*. He must have known that the price of a single bitcoin first reached parity with the U.S. dollar in 2011. Had continued to rise, but was mostly unknown, until the events in the tiny island nation of Cyprus in 2013 caused the price to run above $250 a coin. More volatility followed, but by the end of 2013, the price had hit $1,000.

And then it had crossed $10,000 in November of 2017, then doubled over the next month to $20,000—before sliding back down to where it sat today. It was impossible to know where that price would go from here, or even what, at the moment, Bitcoin really was. A commodity in the midst of a bubble? A new currency? The future of money? A new system, one that would usher in a new, more decentralized world?

Whatever it was, it had been *something* for a few years now, since 2009, and *he* hadn't seen it happening, or he hadn't taken it seriously enough, or he had simply chosen to stay on the sidelines.

But other people *had* seen it happening and *had* taken it seriously. Certain people had not only been accumulating bitcoin, but they had also been instrumental in its incredible rise.

He began to type again.

"One of the most interesting questions in technology right now is about centralization vs. decentralization. A lot of us got into technology because we believe it can be a decentralizing force that puts more power in people's hands. . . . But today, many people have lost faith in that promise. With the rise of a small number of big tech companies and governments using technology to watch their citizens, many people now believe technology only centralizes power rather than decentralizes it."

Ironic, how fast technology could turn on its head, how a revolution could suddenly become what it was supposed to be fighting against—the Establishment—a centralized monopoly, a data cartel, holding the world's data hostage.

"There are important counter-trends to this—like encryption and cryptocurrency—that take power from centralized systems and put it back into people's hands. But they come with the risk of being harder to control. I'm interested to go deeper and study the positive and negative aspects of these technologies, and how best to use them in our services. . . ."

Encryption and cryptocurrency—the type of *counter-trends,* digital barbarians at the gate that could dismantle empires.

But the truth was, revolutions were a lot like entrepreneurial ideas. They could spring wholly built from a creative source, a brilliant mind: maybe a boy genius in a hoodie and flip-flops. They could be co-opted, borrowed, changed just enough to seem unique. They could be subverted—on purpose, for reasons of profit—or involuntarily, a victim of their own growth, their cells becoming cancerous. Revolutions could even be stolen.

There was no way to know what would come next; whether he was just writing a mission statement to try and mollify his growing number of detractors, tacitly acknowledging the sound of digital tumbrels rolling in, declaring something, or just contemplating.

Either way, he hit a few more keys and posted the statement to his blog, instantly sending his words to more than one hundred million followers, a fraction of the 1.5 billion people who logged into his company every day.

Then he turned off his computer and watched the screen as it went dark.

Epilogue
WHERE ARE THEY NOW ...?

M uch as *The Accidental Billionaires* and *The Social Network* strove to tell the story of Facebook's founding—that first year of inception and adoption—*Bitcoin Billionaires* is an origin story, both of the characters within these pages, and of the cryptocurrency itself. We've watched Facebook grow and change over the past decade, and similarly, it will be interesting to see where Bitcoin goes. In my opinion, the story of this new era of cryptocurrencies is just beginning.

One of the greatest strikes against cryptocurrencies has always been their volatility, which the past year has only served to highlight. Since I started writing this book, the price of Bitcoin has declined more than seventy percent; at the same time, the crypto industry has grown by leaps and bounds, with new companies aimed at servicing, profiting from, and building on this novel technology that springs up every day. The blockchain is everywhere, and Bitcoin knows no borders; Bitcoin believers in nearly every country in the world continue to HODL (hold), even as Wall Street struggles to understand where crypto fits within financial structures that seem more antiquated every day.

There is no doubt in my mind: the Bitcoin revolution is real, and cryptocurrencies are here to stay.

As of this moment, Tyler and Cameron Winklevoss still remain Bitcoin Billionaires. Together they are the CEO and presidents of Gemini, their crypto exchange, which now has over two hundred employees and is growing by the day. Gemini has been described as the most regulated crypto exchange and custodian in the world, and on its own is thought to be valued at well over a billion dollars. The twins are also early investors in Ether, Zcash, Filecoin, Tezos, and many other cryptocurrencies.

Tyler and Cameron continue to be Bitcoin's biggest advocates. They believe that though Bitcoin has come a long way since its infancy, there is still a long way to go. If, as they believe, Bitcoin is truly gold 2.0, it is still radically undervalued. Gold is a seven-trillion-dollar market; Bitcoin, currently, is valued at only a fraction of that amount.

Whatever happens next, there is no doubt that the Bitcoin story is far from over. Moreover, the technology behind Bitcoin has only barely begun to infiltrate the financial, technological, and online worlds. The technology that makes Bitcoin work—the blockchain and crypto private keys—has the potential to decentralize not just money but also *data* in a way that could "give the internet back to the people"—freeing user information from the siloed monopolies of Facebook, Google, Amazon, etc. The irony is that Bitcoin and its hashes may very well do what Facebook so spectacularly failed to do—protect its users' data from hackers, misuse, and overarching authority, and allow a form of online communication that is entirely and truly free.

Roger Ver has officially given up his U.S. citizenship and currently splits his time between St. Kitts, Japan, and the rest of the world. A huge voice in the crypto world and a controversial figure online (with over half a million followers on Twitter), at the moment Ver is involved in what has essentially been described as a civil war in the Bitcoin community; Ver and a group of like-minded Bitcoiners have broken off to form "Bitcoin Cash," which takes the cryptocurrency in a different direction in terms of scaling and block size, with a goal of turning it into something that could more easily supplant cash.

Ver continues to invest in crypto-related companies and spends much of his time running Bitcoin.com, whose team has recently surpassed a hundred people. Bitcoin.com endeavors to build the tools to allow anyone to interact financially and without government supervision with everyone else in the world.

Erik Voorhees currently resides in Denver, Colorado, and is the CEO and founder of a cryptocurrency exchange company called Shapeshift, which allows customers to exchange one form of cryptocurrency for another instantaneously. Originally, the company did not collect personal data on its users, or hold any of the currencies in its accounts. An article in the *Wall Street Journal* published September 28, 2018, entitled "How Dirty Money Disappears into the Black Hole of Cryptocurrency," alleged that as much as $9 million in illegally obtained funds had been "laundered" through Shapeshift, as part of $88.6 million of fraudulent funds moving through a total of forty-six crypto exchanges; Voorhees refuted the report, maintaining that Shapeshift uses "blockchain forensics" to weed out money launderers and that *Wall Street Journal*'s reporters didn't understand the data.

After being introduced to Bitcoin by the Winklevoss twins, banking heir Matthew Mellon rapidly became one of cryptocurrencies' biggest advocates, building a massive fortune first in Bitcoin, then in the cryptocurrency XRP—a digital currency developed by the company Ripple in 2012. On April 16, 2018, at the age of fifty-four, Matthew Mellon passed away suddenly on the way to a drug rehab center in Cancun, Mexico, where he hoped to overcome an opioid dependency. At the time of his death, his crypto fortune was valued at somewhere between five hundred million and a billion dollars.

After the U.S. Court of Appeals for the Second Circuit upheld his conviction and sentence in May 2017, and the Supreme Court declined to consider any further appeal in June 2018, Ross Ulbricht, now thirty-four, is currently serving a double life sentence plus forty years without the possibility of parole for the crimes of money laundering and conspiracy to traffic narcotics by means of the internet. There are many in the Bitcoin and libertarian community—including Roger Ver—who see Ulbricht as a martyr who has been unfairly jailed. Ulbricht will most likely die in prison.

Charlie Shrem served nearly a year at Lewisberg Federal Penitentiary in Union County, Pennsylvania, after which he was transferred to a half-way house in Harrisburg. While at the halfway house, he washed dishes at a local restaurant. He was released on September 16, 2016. Sadly, Charlie has no contact with his family. He remains friends with Erik Voorhees. Since leaving prison, Charlie's relationship with the Winklevoss twins has remained unsettled. On November 1, 2018, a federal suit was unsealed accusing Charlie of owing the twins five thousand Bitcoin, which they claim he stole from them in 2012. Charlie has denied the charge, his lawyer Brian Klein telling the *New York Times* that "nothing could be further from the truth. . . . Charlie plans to vigorously defend himself and quickly clear his name." The suit is ongoing.

Almost a year to the day after his release from prison, on September 15, 2017, Charlie married Courtney. Together they've made a life for themselves in Sarasota, Florida, which includes time spent on Charlie's boat. The boat is named *The Satoshi*.

ACKNOWLEDGMENTS

I am immensely grateful to Noah Eaker, Lauren Bittrich, Marlena Bittner, and the entire team at Flatiron Books and Macmillan, who have helped me turn this incredible story into one of the most fulfilling writing experiences of my career; likewise, to Eric Simonoff and Matthew Snyder, agents extraordinaire.

I'm also extremely thankful to my numerous sources, without whom I could not have written this book, and to the group of main characters, who opened themselves up to me and were generous with their time, experiences, and expertise.

As always, I'm thankful to my parents, my brothers and their families, and to Tonya, Asher, Arya, and Bugsy, for putting up with me talking nonstop about Bitcoin for the past year and a half.

BIBLIOGRAPHY

Bertrand, Natasha. "The FBI staged a lovers' fight to catch the kingpin of the web's biggest illegal drug marketplace." *Business Insider*, Jan. 22, 2015.

Carlson, Nicholas. "'Embarrassing and Damaging' Zuckerberg IMs Confirmed By Zuckerberg, The New Yorker." *Business Insider*, Sept. 13, 2010.

———. "At last — the full story of how Facebook was founded." *Business Insider*, Mar. 5, 2010.

———. "In 2004, Mark Zuckerberg Broke into a Facebook User's Private Email Account." *Business Insider*, Mar. 5, 2010.

Chrisafis, Angelique. "Cyprus bailout: 'people are panicking, they're afraid of losing their money.'" *Guardian*, Mar. 17, 2013.

Cutler, Kim-Mai. "Mt. Gox's Demise Marks the End of Bitcoin's First Wave of Entrepreneurs." *TechCrunch*, Feb. 25, 2014.

Dabilis, Andy. "Bailout Cuts Cyprus Bank Accounts, Withdrawals Barred." *Greek Reporter*, Mar. 16, 2013.

Eha, Brian Patrick. "Can Bitcoin's First Felon Help Make Cryptocurrency a Trillion-Dollar Market?" *Fortune*, June 26, 2017.

Epstein, Jeremy. "What you may not understand about crypto's millionaires." *Venture Beat*, Feb. 10, 2018.

Forbes, Steve. "Why a Cyprus-Like Seizure of Your Money Could Happen Here." *Forbes*, Mar. 25, 2013.

Fox, Emily Jane. "The New York bar that takes bitcoins." *CNN Business*, Apr. 8, 2013.

Freeman, Colin. "Cyprus dreams left in tatters." *Telegraph*, Mar. 24, 2013.

Frizell, Sam. "How the Feds Nabbed Alleged Silk Road Drug Kingpin 'Dread Pirate Roberts.'" *Time*, Jan 21, 2015.

Jeffries, Adrianne, and Russell Brandom. "The coin prince: inside Bitcoin's first big money-laundering scandal." *Verge*, Feb. 4, 2014.

Markowitz, Eric. "My Night Out with Bitcoin Millionaire and Proud Stoner Charlie Shrem." *Vocativ*, Dec. 5, 2013.

Matthews, Dylan. "Everything you need to know about the Cyprus bailout, in one FAQ." *Washington Post*, Mar. 18, 2013.

McMillan, Robert. "The Inside Story of Mt. Gox, Bitcoin's $460 Million Disaster." *Wired*, Mar. 3, 2014.

———. "Ring of Bitcoins: Why your digital wallet belongs on your finger." *Wired*, Mar. 18, 2013.

Mibach, Emily. "Last call for The Oasis—beloved Menlo Park pizza, burger, and beer joint closes." *Daily Post*, Mar. 8, 2018.

Osborne, Hilary, and Josephine Moulds. "Cyprus bailout deal: at a glance." *Guardian*, Mar. 25, 2013.

Popper, Nathaniel. *Digital Gold: Bitcoin and the Inside Story of the Misfits and Millionaires Trying to Reinvent Money*. New York: HarperPaperbacks, 2016.

———. "How the Winklevoss Twins Found Vindication in a Bitcoin Fortune." *New York Times*, Dec. 19, 2017.

———. "Never Mind Facebook; Winklevoss Twins Rule in Digital Money." *New York Times*, Apr. 11, 2013.

———. "Winklevoss Twins Plan First Fund for Bitcoins." *New York Times*, July 1, 2013.

———. "Charlie Shrem and the Ups and Downs of BitInstant." *Coindesk*, May 19, 2015.

Roy, Jessica. "It's All About the Bitcoin, Baby." *Observer*, Apr. 30, 2013.

Vargas, Jose Antonio. "The Face of Facebook." *New Yorker*, Sept 20, 2010.

Winklevoss, Cameron, and Tyler Winklevoss. "Bitcoin, the Internet of Money." Value Investor's Congress presentation. New York, delivered Sept. 17, 2013.

———. "Money is broken; Its future is not." Money20/20 conference presentation. Las Vegas, NV, delivered Nov. 3, 2014.